Lyndall Gordon is the prize-winning author of six biographies, including *Lives Like Loaded Guns: Emily Dickinson and Her Family's Feuds* and *The Imperfect Life of T. S. Eliot*, and also *Shared Lives*, a memoir of women's friendship in her native South Africa. She is a fellow of the Royal Society of Literature, and lives in Oxford where she is a fellow of St Hilda's College.

'*Divided Lives* will become a classic in the history of how women's lives evolved at a turning point of our times' Paula Deitz, editor of the *Hudson Review*

'Literature is where their relationship blossomed and where it is now preserved . . . as racy as a novel' *Guardian*

'Prose both lyrical and meticulous . . . beautiful' Juliet Nicolson, *Evening Standard*

'A beautifully written and troubling memoir' *Independent on Sunday*

'A sensitive exploration of the complexities of motherhood and daughterhood' *Sunday Times*

'This quietly devastating book takes us into many strange terrains but it is to the "inner life of that room" in Cape Town that Gordon finds herself returning. It was there she fountained into one of our most sensitive writers' Frances Wilson, *Mail on Sunday*

'Gordon's purest strength as a life-writer is her intuition, where the reader has to bring to a work "her own unvoiced life" . . . Women's lives often end up sinking like dresses in a lagoon, pushed down by the rudders of ignorance and neglect. Lyndall Gordon's writing inflates them with life-saving breath which allows them to float and sparkle in the sunlight of r

D0363026

Also by Lyndall Gordon

THE IMPERFECT LIFE OF T. S. ELIOT

VIRGINIA WOOLF: A WRITER'S LIFE

SHARED LIVES (A MEMOIR)

CHARLOTTE BRONTË: A PASSIONATE LIFE

HENRY JAMES: HIS WOMEN AND HIS ART

VINDICATION: A LIFE OF MARY WOLLSTONECRAFT

LIVES LIKE LOADED GUNS: EMILY DICKINSON
AND HER FAMILY'S FEUDS

Divided Lives

Dreams of a Mother and Daughter

LYNDALL GORDON

virago

VIRAGO

First published in Great Britain in 2014 by Virago Press
This paperback edition published in 2015 by Virago Press

1 3 5 7 9 10 8 6 4 2

Copyright © Lyndall Gordon 2014

The moral right of the author has been asserted.

All rights reserved.
No part of this publication may be reproduced, stored in a
retrieval system, or transmitted in any form or by any means, without
the prior permission in writing of the publisher, nor be otherwise circulated
in any form of binding or cover other than that in which it is published
and without a similar condition including this condition being
imposed on the subsequent purchaser.

A CIP catalogue record for this book
is available from the British Library.

ISBN 978-1-84408-891-1

Typeset in Bembo by M Rules
Printed and bound in Great Britain by
Clays Ltd, St Ives plc

Papers used by Virago are from well-managed forests
and other responsible sources.

MIX
Paper from
responsible sources
FSC
www.fsc.org
FSC® C104740

Virago Press
An imprint of
Little, Brown Book Group
100 Victoria Embankment
London EC4Y 0DY

An Hachette UK Company
www.hachette.co.uk

www.virago.co.uk

For Pip

Contents

1

'Sister'

I'm to be my mother's sister because she wants one so. My part is to be there if she's ill. At four years old, it's a privilege to have this responsibility instead of trotting off to nursery school like other children.

My mother looks back to the wide-open dawns of her

childhood because these days she has to be drugged as soon as she wakes. The powders dull her, she explains, a temptation not to take them, and no one knows if she does or not. Morning is the darkest time of her day.

Suddenly she calls in her danger-voice, 'Help, oh-h, help me. Quickly!'

It's a test she might fail; if she does she might go mad, or worse. I fly to her side and find her on her knees or crouched on all fours. I grab the glass jug on her bedside table and toss water in her face. It doesn't matter if it splashes the bed or spills over the floor. If she doesn't revive I must dig in her handbag for the large blue Mason Pearson hairbrush and push its bristles into her wrists. I never do this hard enough. Is this because I don't have the strength or can't bear to hurt her? She wrenches the brush from my hand and drives the bristles back and forth across her wrists – until she comes round. Sooner or later she will come round. Then she pulls herself up from the floor and lies on her bed, moaning. Lenie, the cook, hears the commotion, and comes pitter-patter on small feet. I'm relieved to see her, and ashamed too for Lenie to see Madam so. Lenie sucks her tongue in dismay and brings a cup of sweet, milky tea. Lenie never says a word, but has her share in our helplessness. None of us say a word. It happens, and we go on till the next time.

My mother is slow to get up, slow to dress. She runs the tap and splashes her face, on and on to the measure of slap, slap, drip, slap, slap, drip to counteract the miasma of the powders. Then she draws seamed stockings over her feet and hooks them on to the four straps dangling from the belt around her waist. All her underwear, including the silky petticoat, is purest white. Her smalls are washed separately every day; nothing unclean touches her skin. I'm waiting for her to finish, but her dreamy slowness makes me restless. I go off to the nursery to dig into the toy cupboard behind the ruched green curtain patterned with a thin red thread. Across the passage I hear her dialling the telephone, her finger in the hole, a whirr to the number then the varied slide of the returning dial; and then her housewife voice, wearily dutiful as she gives Mr Romm the grocer or Mrs Bass the fishmonger an order to be delivered to Lenie (since my mother rarely visits the kitchen). Mrs Bass, leaning over her counter with her gap-toothed smile, has the ready-to-please manner of South African service. She spares the time to answer my mother's many questions as to quality and freshness.

In the forties and fifties, husbands of housewives have a right to complain. My father Harry is easygoing and enjoys (as my mother puts it) 'fullness of life', but he does grumble if breakfast does not appear as he ties his shoelaces, putting one foot and then the other on the *riempies* of his dining-room chair. The grumble isn't made to Lenie but to his wife, who has nothing to do but take charge of the servants and yet, at this moment, is reading Wordsworth and reaching out to a girl who 'dwelt among the untrodden ways'.

Harry's grumble is routine; he's looking forward to a lawyer's day, ready for his next case as in youth he'd stood ready, swinging his arms in his one-piece racing costume: the first whistle took him to the brink of the pool, toes curled around the edge; at the second blast his arms swung back, knees bent, tensing his shoulders for the dive; and then – GO. Other whistles blew him about the pool in games of water polo. The secret of water polo, he tells me, is to tackle an opponent under the water where the referee can't see.

In childhood my mother, as Rhoda Press, lived in a different world, a barely populated place called Klaver (more commonly called Klawer) on the border of Namaqualand, which stretches along the *Weskus,* the harsh west coast of the southern tip of Africa. It has low rainfall, and at that time, before irrigation schemes, looked like the parched landscapes of the Bible. She recalls how 'I opened my eyes on a shepherd's world with flocks of bushes stretching to the curve of the veld.'

The horizons of Namaqualand are often so cloudless you can see line upon blue line of mountains and, looking up at night, a river of stars. In 1917, when Rhoda was born, Klaver was little more than far-flung farms at the end of the railway line that ran more or less parallel to the coast. By the time I'm born, in the forties, the railway has been extended some way beyond Klaver, but it never reaches what is now Namibia to the north.

I am to be a channel for my mother's life and writings. It's impossible to remember at what age this emerges into consciousness. All that can be said with certainty is that a sisterhood of child-carer changes during my schooldays into a sisterhood of poems and stories. She reads Emily Dickinson to me over and over. There seems no divide between the 'Colossal substance of Immortality' in the visionary poets she loves – Dickinson and Emily Brontë – and her own desk-drawer poems. These she reads aloud with modest disclaimers.

Let me be clear: my role has less to do with love than reliance. I am not lovely; I am heavily freckled; not a light spray, but splotched all over despite the floppy-brimmed hat on my head. When the sun is at its zenith each December, impeccable Aunt Berjulie, who was brought up by her own impeccable aunts in Northern Rhodesia, comes down to the Cape. In well-matched outfits from John Orr's in Johannesburg, Aunt Berjulie never fails to alert my mother to my uneven teeth and ruined face. My mother, whose darker skin is unmarked by sun, never thinks much about looks. This makes it comfortable to be with her. I'm a conscientious child, not winning, not brainy, but exercising an earnest intelligence – not the most attractive of qualities, yet it includes attention to phrases like 'the river of stars' and 'the curve of the veld' that fountain from my mother. And I am there; she feels close to those who have shared what she calls her 'attacks'. There are others she loves more: my brother Pip belting out 'Great Balls of Fire'; her Pooh-Bear brother Basil, with a healthy appetite and is inclined, his sister teases, to think it 'time for a little something'; and then there are her schoolfriends, maternal Auntie Monica and practical Auntie Lilian. All charm her as different while I am like, and in that sense an extension of herself.

A channel, then. My mother never explains how this channel is to be dug between her shut-off invalid existence and some far-off future when her voice will emerge.

Nor, given our reversal of roles, does she foresee a divide. It never occurs to her that separation will ever be necessary. In fact, it's part of her appeal for me that the common course of existence plays no part in her dreams.

Mothering may be the strongest bond most creatures experience, and the acts of separation from that bond shape our lives. For me, a daughter caught up in the crises of illness, this divide must be deferred.

2

Mothers

My name is an embarrassment. If only my mother had called me Linda, or any other common name.

'Stand up and spell it,' teachers will say on the first day of the school year.

They never recognise the name of the singular woman in Olive Schreiner's novel, *The Story of an African Farm*. Nor can any teacher know that it marks me as my mother's creature. My name comes from Rhoda's other life, called up more fully in the memory-dream she inhabits. The Lyndall of the novel is a curiosity of the veld: a woman shaped by unstoried spaces where the curve of the earth can be seen on the encircling horizon. I pull the book from the shelf and glance at its opening line: 'The full African moon poured down its light from the blue sky into the wide, lonely plain.' Vaguely I take in an embrace of nature and solitude. Rhoda is not particularly drawn to the politics of the heroine's turn to the feminist cause. What matters is her authentic nature: a woman without a mask, rising from a bedrock of stone and bush.

Later, when I read the novel, I recognise my mother in the perceptive girl, a rarity amongst the farming people about her, and echo my mother's empathy for the solitary shepherd boy Waldo – with his philosopher's name – a dreamer too innocent for this world.

Rhoda's secret self is partly open to detection, through not-so-buried signals like my name. A poem she reads aloud remembers 'children's voices chipped out of silence' when her brothers, Basil and Sydney, dared her to tread the single track of the railway bridge above the Olifants River. There are only three trains a week, night trains due at dawn, but the children work up their dread of an engine, a dark face looming around a curve on the approach to the bridge. They imagine far-off, then near, the puff and clank of a piston. Safety, she tells me, is possible in the form of three, square bays at intervals along the bridge, each just big enough for a person to stand back from a train thundering along the track, and Rhoda makes her advance from one to the next; then leans over the rail to gaze at the drop to the river below.

This scene fills out Rhoda's courage to go on in the face of oncoming attacks. Her fear is my fear for her precariousness. Yet, as a dreamer, she can dissolve fear and, in a poem she writes, can hear 'in the hollows of space / where the wind scoops bliss / the eternal ocean of the universe.'

A timeless landscape, pulsating with import, means more to her than the present where she performs as she must from day to day. It's as though she's protected from what her beloved Wordsworth called 'the prison house' of grown-ups. He too believed the soul must be sustained by memory's allegiance to the child who comes trailing memories of pre-life.

'One morning in school,' she says in her story-voice, 'I saw a crowd of children round the tin lavatory whose door stood open. As I approached there was laughter. On the high wooden seat sat a little girl with her legs dangling and her drawers round her ankles, half way from the ground. Her eyes were helpless before the mocking crowd. This was my first acquaintance with cruelty, and though it remained with me I did nothing about it.'

My mother bathes such scenes in reminiscent tolerance but now and then memory does throw up brutal scenes, which she does not hesitate to reveal to me. If we listeners were not colluding in the dream of Klaver we'd say this: it was a place of violence. Violence against the weak. Mr Biebek, who called his wife 'Girlie', beat her – but, people said, that was a husband's right. At one of the gangers' cottages along the line, a railway worker chased his son round and round the house with a whip, the boy's thin neck-bones straining as he ran. This boy died young, and that is all people recalled in after years: the fact that his father whipped him, and that he died before he grew up. It was, they said, a father's right. 'What can you do?'

But cruelty can't explain why this woman says 'Klaver ... Klaver ... Klaver' all her life. She hadn't seen a bald dorp under the glare of the sun; she had seen the source of all life. Once, there was mystery here. The wind in the gum tree, the snake in the lucerne patch, the twofold *mielie* shoot in the saffron earth, the swallows' mud-nests under the corrugated roof of the stoep, the air of winter mornings (so cold and pure it burns the nostrils), the nursery by candlelight, their father's tales and Yiddish lullabies, will hold for Rhoda – and for her more worldly brothers – the source of some power that propels their lives, as though the God of the Hebrew Bible walked with them in that wilderness when they were young.

'An impress of the everlasting' came to her first when she was six. She repeats the story to me in her memory-voice, throbbing with import when she's not reading or jotting down a poem and wants a listener, and I'm standing there next to her bed, looking down at her to check if she's all right. She won't simplify her words, as other mothers might. A poet expects her listener to catch on, so phrases like 'impress of the everlasting' come my way. Her memory-voice sounds so inward, she's almost murmuring to herself.

Six years old, in Namaqualand, she was sweeping the silky brown sand off the stoep in the early morning. 'I looked across flocks of bushes to where, in the far distance, sun-shafts, like pillars of gold-smoke, moved on the face of the veld. The light and its smoky breath flooded my being.'

For all Rhoda's readiness to share these memories, she shuts the door on others.

'I can't tell you . . . ' she stops short at the onset of illness or what she understands about its nature. And she never follows on from hints of a sad love affair before she married my father.

Why can't she tell, I wonder. Are there things in her past too bad for a child to hear? Am I lucky to be spared a fuller sisterhood? Like a sponge I sop up these hints of suffering, then turn away to do a puzzle on the round nursery table or open a jokey picture in *Winnie-the-Pooh*: the motherly Kanga inflicting a bath on Piglet, who has dared to take the place of baby Roo in her pouch. It's a relief not to read my mother's downcast face.

My brother Pip recalls 'our lying-down mother'. She leaves hands-on care to servants, harassed by her mother who, as Rhoda protests, 'interferes', disrupting the household when she tidies the pantry till one in the morning. Annie Press, our grandmother, is on the watch as the housemaid turns out the rooms every morning. Has the maid swept every particle of dust blowing into the open windows from Lion's Head, the mountain above us? Has the washerwoman fetched the sheets from the top room? The washerwoman's lips are pressed together as she kneels over the tub and pegs sheets out in white swathes, flapping in the wind with gunshot sounds until they stiffen in the sun.

Granny knows that you can't leave running a home to the maids, as she tells Harry her son-in-law, whom the servants call Master (as all South African servants call the man of the house). Our father, too breezy to notice what anyone can see, that Rhoda's respect for servants is more effective, backs Granny's reign. There's audible bustle when guests arrive and tea is not served at once. Lenie mutters '*gits*' quietly over the oven as she takes out her Lenie-cake, to be iced with deft pats and strokes into delectable peaks. Lenie is a church-going, single woman in a starched white cap and apron, whose modesty is not lost on my mother. She has read the New Testament as well as the Hebrew Bible, and sides with Christ's defiance of worldly might: the meek shall inherit the earth.

'Lenie is a saint,' my mother declares.

For all their differences of faith and occupation, as well as the colour bar, Lenie and my mother are suited as moral beings. So Lenie puts up with Granny 'for Madam's sake', and one or other servant agrees out of the corner of their mouths.

Granny whips the cups off the tray Lenie has prepared so that she can replace the tray cloth with one she's embroidered in green stem stitch with pink lazy-daisy loops for the petals. I trace the petals with my forefinger and ask Granny, 'Will you show me how?' I want to touch her skeins of silky embroidery thread, confident that Granny will let me choose the loveliest colours.

Granny's interference seems to me mere fuss, a bit of a joke. Less so to her daughter.

'You see her as she is now,' Rhoda confides behind her closed door. 'You don't know how powerful she was when my father was alive. He never called her anything but "darling", and let her have her way.'

Rhoda idolises her father, a 'sensitive man, a Press'. His character as a Press is another clue to who she is. She is decidedly not a creature of her mother, wholly an issue of her father, a reading, thinking man with an intelligent capacity for suffering. He came from Lithuania, like almost all of the hundred thousand Jews who migrated to South Africa. At thirty-six, after twenty years in the back veld, he visited Cape Town and fell in love with auburn-haired Annie, aged twenty-two, who kept house for her widowed Papa (pronounced 'Pupper') and in her fondly insensitive way bossed four younger brothers and sisters.

When Rhoda tells the story of her parents' courtship she defends her father's superiority, even though, as an immigrant, he'd driven about the veld in a mule cart.

'There are no class distinctions amongst Jews. We are equals in the sight of God.'

She speaks to a child as to an adult, yet I'm aware of things elided from her stories of the past. When I'm older this unease can surface as words that I keep to myself, knowing by then how deftly she translates her preference for her father into myth and principle.

Annie and Philip Press married in December 1914, and for some time Annie continued to preside over Papa's comfortable house on Maynard Street in town while her husband continued up country. It was only after the births of a son, Basil, in 1915 and a daughter, Rhoda, in 1917 that Annie joined her husband at the end of the railway line.

This was the setting for Rhoda's romance with her father – dubbed 'Sir Philip' by farmers in the region, as she asserts too insistently to be convincing. So, as 'our lying-down mother', she fills out the memory-dream into which she wanders away from household routine. On the edge of Namaqualand her father sings by candlelight to four children. Her mother holds dances in the cleared dining room of the hotel; she hangs cheeses from the ceiling of her separate kosher kitchen; and

Engagement photo, *c.* 1914, of Philip Press from Lithuania
and Annie Hoffman, born in Johannesburg, 1892

receives a gift of home-grown tomatoes from 'the Giantess'
who farms in the *kloof* in the Matzikamma Mountains behind
Klaver. Rhoda remembers the gloaming light on the oranges
deep in the *kloof*, a waterfall and the stinkwood furniture: a long
black table, so polished it reflects three bowls of violets.

But Annie damped this down with calls to the nanny to
smarten up her daughter and brush her hair. Annie's crassness
knew no bounds. Rhoda likes to repeat her mother's put-down
of the Parthenon during a tour of Europe: 'I'm sure to *crich*

[toil] up there to see a *Goi-ish-ke* cathedral.' Granny's Yiddish is limited to a few dismissive words, and distorted by the vehemence of a South African accent.

'You're only a *pfefferil* [peppercorn]': her emphatic fs blow me away if I offer an unwelcome opinion.

Granny has no idea what others think or feel, and this makes her a very happy person. A child can nest in this easy insensitivity. There are no undercurrents of need. Her chat has the confidence of a woman at home in her life.

When Annie reaches her eighties her daughter asks her, 'What was the best time in your life?'

'Now, of course,' is her answer.

Basil (left), Sydney and Rhoda, *c.* 1920, in front of the hotel built by their father when the railway was extended to Klaver.
'Three Little Pigs' is Sydney's caption in Rhoda's album

This absence of reflection comes to me as comfort. I associate it with the plumped-up pillows and puffy eiderdown of my grandmother's high double bed, which I share during her long stays with us. She's soft when she unsnaps her corset, warm and round with long breasts from feeding children. I lie at rest, released from the tension of my mother's face, her fear of that beast lurking in the corners of her room, the blue brush with its strong bristles, the jug of water waiting at her elbow, the glass and pills that she may or may not take.

Granny's domain is the large front bedroom, which for some reason we call the top room, though there's no upstairs. The top room is furnished in Rhoda's feminine style. A white muslin bedspread with gathers at the side over a pale pink under-slip covers what was Granny's marriage bed, and where she gave birth four times, tugging (she will tell me when I'm old enough to hear) on a sheet tied to the post at the foot of the bed. There's a rose carpet, and above hangs a curly chandelier painted a faint white.

For a brief spell, it had been our parents' room, before an attack happened there. It was prompted, Rhoda hints, by an unwilling move from Rhodean, her family home since they left Namaqualand. In 1945 she was taken from shady, old-fashioned Oranjezicht and stuck in the glare of Sea Point, with coloured lights strung up on a sea-front hotel and cocktail parties in its palm-filled garden. It suits Harry to be close to the beaches, where bodies stretch out under the sun, turning from back to front or front to back as on a spit. Displaced amidst housewives who invite her to morning cards, Rhoda withdraws into Wordsworth's 'bliss of solitude', fortified by *The Bible Designed to be Read as Literature*.

Harry is cock-a-hoop because he's acquired a house for five thousand pounds. It doesn't occur to him that it's not such a scoop if his wife dislikes it. Too ill to view the house in time, she's dismayed to find herself planted in a thirties box with little natural light, darkened further by a hideous red curtain at the end of a passage. Our house, 11 Avenue Normandie, is in an area of Sea Point called Fresnaye. The avenues, named in the seventeenth century by Huguenot refugees, rise perpendicularly up the increasingly steep slope of Lion's Head. My mother confides that her secret name for our house is 'Upwards'. Secret it has to be, because a way-station on an allegorical climb would be out of place in a suburb where houses and streets have European names like Bellevue and King's Road.

After the top-room attack, our parents move to a back room opposite the nursery. One night in the nursery, I wake to sounds never heard before. Not, this time, a call for help, but almost inhuman cries, coming from my mother. I know at once this is the thing she's feared: the full-on, unstoppable thing. Between the cries, there's our father's courtroom voice. This time I don't run to her, but lie petrified. Am I a coward to leave it to our father, who can't console her? No one can. No doctor is called; Harry is handling this on his own, trying to quiet her. The cries die down and the next day my mother is sunk in a half-daze. She can barely speak, and escapes from time to time into sleep. I tiptoe to see if she's all right. If I don't open the door softly she will stir and cry, 'Oh, NO-O-O.' The feminine touches to her room, the white moonflowers in a dainty vase, the rose lampshade and the pale pink bed-jacket knitted in a lacy pattern, are futile against the attack of the beast.

After our parents vacate the top room, Granny installs her glass-topped dressing table with an oval, swinging mirror and her massive three-door wardrobe packed with hats, sunshades and a fox fur with paws, bead eyes and snout. It has a strange, chemical smell when I put my nose to it to feel its softness.

On summer nights, with windows open to the murmur of the sea and the salt-smell of seaweed, moths and brown, hard-winged Christmas beetles fly towards the lamp. When I hear the click as one knocks blindly against the wall or wardrobe, or see the flutter of a moth, I cry and duck.

'It can't hurt you,' I'm told, but I flee all the same.

'Wait, I'll catch it,' Rhoda says, cupping her hands. Gently, she carries the fluttering creature to the window, opens her palms and frees it into the night.

She takes seriously the Commandment: Thou shalt not kill. Her respect for creatures is in keeping with a creative spirit that rolls through all things. She draws out what she expects to find in all small children: a moral sense, untrammelled as yet by the prison house.

Her absolutes are as striking as the poems and psalms she reads aloud, and I puzzle over certain contradictions: the sticky fly-papers, for instance, dangling from the kitchen ceiling, stuck about with the black spots of dead flies. Though the kitchen is not my mother's scene, she must have seen them. Or does she block from her line of vision what she doesn't care to see? And although we are by no means rich, and although too my mother, cherishing books and memorabilia, scorns 'shop-bought' – mass-produced – goods, she does buy the best when it comes to quality of clothing or linen or food. Money, I slowly realise, can't be as irrelevant as it seems in a house filled with women – grandmother, wife, daughter, female servants – where the man of the house leaves for the office. Rhoda's three brothers are 'in business': they have a growing chain of clothing and houseware stores called Edgars, yet Rhoda exempts them from her abhorrence of getting and spending. For she loves them, and more: she's proud of their enterprise, and overrides her contempt for commerce with praise for her brothers' probity.

As a girl of my generation, from whom little is expected, I'm imbued with my mother's liberating counter-commerce ideals, reinforced by her younger brothers' veneration of books. For many active men in our provincial society, books mean little:

snippets in the *Reader's Digest* for white males like my father or, for black youths in the townships, the *skiet en donder* routines in high-rise cities across the ocean. Aspiring men choose to be doctors or lawyers or accountants, hardly ever scholars or editors or writers.

My father is the son of a dairyman. His school, the South African College School, is lucky enough to have its own Rhodes scholarship to Oxford. Sport is a condition of this scholarship, and since the top boy in his class plays no sport Harry, who comes second, is in line to win it. He has no regrets for deciding not to apply. Bright enough, confident, articulate, yet with no taste for superfluous learning, he shares the view of his mother that Oxford is a luxury he can't afford. For Thekla, a British university is off the map. She comes from Latvia. Small, pretty, her white hair neatly combed away from her face and secured with hairpins, she admires three grandsons, Peter, Gerald and Neville, who greet her with smiles and good-natured ease.

'Good boys, well brought up,' Thekla nods over their heads to their mothers who are her twin daughters.

I'm a little dashed not to be included in Thekla's favour, and have no hope of a share in the neat features of my father's family. To my uneasy feelers, Thekla appears on the lookout for lapses when it comes to Ps and Qs.

Gerald, Peter and Neville are the handsomest boys I've ever seen. My father has that same kind of masculinity, born of the beach, sun, jokes, normality. Gerald is two years older than I. At his house, 21 Avenue Protea, higher up on Lion's Head, he asks, 'Shall we play rude doctor-doctor?' and introduces a twist of plasticine to my bottom. My mother is appalled and reproachful when she discovers it at bath-time. All the same, I'm ready to play again. One summer afternoon we cool off in the sprinkler on Gerald's back lawn. I haven't brought a bather, so wear

one of his. He invites neighbouring boys to inspect a naked girl.
I'm game to show off in a hollow of the hedge where no one
else can see.

Gerald is with my mother and me when we go on a ten-day
holiday to Monica's vineyard. It's on a hill in the wine region
of Stellenbosch. We play in the long, sun-stroked grass on the
summit of the hill, but one morning wake to find an infestation
of moths all over the farmhouse.

'Would you rather die or have fifty moths on you?' Gerald
asks.

It's hard to choose. 'I want to go home,' I beg my mother.

She gets up and encloses a moth in her palms, then slowly
opens them to show how beautiful the creature is with its folded
wings. When it's still, I concede its beauty, but when it grows
frightened and flutters, I scream and run.

Back home I hear on the wireless a different tale from the
domestic or orphan's stories my mother tells. 'The Adventure
of the Speckled Band' by Conan Doyle is my first horror story,
enhanced by sinister sound effects. They tune up my fears of
insects with a new fear of poisonous snakes. Might a snake, like
the one in the tale, slide through the high-up ventilator leading
into the top room from the stoep where, in summer, lizards
cling like scaly hyphens to the walls? This becomes my pet fear;
Lenie has to check under the bed to make sure no snake lurks
there. A nightmare sends me rushing to my parents' room. It's
dangerous for my mother to be jolted awake so I am told to
wake my father very quietly, to say, 'It's me' and to get into his
bed. After a while his arm feels like iron under my head, and I
slide out and return to the top room. The worst that can
happen is to hear my mother groan, 'Oh NO!' It means I've
woken her to an actual nightmare: fear of an attack. Her terror
is lodged in me.

There's a different dread on Sundays when I'm taken for a

stroll with my father along the bustling seafront. Here I'm exposed to comment on my face when my cheery father turns away, every so often, to greet people who listen in to his Saturday radio broadcast on *Sports Roundup*. As soon as I'm idling on my own, children, from a safe distance, yell 'freckle face'. Is that me? It has to be, for who else – certainly no one in sight – is so splotched with brown marks? These children assure me of a disfigurement others pretend not to notice.

Afterwards we visit Thekla in her flat in Gloucester Court, on the beach front at Three Anchor Bay. I sit on the edge of a stuffed chair, wary of touching the white crocheted covers protecting the headrests and arms of the lounge suite. Chopped herring is offered. It gives off a sour smell. I can't put the fishy mush in my mouth, so a wish to please compels me to accept one of Thekla's *taiglach*, though it looks like poo: a sticky brown kind of doughnut cooked so hard that milk teeth can only scratch at the surface. I lick it tentatively. Sugar. Unmelted crystals rasp my tongue. It's like licking a sugared rock.

Thekla has an air of no nonsense, a kind of not listening – different from my mother, who may be dreamy but can be relied on to take note of real trouble. Some years before, Thekla's daughter had a row with her husband when they were new to marriage. I picture his blazing red face as he shoves Aunt Lena out of the house and locks the door. No answer when she rings the bell and calls to be let in.

'What could I do?' Aunt Lena relays this scene to my mother, who feels for the wrongs of women. 'I ran home to my parents. My mother didn't want to hear: "Go straight back," she said. "That's your home now." That taught me a lesson.'

To manage on a modest income from the dairy, Thekla had trained her five children to switch off unnecessary lights and limit hot water in baths. Harry calls Rhoda's attention to waste. She listens patiently to Thekla's grumbles, and explains to me afterwards that surviving, for Thekla and her like, has been too hard to take a wider view. She means a wider view of all she herself cares for: the arts, nature, horizons to be crossed – the travel now closed to her.

Lying in bed with her windows wide open and whenever she ventures outside the house, she opens my senses to what is time-less: the roll of the sea; the rocky crag of Lion's Head rearing above the avenues bumping up its lower slope. Rhoda is awake to the stir of thoughts and feelings in the smallest child. It isn't instinctual or textbook or imitative mothering, and nor is it the busy nurture of mothers today. Mothers of her generation aren't busy, and Rhoda's invalidism allows her to be less busy than most. Contact is not a matter of quality time; there's quiet, a readiness on hold so that a spark can fire spontaneously. Then Rhoda's blue eyes glow, she sits up, looks intently at the child and stills the child's attention as she switches into narrative mode. Family stories pour out. This telling is a ritual: it's not the biographical search for authenticity that I learn later; it's a re-telling, shoring up family myths that declare where we come from and who she is.

Rhoda mythologises the past of her father's family, helped by its distance in the Old Country. 'My father sometimes lamented that his children lived in a different world from his.' Philip Press (in Lithuania the name was Pres) came from a town called Plunge or, in the form he used, Plungian. 'Plum Jam', his chil-dren would joke. Rhoda pictures the inhabitants of Plum Jam as rare and gentle beings singing Yiddish lullabies. She sings her father's lullaby about raisins and almonds – *rozhinkes mit mand-len* – in such plaintive strains that we indulge in rather pleasurable sadness.

The facts, discovered later, are that in 1941 the Nazis rounded them up with the help of Lithuanian neighbours, shut the entire

community of eighteen hundred Jews in their wooden synagogue for two weeks without air, food or water, and then shot
the survivors into three great pits they'd had to dig for themselves in Kausanai forest. It's only one of numerous killing fields.
Three generations later my journalist daughter Olivia, sent by
a magazine to trace her family, will visit the pits surrounded by
silver birches. Olivia, weeping, will light candles there and keep
the matches to this day.

Philip Press, an immigrant, felt that his children lived in a different world.
Surrounded here by his South African wife and children, from left:
Hubert, Annie, Basil, Rhoda and Sydney

Olivia, right, lights a candle, accompanied by Jacob Bunka (left) and
his wife (standing). The only Plunge Jew to survive, Bunka
was away in 1941, fighting in the Russian army

In the absence of facts, Rhoda retells her father's memories.
Even Press poverty is romantic in her eyes: her father's mother,
dropping her hands in her lap when she's unable to afford more
thread to sew caps for country fairs. As a boy, when he was ill,
his father brought him one grape.

'One?' I ask, thinking of a mound of golden *hanepoot* grapes
on the autumn table. Amongst the vineyards of the Cape such
deprivation is strange.

'In that cold, northern world one grape was luxury,' Rhoda
says gravely. I see the scene but can't get inside it. She believes
the intensity of her otherness comes from those far-away people
with expansive souls.

Her mother's family, the Hoffmans, are decidedly not soulful. They sing together at the piano, 'ta-ra-ra-*boom*-de-jay'; they rollick through songs of the Anglo-Boer War ('We are marching to Pretoria'). As children, they and their parents took off in the reverse direction: they caught what they claim to have been the last civilian train out of Johannesburg bound for Cape Town, a thousand miles to the south, where British troops were landing. Their father, Jacob Hoffman, imported British woollens, suitable for the rainy winters and windy nights at the Cape.

The three Hoffman sisters in Cape Town:
Annie (top), Minnie (left) and Betsie

His jolliest daughter is the youngest, Auntie Betsie, whose fingers perform extra trills on the keys; her bracelets tinkle as she
bounces up from the final chord. Rhoda loves her aunts but
thinks their eldest sister, her mother Annie, small-minded.

'Why are you reading?' her mother asks. 'You're not in
school.'

Little is said of Betsie's eldest daughter, my mother's cousin
Cynthia, who lives in England. Photos show her to be in the
Hoffman mould, and yet she doesn't entirely fit that mould.
Buxom, tightly packed into a uniform during the war, Cynthia
married an Englishman and now writes stories – romances set
in the Namaqualand of her childhood – that are broadcast on
the radio. Because Cynthia's stories are read on the BBC's Light
Programme, Rhoda dismisses them as light-weight. I don't
know if she read them or not. I think not, because Rhoda,
along with the rest of the family, shuns Cynthia for marrying
out of the faith.

When her name comes up, they say in told-you-so tones,
'Poor Cynthia has to scrub her floors.' Servants' work, that's
what comes of marrying an Englishman like tall Mr Hind.
Photos of him in army uniform had revealed little – or little
satisfactory to Cynthia's family back home who assume that she
writes for pocket money, which this husband can't provide.

Her parents relent when Cynthia produces a baby. I'm eight
years old when she's invited to bring little Michael Hind home
on a visit. He's adorable, with a round moon face and fluffs of
white hair. I want to seize and squeeze him in my arms, but he's
glued to his mother's lap, wary of strangers inspecting him,
Cynthia's English-looking child. Grown-ups' talk of scrubbing
floors in straitened, post-war England has led me to expect a
downcast Cynthia, but she's sturdy and humorous. To her, I'm
neither a child-confidante, as with my mother, nor a *pfefferil*, as

with Granny Annie, nor plain and awkward as with Granny Thekla. Cynthia talks to me like a motherly friend.

In after years, when I'm grown-up and a writer too, Cynthia makes a low aside at a family party on a stoep one starry night at Basil's house: writing, she says, has been her delight, though none of them, including Rhoda, take any notice. This isn't an instance of jealousy, because that's not part of Rhoda's character. I think it has more to do with her myth-making. Cynthia won't fit Rhoda's bifurcation of hereditary traits to prove how exercise of the mind derives exclusively from her father's side. Of course, it's common enough for people to define family in this divided way, but Rhoda's stories are repeated with so much conviction that her myth has prevailed.

As a child I'm filled with my mother's barely veiled boredom when men jabber about business, the same boredom that deadens the air around my father when he and swimming cronies put heads together over stopwatches. I will never settle for such a man, I promise myself. And then I glance in the mirror and see that I may have even less choice in the matter than my mother did.

I watch her put on make-up, as she stands short-sightedly peering at her serious blue eyes and high nose in the mirror of the three-corner cupboard in the bathroom. There's rouge in a small round pot and a tube of red lipstick. Too red. It's like putting on a mask before she can be seen by a visitor, who might at any moment pop in, or even by the gardener or the women who come to the door seeking work.

'Are you reliable?' she asks. 'Do you have a reference?'

And then the woman fumbles in her bag and holds out a battered bit of paper. If it's a man, it's shaming to see the excessive humility of his hunched shoulders as he cups both hands to receive the ten-shilling note my mother offers. Before the bell starts ringing, my mother parts her hair on the side and puts a finger along the unruly bits to make them wavy not wiry. She pats down and scrunches her brown curls, and if not in a hurry, rolls up a lock in a bendy brown curler to make it behave.

If favoured friends arrive, my mother exerts herself. She gets up and rather tiredly slips on a dress. Her thinness looks frail but passes for feminine delicacy in the turquoise muslins or shades of tea-rose she likes to wear. I trail along as she carefully clicks open the side door of my grandmother's Edwardian tea trolley, with its brass trim and rounded glass, which stands in our dining room. And gently, one by one, she lifts out a set of fragile teacups, thin porcelain with pink and mauve sweet peas on a faintly blushing background. My mother prizes this design for dispensing with the vulgarity of gold rims. Her word for over-decoration is something like 'berahtig' – sounding the 'g' with friction at the back of the throat, as in the Afrikaans of her early schoolroom. I think she's inventing her version of a Yiddish word without knowing Yiddish. Once she'd make a word her own, I and other listeners must lend our ears as best we can.

She relishes words that are expressive, pausing over them, rolling them around her tongue, including the humorously rude or pithy words in the tales of Chaucer's fourteenth-century pilgrims – 'likerous', more expressive than 'wanton', in the portrait of the eighteen-year-old wife in the Miller's tale, who has a 'likerous' eye. It charms me when my mother, telling a story, takes on a character unlike her own: the lasciviousness of the Miller's wife or the punitive hatred of Jane Eyre's guardian, Mrs Reed.

No one outside the house would know that she's ill. I watch a brave performance, her role as wife and mother and what goes with it: household, nursery, guests, servants. Concealed in this casing, along with illness, is a many-shaded freakishness that co-exists with her visions.

With Rhoda on the windy shore at Muizenberg

I partake of the freakish aspect, am shaped by it, yet have no access, as yet, to its secrets. Meanwhile, I lean on the insensibility of Granny Annie and my sporting father who provide a cast-iron armour of normality. The daily marvel of their oblivion is the ease with which they don't see what they don't have to see. I'm less adept at concealment than my mother. The deception of normality – barely convincing as I know it to be – makes me ill at ease with Granny Thekla and other members of my father's family.

My mother broods darkly, in a way that can provoke an

attack. Although it's not possible to press her with questions, the extremes of her self-portrait leave a gap between the other-world illumination of her childhood and what she terms, in her cryptic way, 'suffering' and 'illness'. Each word comes freighted with explosive: the danger of what actually took place. It's her way to hint – a nightmare journey to Europe; misguided doctors; a young man who died – so that I peer ineffectually through a fog of unfocused feeling made up of pity with a pinch of alarm. If only I could calm her; give her pleasure. In a small way it contents her that I fall in love with *A Child's Garden of Verses*: I know by heart 'how do you like to go up in a swing', and 'on goes the river', bearing the child's paper boats to 'other little children' who'll 'bring my boats ashore', and the invalid child who lives in his imaginary 'Land of Counterpane'. My mother is drawn to writers like Robert Louis Stevenson, who contend with illness.

All she will say about the onset of her own illness was that it 'befell' her at the age of seventeen, and that it was bound up with a bereavement. Who was it she had lost? There is an air of things that happened before I was born, an air that her real life is over – as though her lips are kissing her hand to a person I can't see.

3

'Illness Was My Teacher'

The first week of July 1944: I'm told a baby is due. At the age of two and a half, I accompany my mother to a one-storey nursing home in the Gardens. On a glassed-in stoep there's a row of prams. In each lies a newborn, and while Rhoda talks to Matron I skip from pram to pram, in love with the babies whose eyes squint up as I loom above them and bend to look. It's hard to choose, but at length I settle on the one for me. When Rhoda emerges, I too am ready to go, my hands curled round the handle of the pram.

Matron's determined fingers are prising mine off the handle, and then I'm crying because she won't let me take my baby. The cries gain in volume along Upper Orange Street, as the bus climbs the lower slope of Table Mountain. All the way I'm wailing 'Where's the baby?' to my shushing mother, who's seated with a cauliflower atop her pregnant mound.

At this time, before our move to Sea Point, we live with my grandmother, Annie Press, at Rhodean, in the mountain suburb of Oranjezicht above the town. While Rhoda is away at the nursing home, I trot beside Granny down Forest Road, which falls steeply towards the Reservoir. Granny, her pale auburn hair neatly waved, wears a mauve linen dress, buttoned down the front. It has padded shoulders, like the outfit Granny wears when she marches in Adderley Street with the WAAFS.

'I was the only one in step,' Granny reports proudly.

Rhoda often repeats this, laughing. She has a hoard of stories pointing up her mother's blithe oblivion.

I'm content next to the confident swell of Granny's chest and her purposefulness, for she's carrying a jar of home-made chicken soup, the panacea of Jewish mothers. It's to build up her daughter's strength after the birth of my brother Pip. Granny exudes bounty and optimism. But soon after Rhoda returns to Rhodean with the baby, she's beyond the reach of comfort. There's a hush around her.

My grandmother tells me not – *not*, her forefinger raised – to go into my mother's room in the mornings. I stand in the passage outside her door, afraid that something is being done to her – too awful for a child to know. One morning the silence is so heavy that I manage to turn the handle with both hands and burst into darkness. The curtains are drawn against the invading sun. As my eyes adjust, I see my mother prone on the bed, face down, and a stranger leaning over her. What's going on turns out to be massage. Relief runs down my open throat and dangling arms, the first of many occasions when a hush around Rhoda is scarier than fact.

My father, wearing trousers with a funny name, white ducks, reports to Granny that Rhoda 'gave way' in the doctor's office. She fell down. The doctor says she might get well if she goes away; the hushed word 'Valkenberg' crosses the air between the grown-ups. I wonder anxiously if my mother will go far away and not come back. 'If she can't control herself,' they say.

When I'm older she will tell me a lot more about that day in

November 1944 when my brother was four months old: the day she believed that she was mad.

She speaks eloquently, as though she's told this to herself many times. 'Hope died. I lay on the bare boards of the back-bedroom floor. To lift myself seemed as impossible as lifting one's dead body from under the earth. But I forced myself up, and saw a hooded moon through the window above the back door.

'I went out and looked at the grass, the phlox growing in the garden and the contour of Table Mountain against the sky. Then I walked into my bedroom where Auntie Betsie was drying Pip after his bath. I lifted my baby, and walked up and down singing to him a farewell tune. And during that song, "It" passed away and I was released. To be free of terror was strange as a dream.'

So she didn't have to go away.

Our rented house in Cromer Road, Muizenberg, where we spend the summer, is called Sun Blest. It has a trellis with a creeper over the front, which shades the stoep and keeps it cool. The stoep runs round the house to one side, where the nursery I share with Pip opens on to it through folding doors and shutters. Sunlight slants through half-open shutters onto the floor. Two years later I watch the play of light from my bed, because Pip, aged two and a half, and I, turned five, have temperatures.

The local doctor, interrupts the dreamy haze. He orders my mother to take off my pyjama bottoms and put me on a pink potty. 'Make a weh-wee,' he commands in a funny accent, bending down and fixing his eyes on me. I feel stripped, and hate him too much to produce what he wants.

After he goes away, my mother comes back to the nursery with a fat book under her arm, the book she's reading all summer: *Joseph and his Brothers* by Thomas Mann. Sitting on my bed, she tells the story of Joseph and his coat of many colours. In the first

volume, she says, Joseph is thrown into a pit. A shaft of sun pen-
etrates the shutter, and I can see from the cast of Rhoda's face that
she's in a pit of her own. Joseph is lying at the bottom, thrown
down and left to die by jealous half-brothers. It would have been
the end of him had not God brought him up out of the pit.

The narrative goes on, a serial, day by day: how traders find
Joseph and sell him into slavery, and how Joseph, as prophetic
dreamer in the house of Potiphar, rises to become a power in
the land of Egypt. My mother looks tired but I beg her not to
stop. As she yields and takes a fresh breath, 'and then ... ' –
breath – 'and that's not all ... ', she looks intently into her listener's eyes, and yes I'm listening all right. Pity, which includes
pity for the teller, carries the story through my veins: the darkness of the pit, the horror of Joseph to find himself there (he,
his father's adored child), and the power of dreaming.

With each additional 'and' of biblical narrative, the story rises
to crisis, and behind it beats the ancient family tension of two
mothers: wives of the patriarch Jacob, who happen to be sisters.

I'm troubled by the fate of Leah, the elder of the two and
mother of the murderous brothers. Knowing that Joseph is des-
tined to be saved, I'm sorrier for Leah, who wasn't chosen
because she wasn't pretty. Plain, unwanted Leah with her weak
eyes – a handicap in the ancient world where there's no such
thing as spectacles. Jacob worked seven years for Leah's pretty
younger sister Rachel, and when, as he thought, Rachel was
given to him in marriage, he removes the bridal veil and discovers Leah. Tricked, Jacob has to work another seven years for
the bride he really wants.

Rhoda's sympathies lean to Rachel: her sensitivity and physical fragility, making childbirth difficult, and leading to an early
death as Jacob and his retainers travel with their flocks through
the desert. Jacob grieves for Rachel and dotes on her two sons,
Joseph and Benjamin, stirring hatred in Joseph's brethren.

'But Leah . . . ?' I remind my mother, who allows and some-times invites a child to reach into the story.

She stops to think. What she sees is a wife who tries to win Jacob through her fertility: many strong sons, the preferred gender. The name for Leah's first baby, Reuben, is a call to her husband: 'Re-u! Ben! See, a son!'

Rhoda is matter-of-fact about the fecund Leah. She hastens on with the chosen son: Joseph guided in his dreams by the hand of God. It's a story of the innocent victim and his ulti-mate transcendence. The crease between her brows, the intentness of her inward eye, tells me there's more to the story than the story. Her voice resonates with private import. Dreaming is prophecy, and prophecy is power. Political power for Joseph; inner power for Rhoda, a compensation of sorts for the blight of illness and the constraints of an existence between Rhoda's mother and husband who are temperamentally untroubled, content to manage around this dark space they will not attempt to understand.

At Sun Blest my mother stands at the front door with her husband's parents, his twin sisters and their handsome boys. Civil too. They need no prompting to thank Auntie Rhoda for tea. Neither mannered nor careless, they carry themselves already with a manly ease that makes me shy. The sheen of their future popularity daunts me and I try to look away, expecting to remain unchosen. It's enough that such boys should grace our garden: I see them from an inner space, which I'd die rather than reveal, and look to my mother for the conviction she brings to this space by way of poems and tales. As a reader, she's at liberty to live all over the place, and I follow where she goes. She takes me to places where females long in vain for love, sac-rifice themselves and find themselves defeated: Hans Christian Andersen's little mermaid and his little match girl, or the far

At Sun Blest. Rhoda (on right), ill, made an effort with
visitors Granny Thekla and Grandfather Louis (back).
In the centre is Granny Annie, holding Pip

north where Gerda must travel to melt the ice in the eye of her
beloved with her warm tears.

Our visitors are not in the know about Rhoda's illness, nor
could they have told from looking at her. She wears a cotton
frock, striped blue to match her eyes, with a wide collar.
Tendrils of curly hair blow about her head and, as the camera
clicks, she's putting up a hand to smooth her flapping collar.
That's what others see, but I've learnt to detect the effort she
must make to appear normal.

On the stoep Pip is reading *Tootle* upside down: the story of a merry little engine with a top hat of a funnel who goes off the rails. Like Pip himself, later, when he's running in a little boys' race at Clovelly, our father's golf club. Pip's so braced against the wind, ribs lifted and face back, arms pumping from side to side, that he will veer off course into watching clumps of parents.

I'm jealous of Pip because he's smiling and lovable in his miniature-man pullover designed by Auntie Betsie's daughters, Berry and Garda, who have knitted the letters PIP in white wool into a blue front. The letters stretch over his swelling pigeon chest, and as we walk along the promenade strangers call out 'Hullo, Pip!'

That summer when I'm five, I run away. Without a plan, I set forth one afternoon past the faded, peeling bathing boxes, past Tubby's hot-dog stand, under the raised booms and past Muizenberg station, in the direction of St James with its tidal

Pip and me on the seesaw at Tubby's beach,
near the railway station at Muizenberg

pool, appealing to children because it's tamer than the open sea. The narrow coastal road at the foot of the mountains runs so close to the sea that my route is simple to follow: the waves to the left; grand houses to the right (including, tucked amongst them, Rhodes's thatched cottage, preserved as a museum – a landmark on drives but hardly visited by summer visitors who come down in droves from Johannesburg). I whiz along in a mood of adventure, exhilarated to be on my own. Another little girl is playing on a swing in the garden of a big house. I cross the road, open the gate and call out, 'Can I come and play?' And then, happily, I swing up and down to lines my mother has read aloud so often I know them by heart:

> How do you like to go up in a swing,
> Up in the air so blue . . .
> Up in the air and over the wall,
> Till I can see so wide . . .

Flying on the upward beat, pumping higher with bent knees, what I'm seeing is not the quiet countryside observed by Robert Louis Stevenson. I see the heaving ocean, its curling waves with exquisitely menacing undersides of palest green as they rise to their crest and crash back into troughs of dark blue. Our father was out there on long-distance swims when he was young. Women swimmers must have outdistanced him because he's still peeved at women for an unfair advantage: a layer of fat under the skin that keeps them warm.

I swing until John, the Xhosa gardener, finds me and carries me home on his high shoulders.

The rituals of Muizenberg are fixed. In the afternoon the wind comes up and blows the sand about, so it's a morning place. In the morning we swim in the sea, and at lunchtime I throw on my sundress over a damp costume and forget to rinse it. Salty costumes, gritty with sand, hang over the rails of the stoep and dry in half an hour. We stamp the sand off our feet outside the front door, or, if it's caked on our calves, rinse them under the garden tap. The sea makes us hungry, and Lenie serves the main meal of the day at lunchtime: grilled chops and peas, followed by fruit salad. After lunch my mother breaks off an oblong of Fry's chocolate and nibbles delicately.

'Eat slowly,' she says, handing over a piece, 'and if you wait ten minutes the urge for more will pass.'

On weekends, if Rhoda is too ill to get up in the morning, our father, barefoot, his knobby toes slightly turned in (he claims this helps in swimming races), leads the way to the beach, stopping for ice-creams. Pip and I lick them under our white

Our father, Harry, went barefoot whenever he could.
On summer weekends he often took care of us

hats, held in place with elastic under our dripping chins. Granny, in her wrap-around beach gown, drapes towels across our chests. When the door closes on my mother, there's this support system, carrying me from that secret space of trial to the norms of the seaside.

During the summer months of December and January, Jews congregate at Muizenberg: the fortunate descendants of refugees from Lithuania, and more recent refugees – the last to escape before South Africa blocked immigration in 1933 – who come together to shake heads over nightmare rumours from Europe and sing yearning songs like 'My Yiddishe Mamma'.

The hot breath of sentiment makes me squirm. I can't admit that 'My Yiddishe Mamma' leaves me cold, since my mother and others accept that sentiment is called for, if only as respect for refugees. But to take it in feels like manipulation, something I will never manage to tolerate, whether it be these plaintive strains or the words of ads or pop songs. My body seizes up against their insistent, hypnotic beat. It feels as instinctual as a different rhythm in the blood. Generally, for my mother, the sounds of untruth jar more, as though nerve endings detecting what's false stand to attention.

In the privacy of her room she tells me what she can't say to others: how fiercely she rejects false authorities, doctors who don't admit their ignorance of her condition and professors who say what critics say. Once, she relates, she made the effort to sit in on a professor's class on T. S. Eliot, because she loves the poems so; and he, the head of English at the university, said there, in front of the class: this woman is not schooled in the New Criticism, ergo, she's reading wrongly. If you are a house-wife in the forties, if you live where she does, there's no place to say what you think. Only in your own room; only to a lis-tening child.

Was it solitude that developed her sensitivity to truth? This question comes only later when I read Virginia Woolf's essay 'On Being Ill': 'what ancient and obdurate oaks are uprooted in us by the act of sickness'. She makes bold to seize one gain of long illness, its potent subversiveness.

On rare afternoons when my mother is up to it, she takes Pip and me to one or other of the three shelly beaches between Muizenberg and St James. This is a treat because you descend into a white tunnel under the train line that winds around the inlets along the False Bay coast, all the way to the British naval base at Simonstown. The tunnel echoes and magnifies the sound of the ocean; at its far end is a vision of the blue rim of the sea melting into a clear blue sky, and then, as you emerge, there are rocks interspersed with pools big and small, covered with fronds of green seaweed. It's a water-baby paradise.

When she reads aloud from *The Water Babies*, published in grimy Victorian London, I stare at the colour plate of the sooty little sweep, Tom, descending through the chimney into Ellie's gauzy bedroom: the astonishing sight of middle-class comfort. We follow Tom's transformation into a water-baby, along with other fantasy babies in their snug home pools.

My mother suggests that we prepare a water-baby pool for the likes of Tom to discover. I imagine his delight to find a cradle (a rocking shell) waiting for him and inside it a lump of smoothed green glass for a pillow, a silvery 'Venus ear' for a looking glass and curtains made of frilly fronds of green sea-weed.

One afternoon my mother collects a party of children play-ing on the beach and sets up a competition to see who can create the loveliest water-baby pool. I can't now recall who won because winning didn't matter, only an intense absorption, when you become what you make. You hear it in a child's hum – my mother called it a 'cosmic hum'. It's a kind of bliss that has visited me again two or three times in an adult life as a writer – once, tuned to the surges of Eliot's sea-quartet, *The Dry Salvages*.

The shelly beaches are afternoon beaches: no swimming here; the rocks lie close together and sometimes, at high tide, there's almost no sand. The wonder of these beaches lies in their secrecy, smallness and tidal obliteration: no names; no signs; simply steps down to the damp, rather smelly tunnel and a rising anticipation if the tide is low: the chance to hunt the rarest treasures: an anemone waving its salmon tendrils in a rock pool and sucking your finger; a shell with the roar of the sea when you put it to your ear; the Venus ear with its dotted curve and, on the inside, a pearly sheen of silver-grey-pink; and the round green shell of the sea urchin, so fragile it's a triumph to find one intact.

'Close your eyes,' Rhoda says, 'and count how many sounds you can hear.' Concentrating on sound alone, I hear more than one might with eyes open: the gulls of course; the whirr of a fishing rod as a solitary fisherman on a rock reels in his catch; footsteps along the cement floor of the tunnel; the whine of a dog tugging on its leash; the tickety-tack of a passing train and cries coming my way that make me open my eyes to look up at black children in the third-class tail of the train, who are waving from the window as they sweep by.

4

Orphans and Stories

Early readers. Some of Rhoda's library children at the Jewish Orphanage in Oranjezicht in the forties. At the back of the orphanage grounds, with Table Mountain behind them

A short walk from Rhodean is the Cape Jewish Orphanage, filled to capacity during the war. Not all the children are orphans; some have parents who can't keep them; some were evacuees during the Blitz. They are housed in a three-storey building backing on to Table Mountain, and in its shadow. Each floor is in a different architectural style: arches below; columns for the entrance floor, up flight upon flight of steps; and Dutch gables ornamenting the dormitory floor. This melange of designs manages to shut off sunlight from the main hall. Two branching stairways lead to separate wings for girls and boys. There's a largely deserted playing field on one side, which has the look of a space that exists to show what's provided.

No fun to play here, I think as we pass, because it's exposed like a vast, empty tray plonked on a grass slope, a strip of manicured mountain sheering down to Montrose Avenue – too steep for rolling.

Inside, the orphanage is very clean with an odour of polish. The salty, seaweed tang of peninsula air, tossed about by winds, can't blow through small, out-of-reach windows. In my sister role, I accompany my mother who goes twice a week to run the library.

'Librar-ee . . . librar-ee . . . ' she sings up and down the long corridors, putting her head into dormitories with rows of whitewashed iron bedsteads and uniform white bedspreads. Her heels tap-tap along the polished floor.

Children come running, books under their arms. They cluster around as she asks them what books they like. *Biggles*, say the boys. *Pollyanna* or *Anne of Green Gables*, say the girls, who like to read about orphan girls whose opinions disconcert their elders. My mother fires up with eagerness to introduce them to the spark Jane Eyre keeps alive throughout her chilling and starving at Lowood charity school, and to another favourite, David Copperfield, the orphaned victim of Mr Murdstone.

'Mr Murdstone,' she says, drawing out the fearful first syllable, alarm in the cast of her face.

The children's eyes fix in reflected alarm as the bully torments the child; then, from deep within, questions well up. Questions about adult cruelty. Impossible questions because, towards the end of the war in Europe, the Allies come upon the Nazis' extermination camps, and there are no answers for Jewish children. It's enough that Rhoda takes up each question with attentive seriousness. A child who comes to this library has its beak open, ready. Each child gets a kiss when they line up to check books out.

It's not sentimental; more a ritual. 'Have you had your kiss?' Rhoda asks as though it's a right. Some return with a second book, to receive another kiss.

She also asks each one, 'Did you wash your hands?' Books are precious, to be handled with care.

The library is a musty room, long shut up, at the back of a disused wing. This wing, higher on the mountain, is set apart from the rest of the orphanage, and reached by a covered walkway from the dormitory floor. Here are empty classrooms with piles of Bibles, for this back wing had once served as a Hebrew school, and here boys approaching thirteen are prepared for bar mitzvah, undistracted by any outlook on an African mountain three thousand feet high with sunbeams playing across its woods and crest.

My mother, in purposeful mode, trailing children, tap-taps through a dank classroom with a key in her hand. As she unlocks the library the children crowd closer, and help to push open the reluctant door. All at once we're enfolded by what I've thought of ever since as the library smell – print and paper – with its promise of worlds to enter. I associate the enticing smell with books for my mother's generation: all the sequels to *Anne of Green Gables*, running to Anne's children in *Rilla of Ingleside*, where spoilt, lisping Rilla has to grow up when she adopts a baby with croup.

I run my finger over old-fashioned bindings, which have images tooled on them in gold or silver: the intrepid bull terrier from *Jock of the Bushveld* or chums wearing gym tunics in school

With Rhoda in town, *c.* 1945–6, on her way to the library.
She kept records of what the children read in her case

stories by Angela Brazil. Away at boarding school, English girls appear not to miss their mothers because they are level-headed and have their minds on midnight feasts and helping those in trouble. These self-sufficient chums in books I can't yet read and absorb at first through illustration will come back to me at the end of one Hilary term in Oxford in the late seventies, when a student brings a humorous present to his last tutorial: it's an old title by Angela Brazil, *The Jolliest Term On Record*.

*

Colonial settings abound in the old-time books of the orphanage library. I pore over pictures of the paddock at Misrule in *Seven
Little Australians*. These motherless children more or less look after
themselves, especially Judy, a creature of the wild who runs away
from boarding school. In the books I pull from the shelves, colonial girls in nowhere places, with no prospects and disempowered
as the weaker sex, dare to aspire. Their hopeful stories often start
with orphaning: in *Emily of New Moon*, Emily Byrd Starr is taken
in by maiden aunts living on Canada's Atlantic coast: Prince
Edward Island. Emily herself feels like an island, placed as she is
with people who lock away books as lifeless possessions. Or
there's Marie in *That Girl*, by Ethel Turner, who's orphaned and
then treated as a servant by the Australian couple who adopt her.
Marie is determined to be an actress. The novel ends with her
sailing away to fulfil her dream in the mother country. Katherine
Mansfield, sailing from Wellington to London in 1903, and Olive
Schreiner, sailing from Cape Town twenty years earlier, are real-
life versions of a colonial dream.

At the outset, this dream must have looked improbable,
which made their stories all the more telling for a girl like my
mother sprouting on the veld, to be asked – that unforgettable
question – why she's reading when she's not in school. *The Story
of an African Farm* was written in a leaking, lean-to room
assigned to the governess on an isolated farm. Feminist eloquence was not expected in such a place. Nor was it expected
that, under an umbrella, the governess would be writing a work
of literature that would leap provincial and colonial barriers.
This novel proved a sensation when it came out in London in
1883. Such were the narratives that shaped my mother as a girl,
and make her their natural custodian.

She isn't only a guide to reading; the stories she holds out are
also offerings of intimacy with her secret self. At the same time
as *The Little Locksmith* invites me into another world – the New

England of Katharine Butler Hathaway – I can't but see my
mother's closeness to the autobiography of a writer whose
imagination is sharpened by disability. This new book lies in its
plain blue cover next to my mother's bed, and she unveils the
mystery that surrounds the condition of the author as an invalid
child. The little girl is strapped flat to a stretcher for twenty-four
hours a day, and her neck is stretched upwards by a pulley.
Turning her head to one side, she sees a little locksmith at work,
and she feels kin to him because his deformity is what her regimen is intended to prevent.

'He's a hunchback,' Rhoda explains.

The word is never uttered in the author's home or in her
story, but when, at fifteen, she's allowed to get up, she looks in
the mirror and finds that she is, after all, the 'terrible word'. At
the time my mother reads this aloud, her own condition is still
unrevealed to her and a mystery to me. I delight in the bed-life
of this little American girl long ago: her cut-outs; the doll's
clothes she sews, edged with ruffles; her painting hair brown by
gaslight, then discovering by daylight it's purple. I try the experiment but electric light permits no mistake.

Katharine Butler resolves to give her life to writing: she's in
love with what she writes, as well as with her piled-up notes
and peerings into others' faces. None of this can be taken away
because she will not attempt publication. After her hunger for
experience is thwarted by her deformity, she can never again
risk disappointment. To enclose her writing life more securely,
she looks for a place of her own and finds the house of her
dreams in Castine, Maine. My mother partakes of this dream,
with a singing uplift on the second syllable when she says
'Castine'. Though she never sets eyes on the coast of Maine, it's
alive in her as a place where a quirky creature can dwell in possibility. In a similar way Emily, in *Emily of New Moon*, is open
to 'the flash'. My mother recalls her excitement to find a girl in

a book who'd had the same intimation that came to her as gold-smoke across the veld when she'd been a child of six sweeping the sand off the stoep.

I listen as one who's not up to 'the flash'. People remark how I look like my father, a sun-baked, outdoor look of readiness that's common at the Cape. I'm not rare, moonlike and fragile with large, glowing eyes like Emily who means to be a poet and is climbing 'the Alpine path' – taking her gift to its heights – in a sequel, *Emily Climbs*. This has been a model for my mother who, like Emily, 'scribbles' in secret and is suitably delicate with pale cheeks and crisp, dark curls.

From the start, in 1943, Rhoda prompts her library children to write by bringing out a magazine, *Oranjia*.* The idea grows out of Saturday afternoons at Rhodean, where children from the orphanage gather for debates, competitions, jokes, riddles and readings. Rhoda's first editorial declares her belief 'that to cultivate a taste for good literature by reading in youth is to invest in happiness: to provide ourselves with never-failing friends who open their hearts to us, teach us, entertain us, comfort us in loneliness and sorrow, and inspire and encourage us to realise our highest ideals'. She types up the contributions on her home typewriter, and includes her own triptych of orphanage scenes.

'Rachel' is about new arrivals, a thin, agitated girl and her younger brothers and sisters, holding on to one another's baggy garments. The 'big sister' Rachel wails in an exasperated-mother voice that the younger ones never leave her alone. Yet it becomes apparent that Rachel's duties are self-imposed; it's Rachel who follows them about, wiping noses, slapping, settling disputes. In the library, she won't join the other children looking at books and turning the pages of the *National Geographic*. Instead, she starts howling. The librarian promises her 'this will pass' by the

* Though everyone spoke of 'the orphanage', Oranjia was the official name.

time of her next visit, and Rachel licks up a tear. Sure enough, when next she appears in the library her unkempt bush of hair has been washed and tied back, and she's wearing a new dress, which she spreads out to sit. In an artificially polite voice to go with the dress, she returns to 'Miss' a book she'd taken on the quiet – a story of children going off on a ship. It has entranced her, and gradually, as Rachel's cheeks fill out to look like a child, a more natural voice emerges.

The second scene takes place in the orphanage nursery when the littlest ones are going to bed. Routines are disrupted by the excitement of a visitor from whom the children demand 'Story! Story!' The third scene is about a group of dreamy girls in their early teens who adore their dance teacher, Mrs S, and are thrilled to be invited to spend the day with her at her home. One of them, Lottie, is in a fever of expectation – Mrs S might come to know her awakening self – as their train winds to its dreamt-of destination along the ocean. Each of these scenes conveys deprivation through a child's imaginative longing to be seen, recognised, wanted.

One contribution to *Oranjia* is by a boy of ten, Louis Franks. The Jewish community in Worcester, a country town, has invited Louis, along with other children, for a holiday. Elated at the prospect of staying in a family home, Louis gazes out of the train window: 'I followed rivers with my eye until they disappeared ... At one part of the journey we went through a mountain pass.' Then the time comes to return to the orphanage. 'I did not look out of the window coming back,' Louis writes. 'I was too sad.'

On the cover of a 1946 issue is a photograph of Esther, a girl of six with a sprinkle of freckles across her nose and black hair cut in a straight fringe. My mother calls Esther 'a story-book girl', a phrase for her favourites.

What does it mean to be a story-book girl, I wonder jealously.

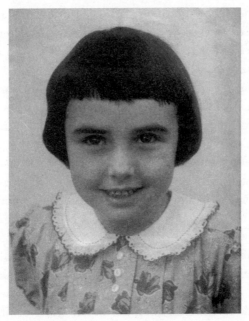

Esther on the cover of *Oranjia*

I'm never one, however keen on stories. Is it because I have a different role as a sister? Introducing me to strangers, my mother calls me 'a long John', a girl too tall for her age. I decide not to grow any more than can be helped. She explains that deprecation is her way of concealing maternal pride.

Two of my mother's special girls impress me because, in their early teens, they discuss the sayings of blind and deaf Helen Keller, which my mother proclaims in the library: 'The world is moved along, not only by the mighty shoves of its heroes, but also by ... the tiny pushes of each honest worker.'

Rosalind, aptly named with her rosy cheeks, has a lift to the corners of her mouth when she concurs in a smiley manner; if her life has been vulnerable, there's no sign of it. Amongst my mother's notes on each reader is praise for Rosalind's 'enthusiastic spirit in seeking new fields, which has improved the quality of her reading'.

Fay Lipschitz, paler, has a waiflike appeal. She's definitely a reader of good books, 'with a taste for humour'. From under heavy lids, Fay fixes her eyes on my mother and chooses her words in a way that suggests her need for a discerning mentor, someone unlike the members of the council who run the orphanage.

Molly Nochemowitz is a childless, older woman on the council, and often about the orphanage. Her affection is on offer, but it comes out so loudly and fiercely that I shrink from her. The boom of her voice announces her presence as she limps up the steps to the hall, looming into view like a monster. In a fairy tale her reddened skin, loose throat and bulgy eyes would warn you to beware. If only we could run away. But my mother stops to commend her. As we walk off, my mother assures me that the orphans do love her. I both trust this and wonder if it's a measure of how bereft they must be. Rhoda sees my hesitation.

'She's a winner of hearts.' Rhoda's pace quickens when she's energised by a point to be made. 'Most evenings, when there's an exodus from the dining room, a ring of children pushes close to Molly. They follow her as the children did the Pied Piper. She charms the older ones with her original opinions, and she can express herself on practically every subject. She charms the younger children by her understanding. "Books-smooks! Dancing-smancing!" she waves me and other visitors off. "Awright we like reading story books, awright we have fun dancing, yet who but Auntie Molly is there every night?" She's there when they need her to stroke their hair and ask, "Your cold is better today?"'

Dancing lessons are conducted by Ren Stodel (the adored Mrs S) who has an upright carriage and wears her hair in crossed-over plaits on top of her head. She teaches the Madge

Atkinson Method of Natural Movement to girls in orange tunics with glossy brown cords about their waists. Barefoot, toes pointed, the girls skip to the rhythm of Dvořák's well-known 'Humoresque', played on the dining-room piano with thumping beats – dah, de dah, de dah, de dah . . . – on a rising scale.

'The dancer listens with her inner hearing,' Ren explains to the girls. 'She feels the rhythm and mood of the music in order to stir in others the depth of emotion awakened in herself.'

After Ren's class, she and my mother, who is well whenever she's with Ren, stride arm in arm down Adderley Street. We go to visit Ren in her thatched cottage, Peace and Quiet, hidden away amongst bush and foliage along a road winding inland

Rhoda and Ren

from the seaside station at Clovelly. It's disconcerting to come upon a husband who is anything but quiet: a grinning, cigar-chomping impresario, Sonny Stodel, who strums his ukulele with head cocked to one side, as though listening to himself while he performs.

Sonny and Ren, who have two boys and wish – so I'm told – they had a daughter, invite me to stay a night at Peace and Quiet. Would my mother have let me stay had she known they would take me out that night to a show at the Alhambra, followed by late-night dinner with the performers at a fashionable nightclub called the Del Monaco? Ren has plaited my hair and pinned the plaits on top of my head in her own style. Only my hair is skimpy and the plaits don't cross to make a crown; they barely meet, but Ren hides this with a bow. I'm amazed by the lavish gestures and kisses of the performers, which spill over onto me, Sonny's newest acquisition. Next morning I'm set to perform on the lawn. He takes off my dress and makes me lie on the grass, toes pointed with hands under my chin. In the photo he takes my face is full of unease: I don't want to be posed in my vest and panties. I want my father to come and fetch me. It's a relief to spy our old Chevrolet flashing into sunlight along the twisty road.

My mother doesn't have to state that she finds Sonny coarse. It's implied when she holds up Ren as a model of wifely forbearance. Wives of that generation don't expect to be known in the ways brothers or friends know them. Their voices are warm with fun in the company of women. But what transforms Rhoda most is to emerge like a mermaid from the waves at Muizenberg on the Indian Ocean or from those on the colder, Atlantic side of the peninsula. For Rhoda, the colder the waters, the more they heal. She's at one with grey days thick with sea mist and great breakers rising, frothing and racing towards her.

*

Photographed by Sonny on the lawn of his house

Back home, at bedtime, she goes on with the water-babies, who are children liberated from the deathly conditions of nineteenth-century child labour. They live together in the chambers of the sea. It's a kind of fantasy orphanage. Water-babies are freer than the children at Oranjia, but like them are subject to visitors. These visitors are moral teachers whom I don't much care for. Mrs Doasyouwouldbedoneby hands out sweets to well-behaved children. Next comes Mrs Bedonebyasyoudid, who pops a pebble into Tom's mouth when he opens it to receive the sweet he expects. The shock and physical hardness of that pebble, as I

take it in, is fixed in memory once and for all. In after years it
will come back, when I'm seventeen and trying out dreams of
love (shaped by thrilled replaying of arias from *La Traviata*). It's
late one summer night, January 1959, and I'm kissing a boy of
twenty on our stoep, semi-curtained by vine leaves and unripe
grapes. Startlingly, he passes a peach pip into my mouth. His
green eyes glimmer through the dark, inviting me to share the
joke, but I'm taken aback, and literally step back.

Unlike our father, Rhoda lives almost entirely in books, an
inner life she keeps intact, separate from her outward identity as
Harry's wife. In her housewife aspect, she often appears defeated
and in need of awareness – even a child's awareness. If she
absolutely has to go into town – to the dentist, say – she takes
me. I hold her hand as much as she holds mine. Dressed for
town, she's made-up with red lipstick and walks rather hurriedly
in a Swiss Hanro suit and a mannish felt hat; at her side I'm
ridiculous in a green tweed bonnet with curled-up brim to
match a double-breasted coat. It would suit a doll-child, not
one sprouting freckles. If only we don't meet anyone we know.

During the appointment, she leaves me in a nearby bookshop.
In the children's corner, I sit on the floor, pulling out a book with
pop-up pictures of castles in fairy tales, and another with tags to
waggle so that a lion's mouth opens, his teeth gleam and a red
tongue comes out as he roars. I feel safe there with the books.

When we return home, my mother opens A. A. Milne and
reads aloud about James James Morrison Morrison Weatherby
George Dupree, who warns his mother, 'never go down to the
end of the town / without consulting me'. I'm invited to laugh
at the imperiousness of this little English boy.

But however much I yield to my mother's intonations as she
reads aloud from *When We Were Very Young* and *The Water Babies*,
longings continue to circle around the two bookshop books –
not the kind my mother would buy. As my birthday approaches

I dream that, magically, someone will divine and grant what I want. When Granny Annie tells me to make a wish, her hand guiding mine in cutting Lenie's home-made birthday cake, I close my eyes and choose the toy-books, dwelling on the lion because there's more chance of the wish coming true. I want the pop-up castles even more, but sense that those tiers, wobbling as the page opens, are too wondrous to own.

Another longing is for a baby doll in the window of a toyshop along Main Road at Three Anchor Bay. She's made of rubber, and dangling from her hand there's a miniature bottle to fill with water and feed into the hollow of her open mouth, with an outlet below. I don't like fanciful, dressed-up Raggedy Anns; what appeals is a doll who looks like a real baby. I gaze entranced at the baby on the other side of the glass whenever we pass on visits to my father's parents. And then, one day, my tall, sombre grandfather, an old man of few words, announces, 'You can choose a present.' As he shuffles along Main Road, desire intensifies. Inside the toyshop the darling doll, retrieved from the window, turns out to cost ten and six. Instead, my grandfather buys a tiny one – too tiny to have an inside – for sixpence. Embarrassed by my extravagant choice, I pretend to like the substitute.

Truth be told, I'd known that the life-like doll cost too much before that visit to the toyshop. When I pointed it out to my grandfather I was playing ignorant: the simple child who can't tell the difference between what's affordable and what's not. My pretences fail to match my mother's instinctive sensitivity, for she's told me how, as a child, she'd drawn back from greed.

'Everything lived for me in the light of my father's love,' she says during one of her reminiscences. 'It was just because he gave all that I developed the conscience not to take all. I remember reluctantly returning a gold sovereign, which he pressed out of the spring of the sovereign case men wore on a chain across the chest in those days. I returned it because I felt instinctively it was too much to take.'

It's all too clear that others' instincts, including mine, are grosser. However compelled I am by the rarity of my mother, and by her reading, writing, taste and judgement, my secret self has to acknowledge how much comes from my father: appetite and energy and wanting ordinary things. Above all there's the fascination of what's difficult: I want to be lovable, like my brother Pip who's a laughing baby with a cute nose, pointy tongue and a fluff of fairish hair against my mother's shoulder. In her striped dressing gown, her face lights up as she turns towards him; how tenderly she's brushing his hair upwards into a little curl on top of his head.

In 1989, when St Hilda's College, in Oxford, is about to elect a new principal, the tutor in Roman history, Barbara Levick, suggests that we ask candidates for an adjective or noun describing how they'd wish to be remembered. We elected Elizabeth Llewellyn Smith, who said 'integrity'.

I was old enough by then to admit to a friend, the writer Gillian Avery, that my dream adjective is less high-minded. 'It's "lovable",' I confessed ruefully, as one who knows the time for hope has passed.

'Mine too,' Gill offered, 'but it would never do to admit it at an interview.'

I felt a surge of fondness for her. As a writer, she might have wished to be successful or to be remembered, as my mother (for all her modesty) wished to be remembered after her death. The whole edifice of my mother's married life was alien to the writer my mother felt herself to be. Through writing she escaped to her first world, 'roots clasping native stone'. In a poem she read aloud, the word stone rhymes with home, and home to her was elsewhere, not with us, not with our father.

Rhoda, aged seventeen

Like a tree born in dawn's dark crystal stillness
Roots clasping native stone
My spine, my staff
For I am home.

I understood that home was the timeless face of Creation, and that she felt interfused with the veld, that stark terrain of her primal landscape, as (I'd later learn) Clym Yeobright blends into Egdon Heath in *The Return of the Native*, or as the Brontës blend into the Yorkshire moor. These inhabitants of my mother's bookcase are amongst her intimates.

Her other lifeline is memory: her pre-illness past. She's in her late twenties, and then thirty, and still she doesn't know, or dreads to know, what is wrong with her. In so far as she's beset with uncertainty and mentally alone, she does cross the borderland of deep depression.

5

The Silent Past

It would be untrue to say that, back then, I had no ideas about my mother's illness.

As I grew up, the fog around it did block questions in a way that must have become habitual: the absence of words closed off thoughts, and that would have been all too easy in a house where talk flowed about public issues – racial oppression and legal cases and the declaration of the State of Israel in 1948. A closed-off channel pre-empted questions, even to myself, and I realise now how convenient it became to ease the discomfort of awareness by closing the valves of my attention.

Pip has no recollection of threatened attacks when we were small. Where I have the sister role to stay at her side, Pip's role is to delight. She's charmed and amused by the swelling maleness of his chest, his readiness to sing and even his glee when, bored by our obligatory after-lunch rests, he stands up in the cage of his cot in order to smear poo on the nursery wall. Unlike me, he trots off to nursery school. Our father drives away to his law office in town, so he too is not a witness, or not by day; nor is he told on his return. Nor is my grandmother present in my memory of these times. I'm alone with my mother as she falls on her knees next to her bed or on a rug in the dining room.

Curious to me, looking back, is that my father and grandmother must have known that these emergencies would occur from time to time. Why did they say nothing? Might they have hoped she'd exert more control in the presence of a child? More likely, I think, was their reluctance to imagine what might happen when they weren't there – what George Eliot meant when she says that most of us go about well-wadded with oblivion. She actually says 'stupidity', but that's too dismissive, and her link of herself with 'us' doesn't ring true. It tells us more about the frustrations of George Eliot herself as an intellectual in a provincial society. Harry and Annie were certainly not stupid. Their extrovert high spirits simply overrode the intrusion of troubling thoughts. Their wadding may even have been of benefit. It ensured a cover for anything out of the ordinary.

It will happen quite casually when I'm fourteen that my eye falls on words my mother has set down at the age of thirty-eight.

Mid-afternoon, the house is quiet. The servants, having cleared
up after lunch, have gone to their rooms off the yard at the back.
Wearing uniform, a white panama hat and a green cotton dress
that looks creased and rumpled by the end of the school day, I'm
returning home, through the gate, across the stoep festooned
with heavy boughs of vine, and quietly pushing open the front
door. To the left of the hall is a black, stinkwood bench with
three *riempie* seats, which came from one of the farmhouses in
the *kloof* behind Klaver. In the corner next to it is a round
pedestal table, and on it is 'Love and the Soul', a long body
enfolded by a winged angel by Lippy Lipshitz, the Cape Town
sculptor born in Plungian. Next to it are three lavishly illustrated
books between carved wooden bookends: *The Happy Prince and
Other Tales* by Oscar Wilde, *The Bells* by Edgar Allan Poe and the
plays of Shakespeare. I often stop at that table to look at Millais'
painting of Ophelia singing as she drowns with 'clothes spread
wide, / And mermaid-like, awhile they bore her up'. This time,
I notice that my mother, in her absent-minded way, has left a
half-finished poem there before she closed her door for her afternoon rest. It's usual for her to be sleeping, or trying to and easily
disturbed, when I tiptoe back from school.

As I glance at the poem a word leaps out. The word is
'epilepsy'. Instantly, it hits me: That's what it is.

Until that moment the problems besetting my mother
seemed various: tension, fatigue, anxiety, falling, jerking awake,
sleeplessness and 'dry-sickness' (the last a made-up word that she
associated with *The Waste Land*, and familiar long before I read
that poem). It has never before occurred to me that one symptom could take precedence. My next thought is surprise that
there might be a word for it after all. Something definite; something by then made known to my mother.

I never mention this discovery to her, but it will linger at the
back of my mind as a possibility not to be communicated or

explored. Why not look up the word in a dictionary? I can't explain my incuriosity.

Branded on memory, the scene will present itself, two years on, in another scene that will open up the rest of my life. A student invites me to see a French film. I have just turned seventeen, and the student's name is Siamon Gordon. Afterwards he walks me home and asks about my family. His directness – more than I'm used to – invites direct answers, and impulsively, because medicine is his subject, I blurt out – swinging back and forth on the gate – the secret in our family, and what I suspect might explain it. To utter that word aloud is, for me, more intimate than touch, an exposure of fears for my mother going back to the age of two and a half.

'It's probably correct,' he says. 'There's an irritable focus in the brain. It can spread from one area to another.'

As facts dispel uncertainty, I feel grateful. Jokey though he is most of the time, he takes this seriously.

'Have you witnessed a seizure?'

'No. Only threatened attacks.'

'If a full attack happens,' he warns, 'it could look like your mother is dying, but that won't happen. Sit tight. However desperate she looks, she will eventually come round.' I lock this promise away, to be called upon in time to come. 'Hold her hand,' he advises, 'and comfort her when she comes round, because there is often an after-effect, a miasma.'

Long after, I will find assorted statements amongst my mother's papers: '*Through epilepsy I was stripped down to the foundation-rock from which I was able to strike new sparks. For on the edge of that precipice, any weakness in thought, word, or deed could plunge one into the bottomless pit, there where all vanities and falsities are expunged.*'

Where does the history of an illness begin? A history told to a doctor would begin with a symptom in the sense of malfunction. It's well known that visions can be associated with epilepsy, yet for Rhoda visions were not a sign of disease. No medical term, no ordinary words, only poetic language could reach towards this inexpressible thing, like Wordsworth's 'sense sublime' or the wandering airs that closed in on Emily Brontë when, she said, 'visions rise and change that kill me with desire'. Dostoevsky, himself epileptic, records the exhilaration of this visionary state in his portrait of the epileptic Myshkin in *The Idiot*: a breakthrough into 'a higher existence' when 'there shall be time no longer'. To take in this is to see how far any medical explanation of visions as symptoms must fall short of leaps in imaginative minds.

The diary, written when Rhoda was seventeen, eighteen and nineteen, was found after her death. Pip did the first sifting of her papers: poems, autobiographical fragments, copies of *Oranjia*, stories, letters, notes on the Bible, scribbles on the thin, almost transparent blue paper – you could write only on one side – that our father used to bring home from the office. Pip sorted identifiable batches into large brown envelopes, which he handed over when I came from England, to be kept in my flat perched over the ocean at Saunders Rocks.

A separate, small room on the floor below comes with the flat. It's dark there, cave-like, behind the blinds that close it off from a walkway. Here I unpacked Rhoda's papers and books. In the envelope containing the diary is Rhoda's list of books she was reading during the first two years after she left school. In a separate envelope is an exchange of letters with a young man, starting in the same period, 1935, and extending to the end of 1937. I took the diary and letters upstairs and lay on the window seat to read them, with the waves pounding on the rocks below. Here was my mother as a girl whose life gets rocked by two successive blows.

*

A stranger appeared at her birthday dance when she turned fifteen. A new neighbour, befriended by Rhoda's brother Basil. His name was Lou Freedberg, a tall youth, blowing moodily on the short end of a cigarette as he let fall contrary remarks in the manner of an atheist. His eyes crinkled and he folded his arms, not a twist but one hand clasping an elbow, as he withered an optimistic view of progress. 'Human nature is what it was five thousand years ago.' Rhoda was struck by the sound of cynicism, unheard amongst the men around her: Basil, as benign as Pooh Bear; his friends the Bradlow twins from Johannesburg, mildly humorous; while her father, as an immigrant, could not afford futility. Lou was an intellectual, impressive to a reading girl.

— As a corrective to her taste for Romantic poets, Lou gave her one of the books on her reading list: *The Mysterious Universe* by an astrophysicist, Sir James Jeans. Predictably, what she took away from it were philosophical questions where physics touched infinities. For these were not incompatible with the focus on infinity in the poems of her favourite, Emily Brontë.

She respected Lou as a reader, and twice was drawn to him physically; both times at night when she was caught up in the pulse of sea or wind: once while playing a ball game with a group of friends on a beach, the other time when she was pressed against him in the dicky of a car, while the wind 'blew the stars about the sky'.

It was unprecedented for Rhoda to acknowledge physical attraction. I remembered how she brought up the Virgin Queen in one of what she calls our 'lying-on-beds' conversations in her room. She imagined that Elizabeth's withdrawals when it came to marriage were not primarily a matter of caution or sexual coldness. Nor was Elizabeth exercising her power, rather her desire for expressiveness, which would be terminated by an act as conclusive as marriage. Her idea of Elizabeth's desire came from her understanding of a fuller kind of desire prompted by emotional intimacy, drama and the play of character, which, she implied, the blocked-off husbands of her milieu (their reading confined largely to law reports, finance, sport, war and politics) did not entertain.

Rhoda would have discussed this only with a trusting daughter untouched as yet by the social agendas that accompany reproduction. What my mother never discussed was her attraction to Lou and her conviction that he preferred another.

One Wednesday 7 March 1935, a week before Rhoda turned eighteen, she woke to hear Basil start the engine of his car, the Ashcan, to rattle off to medical school. She sat up in bed and told her schoolfriend Monica, who had stayed the night, to throw open the shutters so that they might call goodbye. And then – suddenly, with no warning – she fell back in a faint.

Fainting took her over all that day. Knowing this and also the fact that she was due to sail for Italy the following day, it is to me bizarre that on Wednesday a girl is fainting all day and on Thursday her mother waves her away at Cape Town docks. My grandmother's oblivion wouldn't have extended to a physical ill. But if she thought a love-crisis had brought her daughter to the point of breakdown, then it would have been reasonable to consider it best for Rhoda to go away. In that case, the voyage would not have been conceived as a jaunt, rather as a cure. As this idea came to me, another fact I've always known seemed to confirm it: Rhoda's travelling companion was not a girl of her own age or someone close to her; it was middle-aged Aunt Tilly from Rhodesia, who was a hospital nurse.

Why was it not seen to be epilepsy, I wondered, turning the pages of the journey. Could it be that the jerking of arms and legs accompanying the worst form of the condition did not manifest initially? 'Faint', the word she uses in her diary, means that she lost consciousness, but there may have been no readily identifiable symptoms when she had that first seizure in 1935. It's easy to blame a victim, and Rhoda would become complicit with a view of herself – implied if not stated – as 'failing'.

Two days out to sea, she remained dazed.

10 March 1935: All the strangeness of a poem by Edgar Allan Poe, all the loneliness of a solitary gull skimming the waves, all the terror of eternity grips me as I look upon this watery waste . . . grey sea and grey sky and a grey dawn breaking . . . utter desolation.

Was this one form of the wasteland experience she'd often lamented to me as a child? Or does desolation often follow an attack? She went in fear of another, and her diary records tight-lipped that this did happen on deck.

Wrapped in a rug as the ship ploughed through the Bay of Biscay, she was reading keenly, dismissing ephemeral publications. Noel Coward was 'disappointing'; A. A. Milne's *Two People* 'too nonsensical'. The emotional nourishment Rhoda craved came from *Othello*. The Moor's suffering and downfall, and his self-punishing death left her 'greatly moved'. Vera Brittain's *Testament of Youth* offered a more resilient answer to the cruelty of existence when a woman loses the man she's loved, and finds the courage to make service to others – Brittain's work as battlefield nurse – a way to go on. 'Slowly absorbed every page from first to last – vivid account of woman's side of wartime.'

Rhoda was away for nearly a year. Aunt Tilly returned to Rhodesia and in July, Rhoda moved to England. There, responsibility for her care fell on her mother's closest sister, Minnie Ross, at 3 Alvanley Gardens, a pleasant house in Hampstead.

This is where Rhoda stayed all through the second half of

1935. Her aunt welcomed Rhoda like a daughter. They looked alike with dark hair and narrow, dignified faces. Solicitous as her aunt was, Rhoda's condition – the attack on deck had been followed by another in Jerusalem and then one in London – was beyond her.

She took Rhoda to three doctors. The fact that they went from one to another suggests that either no satisfactory diagnosis was made, or treatments proved ineffective.

First was a seasoned, somewhat old-fashioned neurologist of sixty-six, Wilfred Harris of Wimpole Street. Included in the history Rhoda gave to Dr Harris was her infection with the love-germ.

'Never mind, Chicken,' he told her kindly, 'we all get that disease.'

In late September Rhoda accompanied her aunt, uncle and their younger daughter Phillis to Het Zoute, a chic resort on the north Belgian coast. Close to the Dutch border, Zoute boasted blond sands, golf, luxury cars, a casino and appearances by Maurice Chevalier and Marlene Dietrich. What happened during that fortnight was silenced until Phillis, now in her mid-nineties, told me. Phillis, aged sixteen, shared a room with Rhoda in a separate wing of the hotel, far from her parents. She had been told nothing of her cousin's illness. One night she witnessed a seizure – the worst yet. Thinking Rhoda was dying, Phillis rang desperately for help. No one came for what seemed ages, and when a waiter did eventually appear he spoke only Flemish.

This instance of failed translation lights up the nightmare Europe would remain in Rhoda's memory: the strains of travelling, the constant fear of public exposure and the blight of helplessness reinforced by the self-blame induced by doctors' talk of hysteria, that diagnosis reserved for women.

A final try, in November, was to consult a Dr Leaky, who

Rhoda looks drawn between her London cousins,
Phillis and Rita Ross. Seated: Auntie Minnie

treated Rhoda through hypnosis. He meant to prove to his
patient that she could train her subconscious to control her
faints, and provided a notice to this effect. Rhoda was to put it
above her bed. The implied diagnosis was self-induced hysteria, a womanish excess, which she must resolve to control. The
onus of a potential cure therefore fell on her. She was persuaded
to believe that if she did not manage to control her attacks she
could go mad.

Two months later Rhoda, supposedly cured, left for Cape
Town. As she drove for the last time through London, to catch
the boat train at Waterloo, she was terrified at the prospect of
travelling alone, with no one to help if she went under.

January 9th, 1936: ... These months have seemed dreams; dreams
that followed close, one upon another ... dreams filled with an
hysterical horror passing that of hell – nightmares of insanity ...

*We passed Westminster, and I saw Wordsworth leaning over
the bridge.*

. . . silent, bare,
Ships, towers, domes, theatres and temples lie
All bright and glittering in the smokeless air.

The Thames flowed quietly by.
Waterloo Station . . . Farewell London . . . I am going home.

When she went to her cabin after dinner, panic and melan-
cholia crept upon her 'like a Thug'. During the night she woke
sharply, wanting to scream yet knowing no one would come.
She felt herself ascending 'a pinnacle of insanity', her body shaking violently with repressed fear. She prayed and recited poetry,
and the panic gradually subsided.

Leaky. Wilfred Harris. Here are names I could look up.
Harris was prominent in the field of epilepsy. Could Leaky be
Dr J. E. A. Leakey, who advocated a 'ketogenic' diet for epileptics in the thirties? Until these names surfaced in the diary, I'd
believed that doctors had been in the dark. This is what my
mother told me, and probably also what she'd told herself
because she, certainly, remained in the dark. But these doctors'
associations with epilepsy, coming up on the computer screen,
suggest that the nature of Rhoda's illness was not wholly a mystery. If Auntie Minnie took her to these respected physicians,
then the possibility of some form of epilepsy was aired. There
must have been a decision amongst the older generation to conceal it from anyone outside the family, and from Rhoda herself.
The secrecy makes it clear that the illness continued to carry a
stigma, particularly for a young woman. It could have spoilt her
chances of marriage. And since the illness carries a genetic element, there might have been a question whether she should

have children. All this would have been mulled over, I imagine, behind closed doors.

Fourteen days out of Southampton, Rhoda woke at six to find the ship gliding past Robben Island wrapped in morning mist. As they docked in Cape Town her parents and her dear schoolfriend Lilian were waiting on the quay. Then she saw Monica, the other member of their schoolgirl trio, getting out of a car and knew all at once, 'I love her.' It was as though some

Rhoda and Monica (left) on holiday at Hermanus.
The last illness-free summer, 1934–5

fount of feeling, sealed for ten months by the artifice of normality, was suddenly unstopped.

Monica was astonished by Rhoda's grown-up look in a green
Tyrolean hat and fox (as though she were still in wintry
London). 'You've changed,' Monica told her. Rhoda thought
how surprised they would be to know that the change was due
to illness.

It was high summer, hot, dusty. Her distanced ear picked up
'uncouth accents'. These sounds, she knew, would grow dear
and familiar again. Her father took her and her mother for tea
at Markham's in Adderley Street. There was a family quarrel,
and for a moment Rhoda felt about to faint, but managed to
control herself. Then they drove fifteen miles to a house on the
dunes at Muizenberg, which her parents had taken for the six
weeks of beach life known as the season. As they neared the
ocean the air grew cooler. There were gold coins of sunlight
on the grey-brown carpet, and the sea, she thought, sounded
for twenty miles along the shore like the roll of eternity.

After lunch, Basil, large, trusty, sprawled across her bed and
she told him how she'd loved Lou, and all she'd had to endure
with her illness. Basil was 'shocked and upset', and wished she
had confided in him before. His presence was balm. She could
lean on him from now on, and he would help her get well.

In her nightie, before she went to sleep, she leant out of
her bedroom window, listening to the 'rhythmic purr' of the
sea across the dunes. And looking up 'at the arch of the stars',
she felt the wind blow the constraints of London away. Here,
at home, she would be free to say what she thought. She
would heal the strained ties with her parents, though as far as
dependence went, Basil had replaced them as a father-
brother.

Basil now brought about the next drama in Rhoda's young
life. First, he relayed Lou's identity to their father, who duly

Rhoda and her eldest brother Basil were close throughout their lives. Clockwise, from top left: Klaver days; Rhodean days; Muizenberg days, 1940, with Basil on leave from Pretoria Hospital; Muizenberg again in the early fifties

Low tide at Muizenberg in the thirties. Back: Phillis, Monica, Rita,
Rhoda. Basil second from right, Lou far right. Front: Hubert

invited Rhoda for a walk to St James. There, over tea, he
assured her that he and her mother would favour a future
attachment. He even suggested that Lou might have been in
love with her all along. Then, on the first Saturday night after
her return, Lou – whom she still believed to be the prime cause
of her breakdown – drove out from town to see her.

Rhoda heard a car come to a stop at the dunes across the road.
Entering the house, Lou's eyes behind his glasses creased at the
corners as he smiled on a girl to all appearance metamorphosed
at nearly nineteen: slim and delicately beautiful in her well-cut
London dress, shorn of ringlets, her bubbly hair smoothed and
short. He fell in love at that moment.

Rhoda decided that she liked him, but was not in love. He
had the watchful half-smile of someone who's not entirely well.
Lou was thin and carried a shadow of paleness under the usual

layer of sunburn. Though land-surveying took him out of doors, his shoulders were a little hunched and his chest a little concave, rather like immigrants from Lithuania, raised on a poor diet, whose frames had not spread and hardened in sufficient sunlight.

Returning at last to Rhodean and her little room with the shutters, which she'd left as in a dream the year before, Rhoda felt 'like a ghost revisiting some vaguely familiar place'.

She and Monica visited Good Hope Seminary, a school founded in the 1870s along the lines of the Girls' Public Day School Trust in England to provide equal education for women. They went to see Miss Krige (their literature teacher, related to the Afrikaans poet Uys Krige) and Miss Stevenson ('Stevie')

Friendships formed at Good Hope were lasting. The top girl, Monica, is second from left, back row. Rhoda second from right, middle row. Lilian second from left, front row. Third from right, front row, is Thelma, who was to illustrate Rhoda's children's book, *Jonah*

who taught Latin. Stevie had birdlike bright eyes and a face like a wrinkled apple. Their teachers kissed them and the girls' 'untainted lips' were 'besmirched' with lipstick. Miss Krige almost wept when she told Rhoda that their literature class had been the happiest she'd ever had. Teachers then (and into my time at the school in the fifties) were not models for their pupils. They were single women, whose professional lives seemed unenviable, unthinkable. Although some found fulfilment in work, motherhood tethered to home was still a pervasive norm. In my mother's time, a girl might earn a bit or she might travel and go out with well-conducted men (it was considered fast to flirt or kiss on a first date) before she settled down to home-making in her early twenties.

So it was that Rhoda's parents could think of nothing better than to start her on a course of shorthand and typing at Underwoods, a secretarial college in town. It was a dusty, crowded place full of silly girls with little to offer in the way of friendship.

Later, my mother will say how she'd longed for higher education at a time when her father, after his losses during the Great Depression, could not afford it. Her parents, though, had managed to send her overseas for almost a year. Restoring her health would have been a priority; not a daughter's education, and in this they were not unusual. None of Rhoda's set went to university.

Why, Rhoda asked herself, did she not find with Lou Freedberg the intimacy that she had with Monica and Lilian? 'His absolute worship seemed strange. I was unaccustomed to being loved, and not a little worried because I believed ... I was not being quite honest – and yet I could not force myself to break.'

Rhoda's father, mindful of her breakdown and unaware of the doubts she confided to her diary, invited Lou to accompany

The trio. From left: Rhoda, Monica, Lilian,
in front of Muizenberg Pavilion

the family on their winter holiday, in July, to Graafwater, in the rough terrain of the *Weskus*, near Klaver.

On Lou's birthday she gave him an illustrated copy of *The Happy Prince and Other Tales* by Oscar Wilde, 'to begin your education in the importance of unimportant things. They prove that cynics write the loveliest fairy stories.' The title tale is about a statue of a happy prince, who in truth never experienced happiness. Viewing misery from his plinth, he asks a swallow to strip the gold leaf covering his body, to give it to the poor. The statue is then torn down, but the lead heart, all that's left when he's melted down, is taken to heaven.

Rhoda and Lou took long walks, not entirely agreeable to

With Lou, *c.* 1936–7, on Clifton Beach (left) and with a river picnic party

Rhoda because they found 'so few points of contact mentally'. Lou's ominous perspective on human history, reinforced by a film they'd seen, H. G. Wells's *Things to Come*, alerted her to Europe's rearmament. To acknowledge what was to come changed her inner landscape. '*The buoyancy of mind I had been building up since my return to Africa sunk as he talked ... The inexorableness of the distant blue hills which had cleansed me, the beautiful silences of the veld which had uplifted me, now overpowered me with a terrible sense of futility.*'

In September 1937 a streptococcal infection found its way into the weak left ventricle of Lou's heart. He was admitted for observation to Somerset Hospital, near Cape Town docks. And then, ominously, he was moved to the main hospital, Groote Schuur. Lilian recalled holding his hand in the ambulance rocking around the mountain curves of De Waal Drive. Later she stood with Rhoda in the corridor outside his ward and heard him scream in pain.

Each day during visiting hours, Rhoda watched Campbell, the night nurse, as she bent over temperature charts under the lamp at the centre of the ward. It was she to whom Lou turned. 'I will never marry,' he told her while Rhoda was there. To Rhoda, he spoke harshly.

Nurse Campbell cared so much for 'dear old Freedie' that Matron, Miss Pike, had to tick her off for favouritism. Miss Pike then moved Campbell to another ward and forbade her to see Lou. Campbell had to glean news of him from other nurses and resort to smuggled letters.

On 15 March 1938 Rhoda turned twenty-one. A birthday letter from her brother Sydney in Johannesburg invited her to join him, promising to look after her. The invitation may have been prompted by awareness of what was coming. On 31 March Lou died, aged twenty-three.

On the day of the funeral, Rhoda sat with Lilian in her father's car. Her mother had forgotten her hatpin, and held up the party because a well-dressed mother couldn't set out for the cemetery without it. When Lilian is old, she will remember how the two girls, in fits of mirth, rolled together on the back seat.

During the burial, Rhoda blamed herself for failing Lou. Listening to the strong whistle of a bird, she felt 'deeply ashamed', but apart from this, no emotion:

I knew positively that Lou was not in the box covered with a black cloth. I felt no emotion whatever. Why should I? I knew this was an unreal conventional ceremony & Lou would have hated it if he had been there and yet I deliberately squeezed out a tear. Inside I felt quite dead & yet I did this because I felt it was expected of me!

*I am afraid I am full of what K[atherine] M[ansfield] calls 'sedi-
ment'. Examined in the clear light of what has happened I know
I was tinkling & vain and grasping at shadows. That is why I failed
him so terribly. And yet for the rare moments when I 'broke
through' and was 'real' he loved me.*

My mother never spoke of Lou, but she did tell me that she
went to live with her brother in Johannesburg 'after a bereavement', and that she was wretched there.

Although Rhoda and Sydney felt and appeared polar oppo-
sites – Sydney, at nineteen, at the start of a high-flying business
career, Rhoda opposed to 'getting and spending' – they were
temperamentally the most alike in the family, with a vein of
originality entwined with moodiness that could make them, for
all their charm and courtesy, difficult. There was a lurking vehemence, a sense when you were with them of having to tread
lightly on top of tremors in the earth.

Sydney intended to be helpful after Lou's death but an ill and
grieving sister would have burdened a young man who was
working every moment and often returned to his workplace at
night. Rhoda would then be alone in his flat, in a city domi-
nated by mine dumps. In the allegorised landscape of her
imagination, Johannesburg was a place of hollow men groping
for gold.

In the winter of 1938, three months after Lou's death, she
sank very low during a bout of flu. *'People say grief goes over.
Right. Perhaps it does. But what has one left?'* Basil came a thousand miles – two days by train – to fetch her home.

I understand now why *The Happy Prince* stood to attention
beside my mother's much-thumbed volume of Shakespeare on
the pedestal table at the entrance to our family home.

6

'Only a Housewife'

They meet, of course, on Muizenberg beach. In 1939 Harry, at thirty, is an attorney, handling traffic accidents and divorce. Traffic is the last thing Rhoda cares to notice. As for divorce, it's off the map for orthodox Jewish women. Orthodox women are observant, attentive to the community, and they look on marriage less as a private story than a ritual of communal perpetuation. If a bride has a poetic bent, it's nice enough as a pastime, but irrelevant to what's expected of a wife. And if marriage makes a Jewish wife unhappy, she learns to put up with it.

As Harry breezes about the beach in his swimming trunks and the cream and blue striped blazer of the South African Swimming Union, divorcées, hair in clenched blonde ridges, wave to him with toothy smiles. He raises a hand and winks back. Winking is almost a reflex as his light green eyes scan the crowd for his numerous acquaintance. Now and then, exuding health, muscles shifting in his shoulders, he bends down or crouches to shake hands with one-time rivals. He has firm views on sporting behaviour. Swimmers sprout up around him.

University of Cape Town Swimming Club, winners of intervarsity 1930.
Harry is second from right, middle row

His passion is sport: swimming, water polo, soccer and baseball.
In the past he'd raced in pools around the country, intervarsity
contests like the annual Currie Cup, and now he manages
teams, sorts out disputes and does running commentaries on the
wireless.

He first spots Rhoda sitting on the sand under a sea-coloured
sunshade, which matches the blue-green sundress spread over
slim legs tucked to one side. Her dark skin doesn't have the
sultry olive tint of the Mediterranean; it's a serious darkness. Her
large blue eyes and a high-bridged nose lend her face a thought-
ful cast. Though she holds a poor opinion of her appearance, it
has dignity, the kind of face that gains distinction with age. Her
poor opinion probably has its origin in her mother's pride in
Sydney, the favourite and the only one of the four to look like
her. He has her fair skin and what my mother calls, a little envi-
ously, 'a chiselled nose'.

Harry is good looking in the sunburnt, South African way,

with hair parted off-centre. His legal office displays photos of Western Province teams, rows of solemn men with arms folded over their one-piece racing costumes, and at their feet the Currie Cup.

Men like Harry play around with floozies as a matter of course and marry virgins – manliness demands no less. In the meantime they slip in and out of divorcées and, satisfied, go their way. In male company they joke about needing the know-how, as though they're Boy Scouts obedient to the motto Be Prepared and in training for their next badge. 'Marie Stopes showed us the ropes' is the jingle of those prepared enough to pack condoms when a team sets off.

Born in 1909, Harry is eight years older than Rhoda, and by the time they meet a veteran in the sheikh role. At fancy-dress parties he would appear in Arab robes, layers of exotic stripes topped with a flowing headdress. In addition, he sports a prickly brown moustache, the current badge of masculinity, and hard knots of muscle bulge in his calves and arms from long-distance swims in rough seas. In his youth, girls hummed an old hit in his vicinity: 'I'm Just Wild About Harry'.

None of this, of course, impresses a high-minded girl like Rhoda Press. Harry, who knows loads of pretty women, has never encountered any as serious as Rhoda. He doesn't quite know what to make of her. Though Rhoda needs a man to protect her, she's unsure if she wants to marry someone so on the go, calling to her to 'shake a leg' if she isn't ready – and she's never ready – when he comes to take her out.

When Rhoda stalls over his proposal Harry picks up the phone and dictates an ultimatum to Lilian, now a legal secretary, who is to pass this on. Either Rhoda says yes, or the offer is off.

This is Lilian's story, and it rings true, yet Rhoda has a different story.

It can happen that some trivial pressure drives a life-changing

Harry meets Rhoda on Muizenberg beach

decision, as in the case of a friend of mine who didn't want to go through with her wedding. She went to my Aunt Berjulie for advice, and my aunt, an arbiter of rectitude, told her it was too late.

'You can't do that to Krafchik.'

Krafchik was the caterer and since then, 'Krafchik' has been our family code for an absurd obligation. What really drove Rhoda to accept the proposal, she told me, was an invitation from Harry's sister Lena, who had given birth to a son. Lena, always friendly to my mother, asked her to be Gerald's godmother. It was not easy to refuse. Yet, since Harry was to be godfather, to agree was to appear a couple. So it happens that Rhoda, unwilling to cross Lena's overture, finds herself engaged.

As a bachelor, Harry has been a habitué of cocktail parties and so at ease, waving, winking, engaged in confabs on the latest scores, that no one noticed he didn't drink. He actually had no taste for alcohol, and I will inherit this – though coming to Oxford in the seventies will compel me to touch a glass of sherry to my lips from time to time. The result of Harry's visibility at cocktails means that my parents receive no fewer than eight cocktail sets as wedding presents. Rhoda will consign them to a cabinet in the dining room from which they never emerge.

The night before the wedding the family tells the bride-groom . . . something. It remains confidential, and my guess is that they didn't say too much. Certainly, whatever they told him came too late for a bridegroom to retreat. So then, the inter-mittently visible illness and the invisible shadow of Lou behind this union.

How much did Harry know? As their first child, I both know and don't know, and the weight of suffering, unspoken but present, makes it nicer not to know as I grow up. I think it's nicer for my father not to know, or not fully, what it's like to live as what Katherine Mansfield calls 'an exile from health', and naturally it's easier not to know whether his wife did or did not continue to grieve for her lost love. And I see now how read-ily I took on my father's unknowing.

So it is that, for years, I turn away and put off the task to be her channel. Was it cowardice? Does emotional cowardice block me even now? 'Winter kept us warm,' Eliot says. It's tempting to wrap ourselves in a blanket of unknowing, for life-writing demands that we come to know ourselves through our subject.

The two are married on 9 April 1940. Rhoda looks dreamy in white satin embossed with hearts. The dress has a plain round neck and girly puffed sleeves. Lilian and another schoolfriend, Marjorie, are bridesmaids, both engaged to marry in June. Monica is not

present because her new husband, Bill, an accountant, is going up north, and Monica has gone to Johannesburg to be near him while he trains in the army. The senior partner of Harry's law firm, Bertie Stern, went up north in 1939. They agreed that Harry should remain in Cape Town to man the office.

After the wedding, Rhoda decides not to go on honeymoon. She stands in her shuttered room at Rhodean, her wedding dress on the bed, as Lilian helps her into her going-away suit, and watches as Rhoda bends to the mirror to put on a little pointed hat with a veil dipping over one eye. She says to Lilian that she's gone through with the wedding, and that's as far as she's prepared to go.

Lilian, another virgin told nothing by her mother, looks forward to marriage with keener anticipation, and assures Rhoda that marriage will do her good. Lil will be waiting when Rho gets back, and they will love each other dearly as before. Rhoda allows Lilian to persuade her to go away.

They go off to the Wilderness, a five-hour drive up the east coast to a honeymoon place on the Indian Ocean. There's a wide white beach, steadily rolling waves and thatched rooms strung out along the shore. Granny had prepared her daughter with a satin nightie and matching gown, and when Rhoda, suitably arrayed, attempts an entrance, she trips over the flowing gown. She often, regretfully, called herself 'excitable', meaning nervy.

In my teens, my mother will relay something of her wedding night as one of her arguments in favour of virginity. She said that her purity so moved her bridegroom that he, a man not given to tears, shed a few when she gave herself to him. She looks on the body as a temple, not to be cheapened by casual use. She never utters the word 'sex', always 'love-making' because, I take it, she includes what she herself may not experience, delicacy of feeling.

My grandmother's own story is calmer and sweeter. Her honeymoon was at Caledon, an inland spa with hot springs that was fashionable in 1914 – Granny was always fashionable. After the wedding, she likes to recall, 'My husband said to me, "Now we'll enjoy the fruits of our love."'

He wasn't a native English speaker, yet found the perfect words. Annie is not attentive to language, yet these words remain with her all her life. The feeling is active, as she repeats it to me lolling in her room at the Balmoral Hotel in the centre of Muizenberg. In her eighties she's still vigorous enough to cross the Beach Road to dip in the sea before breakfast, bending over first to splash her freckled arms.

Her husband was a good man, she wants me to know. He was so good that when he heard that Annie's sister Minnie was pining for their mother (who had recently died), he insisted that

Minnie should join them on honeymoon. Granny was teased when it came out that the sisters had shared the bed (as they'd shared a bed at home) and my grandfather had slept on his own behind a screen. Granny sees fit to confide that she was observing the Jewish law that forbids a couple to share a bed during menstruation.

It's impossible to be accurate about the past. Reports conflict. In a photograph, Rhoda dances along the sand in a bathing costume, arms flung wide. There is also the 'amazing' fact she reports to Basil, 'that after rigorous daily tuition from a determined husband I got my Driver's Licence on Honeymoon!' She rarely succumbs to the vulgarity of an exclamation mark; it is a measure of her surprise. On her return she looks radiant in the expected bridal way, to the noticing eye of a teenage cousin (Auntie Betsie's youngest daughter, Garda). She thinks that Rhoda was happy on honeymoon.

The family's precaution in not divulging Rhoda's history until the last moment does Harry an injustice: he never loves Rhoda any less on account of her illness; he may, in fact, love her more, though it isn't in him to know her as a reflective man might. A more sensitive man, on the other hand, might cope less well than Harry, with his ready optimism. If Rhoda is unwell, he's content to leave her in bed with a book – he rarely requires her company. Her invalidism and his unquestioning acceptance of a condition that neither he nor anyone fully understands frees her to read and write. In no time he's on to the next case, the next match. Leaving the house, he calls in his happy going-away voice, 'I'm off like a dirty shirt.'

Rhoda has no interest whatever in sport, though she does like to plunge in the breakers. The sea is 'pristine', while swimming pools are decidedly not her scene. I watch her after her bath, parting each of her toes carefully, one by one, and patting the crevices with her fluffy white towel in her battle against athlete's foot, which Harry, she complains, picks up in public swimming baths.

Like many outdoorsy South Africans, he likes to walk bare-foot. Pip and I patter barefoot at his side, careful to step over the lines of pavement slabs. In our heads is the sing-song of a superior English boy, Christopher Robin, who warns not to step on the lines because, if we do, *bears* will emerge: burly, shaggy bears hungry for the flesh of little children. Although there are no bears in Africa – no bears in the zoo with its monkeys and lions on the hump of Devil's Peak above De Waal Drive – we've stared in willing suspension of disbelief at these grim, other-world bears in Shepard's illustration for *When We Were Very Young*, before our mother turns the page to the poem we like best because it makes us see ourselves in a humorous light: Mary Jane is 'crying with all her might and main' and refuses her food, though it's *lovely* rice pudding again.

Pip and I side with Mary Jane; we detest puddings second only to stringy rhubarb, and marvel at the steady spooning-up on the part of our visiting cousins out from London, the well-behaved grandchildren of Auntie Minnie. Their no-nonsense English nanny ('a white nurse', in our mother's mock-awed tones) sets out wobbling gobs of pudding on the nursery table at the flat they have taken on Beach Road.

If the cream slabs of Muizenberg pavement get too hot, you can cool your soles by balancing along the stone edging or, better still, walk in the invitingly cool stone gutter, dry in summer. At noon, the tar of the road sears a child's tender feet: to cross the road, we reluctantly put on brown leather sandals with difficult buckles. Our father good-naturedly crouches down in shorts over his dampish swimming trunks (catching cold doesn't concern him as it does our mother) to do them up.

His sheikh costume, meanwhile, is relegated to the top of a cupboard in our nursery. I climb on a chair to fetch it down and

try it on, the layers of thin, striped garments, this outfit being
the offshoot of a torrid novel and silent movie, in which a girl
is carried off into the desert by Rudolph Valentino. I will dip
into this novel later, in adolescence – a few pages are enough to
explain why my mother dismissed it, along with other sex-
hungry fiction of the twenties, which she sees as a response to
the lost generation of men killed in the First World War.

Rhoda's letters to Basil during the forties challenge my memory
of a suffering semi-invalid who lives through books and poems.
With Basil she continues to be the outgoing girl she'd been before
her illness. In May 1940, after her return from honeymoon, she

Rhoda posing on honeymoon at the Wilderness

hastens to assure Basil that she's well and happy in the marriage, 'since you played such a big part in engineering it'. I picture her bored by Harry's sporting chums, yet it's through him that she meets the dancer Ren Stodel, who invites her to watch her Monday class – this then is Rhoda's introduction to the orphanage – and she also meets an advocate, Gerald Gordon, a left-wing intellectual with whom she shares books. They take long, heads-together walks. He's active against racial oppression, and after the National Party comes to power in the late forties he brings out a novel, *Let the Day Perish*, about two brothers who live apart on separate sides of the colour bar. The cover has two Henry Moore-like figures, side by side with hands touching but divided by a line down the centre.

When we're alone, my mother calls it, somewhat disparagingly, 'a social service novel'. This is her phrase for a novel written primarily to protest a wrong, as distinct from literature, even though she shares the author's political views. Later, when I gave tutorials on the poetry of the First World War, I asked students whether propaganda – in that case, against war and war-makers – can be literature? Oxford undergraduates invariably argued that most great writing contains propaganda of one sort or another: a famous instance would be Levin's philosophy in *Anna Karenina*; another would be George Eliot's humanism. All the same, my mother had a point, I think, in her distinction between the primacy of a current issue and lasting art.

My parents stay, at first, in the Mimosa Hotel. It's opposite the Sea Point Pavilion, spread out between the rocks, where Harry swims every day after work. It's a complex of open-air, sea water pools of differing depths – including a sixteen-foot pool with diving boards mounting to a perilous height.

The plan has been to look for a place of their own, but war defers this. In May 1940 Rhoda sees seven giant British ships move 'silently and mysteriously' into Table Bay, escorted by the South African Air Force. Twenty to fifty thousand soldiers from Australia and New Zealand wake up Cape Town. This is their 'last fling'. The future to Rhoda looks 'nebulous', and to act for herself alone seems wrong. For the duration of the war she prefers to stay in her old home in Oranjezicht.

Her high-minded reasons often take precedence over mundane ones, and I suspect that my father's frugality played some part in this decision. They rent a flat near Saunders Rocks for a while, but Rhoda is 'ill' and takes against the setting where it happened. She becomes averse to the sight and smell of the sea, and finds herself happier back on Table Mountain amidst the pines and oaks.

Beloved Monica is there too, staying in her father's house while her husband is up north. Each morning at a quarter past eight the two friends take a long walk through the Avenue lining the Gardens and into town. Rhoda's state of health veers according to her company. Mood plays so large a part, it's a little disheartening, when I come on the scene, to find that I can't cheer her – not in the way of Basil or Monica. They don't have to do more than walk into her room. She loves them so intensely, her spirits soar.

Reading between the lines of my mother's letters, I see a return to Monica as the prime reason for settling back at Rhodean after her marriage. The death of her father in 1941, and my birth later that year, may be further reasons to return to her family home. Her practical mother is there to help, assisted by jolly Auntie Betsie, who comes to town from Namaqualand. In those days, a live-in nursing sister accompanied a newborn home in order to establish its routines and allow a new mother to lie down for the protracted period then thought necessary. With the prospect of three women to nurse her, as well as the support of Basil, on leave from Pretoria Hospital, Rhoda appears content. She remains so for the next two years, despite my 'feeding problems'.

At the time, mothers are still tyrannised by the childcare guru Truby King, who rules against demand feeding, as practised by African women. My mother would have seen those African babies easy at the breast, but like other mothers of her ilk obediently mashes together five vegetables for every meal, to be given on the dot, and denied if a baby is so ill-regulated as to cry at the wrong hour. I don't take to this regimen or to the stuffing, and my mother pictures herself rather comically circling my cot with a spoon while I edge around it, holding on to the rails. My mother has more success with a blue dog, who meets another blue dog in the mirror, and when my mouth opens in wonder she pops in the spoon.

The other tyrant is the paediatrician. The nervous voices of young mothers echo his rulings to one another: 'Dr Rabkin said . . . ' and 'Dr Rabkin thinks . . . ', and one day, when I'm about two, my weary mother is forcing herself to take me to him. There are called-out instructions to Lenie as my hair is brushed into a sausage curl on top of my head and I'm put into my tucked dress. I can remember Dr Rabkin's pallor and long-faced solemnity; my mother's deferential intentness.

When both my grandmother and father are away, she's content to be alone with me at Rhodean. There's 'conversation' and we go for walks. She's safe at night because John, the gardener, sleeps on the stoep outside her room. (Like many Xhosas he's taken a 'white' name as his working identity, a common habit to this day – the assumption being that employers can't get their tongues around a variety of clicks made by the tongue against the teeth or palate.)

It's not until early in 1944 that Rhoda's morale appears to crack. The hormonal run-up to my brother's birth is inextricable from 'illness'. During the summer of 1943–4 Basil was on holiday in Muizenberg and stayed with Rhoda. The letter she writes to him on 19 March 1944 attempts to cover up signs of illness that Basil has seen. 'I must ask you to believe that those nervous explosions you witnessed are by no means normal to me and have completely disappeared . . . ' She takes the onus on herself: the explosions will be under control if she's sufficiently occupied.

'I feel very distressed that I should have allowed you to acquire such a very distorted version of our married life, and especially of Harry,' she goes on. 'I can assure you we have never been so out of harmony before or since . . . I am happy to say that Harry does much good in his own way through little personal acts in which he takes pleasure.'

Basil must have noticed Harry's frugality, for Rhoda defends this: 'As for money, luxurious living is particularly abhorrent to me in Wartime, and . . . I have never personally suffered a single want since my marriage.'

Marriage, as the ideal arrangement for life, is unquestioned. Basil and his friend Frank Bradlow (both in the army and out of contact with women, except for leaves) have told Rhoda that they feel their married friends are one up on them. In warning Basil against his easygoing propensity to fall for any girl who is amiable, Rhoda envies a man's freedom. 'Unlike our sex you have the advantage . . . of being able to Wait and Choose.' Despite all she's said to contradict Basil's impression that her husband has proved ill-suited, that sentence might seem to confirm it.

Housewives like my mother are assumed to be at home, and other wives pop in on impulse. The front door bell can ring at any moment, and Lenie brings tea, a 'cool-drink' (a granadilla cordial) and home-made iced cake. Wives speak detachedly, though not disloyally, of men as needy pets whose antics amuse them. Lilian's husband Bertie Henry, it's said, has never worn pyjama bottoms. Twin beds (as seen in the film *The Red Shoes*) are currently in fashion for couples. Monica, it's said, marks the deliberation with which her husband has to cross from his bed to hers.

Listening to them, I wonder at their accommodation of such husbands as they have chosen: dependable men respected in the community. Is this what the future will hold? Do they expect less than I will want, for I'm under the spell of books with dreaming girls. They too had been under that spell, and lived in those books. What had happened to make them accepting? My mother tells me that she married to have children. That's what wives of the forties say. The romances and desires of their teenage years seem to be left behind in favour of home, family and community. At best they take the position articulated perfectly by Jane Austen when she relates how a mother 'had humoured, or softened, or concealed [her husband's] failings, and promoted his real respectability for seventeen years; and though not the very happiest being in the world herself, she had found enough in her duties, her friends, and her children, to attach her to life'.

This is Lilian's solution as a farmer's wife. At dawn she lays out great tureens of porridge and steaming mugs of coffee for the labourers; come autumn, she's shoulder to shoulder in the apple-packing shed; in summer, when a mountain fire breaks out, she's out there with the men. The farm flourishes; in time they are no longer poor.

After the birth of their second son, a fretting baby who leaves Lilian depleted, Bertie's mother arrives from Edinburgh. An antiques dealer in a kaftan and Moroccan shoes with turned-up toes descends from the plane. Mother, as Lilian dutifully calls this apparition, has brought her daughter-in-law a silver belt and an antique sugar shaker – neither of use on a farm – but then proceeds to ignore her. Each evening mother and son sit down to dinner on their own (Mother's favourite meatballs), and it does not occur to Bertie to draw in his wife.

After Mother departs, Lilian finds herself inert. She loses weight and her well-spring of feeling dries to nothing. Bertie takes her to a doctor in Cape Town. Women like Lilian don't speak readily of their trials. Not many town women would have adapted to a farmer offering rough and barely furnished quarters. And there'd been more to be borne, I learn later, when Lilian gives me a copy of her memoirs. For when, as a bride, she came to Pomona, at large in the kitchen she found the foreman's wife who, Lilian guessed, had served her husband's needs during his years as a bachelor. The most Lilian could do was get rid of that brooding presence; it was not possible to run home from the top of Piketberg Mountain; she didn't for one moment consider it. The only way forward was not to pursue the facts.

Is Lilian's doctor aware of things to know beyond physical symptoms? A consultation that fails to enter into the buried cause of distress can be dangerous, as when Rhoda fell to the floor in a doctor's office and went home to end her life. So it happens that when Lilian turns her head to the doctor's open window on the sixth floor, she wants to throw herself out.

Instead, she takes refuge with her grandmother in Muizenberg. Only unstinting love, the same as Lilian herself has scattered like seeds falling in the furrows in fertile abundance, can extract her from what my mother calls 'dry-sickness' – what medicine might, in Lilian's case, label post-partum depression. It's out of character to abandon her two boys, one a continuously wailing baby, to her brusque husband. After two weeks he asks her to return, and she resolves to do so. What eventually brings her back to life is another pregnancy. She is sure this time it will be a girl. She will grow a creature of her kind who will be a companion.

Where Lilian's maternal nature brims and flows into practical altruism, Monica's maternity is more consuming: it emerges in her twenties as the bedrock of her being, filling the vacant space left by a mother who was put away in an asylum after Monica was born. While Bill, her husband, is up north in 1944, Monica gives birth to Michael. My mother goes to see her, and never forgets the scene that meets her eyes. Monica is standing in a shuttered room with a baby in her arms: as she carries the baby out of the shadow, my mother sees that Michael has Down's syndrome. Monica wraps her maternal nature around Michael, ready to give him her life. Though she goes on to have three more sons, Michael's need for protection takes precedence. As he grows up, he will become my father's most faithful listener to sports broadcasts – a consolation to Harry for my mother's habit of switching off his happy voice.

During the forties, these three friends struggle to come to terms with difficult lots: Lilian off on the farm with a rough man; Monica brooding over Michael; and Rhoda sunk in depression after Pip's birth. They don't meet much, and their twenties go by minus the balm of their friendship. Yet it's during these hard years that each constructs something of her own.

In her unassuming way Monica creates a garden in tiers on the mountain slope high above Bantry Bay. It's a secret garden, invisible behind a suburban house, Bayhead, on Kloof Road. My mother, recovering, breathes in the fragrant tea roses blooming in abundance.

By the time I come to know Auntie Monica there's no sign of the winner my mother pictures in their schooldays: the girl who came first in every subject, the best at games and the lead in a Good Hope production of *Peter Pan*. She's mild with that slightly cut-off look of women feeding babies, and I can't fathom the depth of my mother's attachment. Books are still part of it, and they reminisce about *Testament of Youth* and *South*

Riding not so much now for their portraits of independent women as because they were read in friendship – read by the girls Mon and Rho had been. Nowadays, Auntie Monica is less ambitious than my mother, and quieter than Auntie Lilian. Auntie Monica appears contained in her matronly skirt and cardigan, the unobtrusive, covered-up clothing I associate with Englishwomen in magazines from overseas. No sundress flaunts her flesh; nor does she choose the floaty muslins and organdies that suit my mother's slender form; nor of course the boots and overalls Lilian dons on the farm.

'Mon,' my mother greets her with a joy no one else can give. Mists clear. The curtain rises and her friend flies out of the window as Peter Pan.

Monica's mouth curves into a slow, charming smile as she says softly, 'Rho.'

While Monica cultivates her garden, and Lilian her farm, my mother is 'scribbling'. When she pulls herself together to leave the house, she carries her small wire-bound notebook in her handbag, and sometimes stops in the street to set down a character she's noticed or a line of a poem that comes as she sniffs the sour-sweet tang of the *fynbos* with face uplifted. The challenge is to voice what has been voiceless.

Where are words for extremes of experience? A glimpse of pre-existence or plunges into what was once called the falling sickness co-exist with the veld awaiting a poet's voice. Sealed in a car, cut off from her first world in her suburban marriage, Rhoda spies a gazelle. Native of the veld, its eye meets hers. No language, she intimates, for what that creature feels of terror and bliss:

> *The veld is voiceless*
> *Africa is dumb;*

flat and far as space can reach
mountains that bless
await in the sun
a poet's speech.

In steel machine
and glass we glide;
metallic void and sterile cell
from Great Africa divide.
While a Gazelle –
eye tendrils long –
sucks from sourbush and scent of clod
a poet's song.

I feel privileged to be her sole listener, though my attention does wander: 'gazelle' has a lovely sound but I've never seen one. My mother tells me she has another, secret name, like Upwards for our house. She's Tsviah, meaning 'gazelle' in Hebrew. 'It sounds like my middle name, Stella,' she justifies the choice, 'and I prefer Stella to Rhoda.'

Not to hurt her feelings, I don't admit my indifference to a more ordinary poem she's written, designed for us children: 'Story of a Tree for my children, Lyndall and Pip'. A tree without its leaves, stilled by 'Winter's breath', waits 'secretly and faithfully' for the 'tremor' in the earth that brings on spring. This seasonal story of renewal doesn't touch me like the word 'suffering' (an ominous word on her lips), and again 'suffering'.

Her models come from books beside her bed. One is the journal of Katherine Mansfield who, my mother says, was ill in the south of France, away from home and unsupported by her husband. And yet, for her, illness was a 'privilege' because it opened her eyes as a writer.

This is the challenge Rhoda undertakes: to transmute fear into sight and to find words to unlock those words that 'lie beyond the mouth / locked in the mountain's chest'. Her metaphor is prompted not only by the difficulty of expression but also by modesty. For Katherine Mansfield had genius. Rhoda, laid low at the bottom of Africa, can make no such claim, not even to the child at her side. All the same, I understand in some fashion how sightings along the way come as compensation.

August – late winter 1946. I have something the doctor calls 'trench mouth'. Before penicillin becomes available in general practice, temperatures run high and infections don't heal that fast. I'm in bed for some time, not in the nursery but in my mother's room. I'm impatient for my mother finally to finish splashing her face and giving the orders on the phone. She sits down on my bed with the finality of a down movement mingled with an air of expectancy. Whenever she lends herself to the drama on the page she becomes these characters: bungling Pooh Bear hunting a heffalump; the naughty look in the corner of Peter Rabbit's eye when Mother Rabbit warns him not to go into Mr McGregor's garden; and Betsey Trotwood calling on laughably simple Mr Dick for his opinion as to what to do with her runaway nephew Davy Copperfield.

When I get up and am helped into navy blue woollen dungarees, I wobble. I take a few steps to the open window and see the sea in the distance and smell its salty sharpness mingled with ripening loquats. I'm uncertain whether or not to believe my mother's story that I once spat a loquat pip out of the window, and it grew itself into a tree in the soil below.

A glad day to be up again, and my mother celebrates by reading aloud a new story, 'The Doll's House'. It's about an awakening to snobbery. This could be any suburb, it could be

Sea Point, but it's based, my mother's explains, on Katherine Mansfield's colonial home in Wellington, New Zealand. Here, Aunt Beryl rebuffs two children in ragged dresses, the Kelveys, who are hanging about after hearing boasts at school that Aunt Beryl's nieces have acquired a doll's house complete with furniture. Kezia, the Katherine Mansfield child, smuggles the ragged Kelveys into her middle-class home. Proudly she shows off the doll's house, before Aunt Beryl shoos the children out. Lil Kelvey's cheeks burn, but the smaller girl, filled with wonder, says, 'I seen the little lamp.'

These words of 'our Else' come back to me in my mother's plangent tones, resonant with that child's undamped wonder.

At the end of the war in Europe my mother posts food parcels to an orphaned girl in France. I'm fascinated by my mother's letters to this motherless girl, and decide to write to her myself. My letter is pencilled on the invitingly blank margins of *Winnie-the-Pooh*, covering many of its pages. It's puzzling that my mother should say with a line crossing her forehead, 'You must not scribble in books.' Scribble? To me it looks like a faithful imitation of adults' joined-up writing, and each page is filled with thoughts and feelings.

My mother picks up a stick and draws the letters of the alphabet in the gravel of the Sea Point beachfront. In her poem 'Her Girl' she's laughing with me as we lie, 'close-huddled', drawing faces on the hot, white sand, 'the wind threading our hair / Filled with the voices of the waves'.

A companion poem, 'Her Boy', is more humorous. It starts:

Better than poetry
Are your buttocks

and pictures her boy 'standing so donkeymeek / To let me

peer/ Into your ear.' She records Pip's comment at the end of
'The Doll's House':

> *'That story's sad'*
> *You ruminate*
> *'Until the end –*
> *'But the tip-end's glad.'*

Her scribbles in pencil have rhythm marks to one side. Then
she types a fair copy. She says to Pip and me, 'If the house was
on fire, I'd save first my children, then my typewriter.' It tells me
how much poems count.

7

School versus Home

Little as Pip is, he's a fighter, and he has the courage to act against Nurse (as we call her) from St Helena. Unlike indulgent local nannies, Nurse declares that nowhere has she come across such bad children. How we hate her with her cross face and oily hair under the prim, white headgear of a hospital nurse. Once, when we are seated at our round table, Pip hears our parents' voices in the next-door bathroom and on an impulse breaks out of the nursery to tell them. It's a wild risk. Though they listen patiently to what Pip has to say, they lead him back to her hardening control.

Two years later Pip will come home from his boys' school, Sea Point Junior, with two red lines across his small bottom. Caning, I'm shocked to hear, is to be expected. Once again, it's not a matter for parental protest.

My mother decides that the time has come for our morning companionship to end. I too must go to school, and her choice falls on FPS (Fresnaye Preparatory School) – Mrs de Korte's school, as it's known. My father demurs at the expense, six pounds a term, twenty-four pounds a year, but he's overruled.

Sighing, because it's difficult for Rhoda to rouse herself for an interview with Mrs de Korte, she walks me along Avenue le Soeur, where the High Level bus to town sits, chugging, at its terminus, and then up the steep, cobbled slope of Avenue des Huguenots. It's only ten minutes from our house in Avenue Normandie. There's the resinous smell of the mountain pines – we children pounce on fallen cones and, sitting on the kerb, crack the nutcases with a stone. Nothing is so delectable as chewing a newly extracted *dennepit*, mashed by the stone. Ranged over low walls are the pointed beaks of orange poinsettias or, reaching towards the blue sky, the blue shock-heads of agapanthus. Above looms the rocky crest of Lion's Head.

Sorry though I am for my mother's forced steps, I'm ready to go, eager to belong with other children. Mrs de Korte, with a dark bun, talks gravely to my mother, who is ill at ease. I'm given a tray of shapes to fit into holes and an inviting new box of Crayola crayons: I pick green, and draw a house like the houses I've drawn many times on the sand. My mother tells her friends afterwards in a rather sad, self-mocking voice that she's surprised by my alacrity, as though she'd expected more reluctance to leave our retreat. At such times she comments how much I resemble my father.

That hint of reproach is not only about defecting too willingly to my father's active mode. The retreat she and I shared had offered a pirate's cave of treasures, what might be called an alternative education, but now her secret sharer is to be recast in the standard mould.

At school we are asked to recite a rhyme, and one child after the other picks 'Baa Baa Black Sheep'. I vary this with 'Little Miss Muffet', thinking of the scary spiders from Lion's Head, who pop up on our walls. When I report the choice at home my mother lets loose a displeased 'ohhh'.

In the back garden, ready to leave my mother for the first day at FPS

She shakes her head at so mundane a choice.

'Why not "The Swing"? You know it by heart.'

I can't explain about conformity, and a sense that to choose this poem would appear as showing off.

Almost every other child carries a school suitcase. A satchel is better for posture, my mother argues, but I don't care about posture. Only Denise Sagov has a satchel like mine and, even so, her walk is ungainly. Denise is 'unpopular' – that's the word children use. It's not discussed; it's a fact. And it will stick when we go on to King's Road Junior School at the age of eight, and then, at twelve, to Good Hope Seminary. Denise compensates by bringing to school a giant box of Crayola with enticing half-shades of greys, blues and greens, and though we besiege Denise to try these out, she's no more popular than before.

Truth be told, I don't much like Denise because she boasts, even though there's something pathetic as well as intransigent in such bravado. My mother, who'd been at school with her mother, urges me to befriend Denise, but I prefer the party in power, all the while recognising another kind of outsider in my secret self, to be preserved in silence. My mother's retreat or some instinct warns that it must fade to nothing in public. I'm too sorry for Denise to join the bullies, yet too craven to risk protest.

In our early teens I shy away from parties, but at one or two where I'm an onlooker there is Denise, uninhibited as ever, bopping (my diary says) 'with her mouth open'. Then, at fifteen, Denise comes into her own in the art room. Her boldness takes shape in strongly coloured figures in local scenes, barrow-boys and street musicians slapped onto canvas with lavish strokes, like the paintings of Irma Stern. (I'm familiar with the style because my mother has an Irma Stern: two Xhosa women, one in yellow, the other in orange, leaning towards each other to share a pipe.) Miss Lust, the American art teacher, who tears around in a jeep, cheers Denise on: the bolder the better.

Later, when I return on a visit from New York, Denise invites my daughter Anna, aged four, to her child's birthday party at her old Fresnaye home. The party is too big and too much entertainment is laid on. While I mill about with other mothers, it shames me to hear Denise blasting out above the noise that I'd been her only friend at school.

Still later, Denise (re-named Dunya) emigrates to New York. I hear from anti-apartheid activists Rusty and Hilda Bernstein that she opens her home to them and other refugees during the Struggle. They like her wholeheartedly, and look puzzled – as well they might – to hear how it was at school.

Jane and Dick pat the cat in our reader. The cat sat on a mat. Jane and Dick toss a red ball. My mother says that there were no books on the veld except the reader in her one-room school, and that her imagination 'irradiated' the equivalent of Jane and Dick. I'm less imaginative, bored, and yet content to line up after break and pencil a row of wavery 0s.

Away from school, the houses I draw on the sand are for dream-families with lots of children who act in a world of their own. There's always one girl amongst them, the Judy or Jo March girl, who clashes with adult expectations. These dreams are prompted by *Seven Little Australians* or *Little Women* – orphanage library books whose stories my mother reads aloud, like the humiliating scene where Amy March secretes pickled limes in her school desk, is found out, and has to offer her hand to be caned.

A generation later, when my second daughter, Olivia, starts school in 1984, I recall a scene of humiliation in mid-January 1947. I write it down for her in an exercise book entitled 'Old Stories', which she edits and illustrates.

The First Day at School

Miss Grey, who was small with a red face and grey hair, was our teacher. When we were seated in rows at our desks, and Miss Grey had asked us our names and checked them in the register, she suddenly did something odd. She turned to the blackboard. On it she drew

Two big, round circles.

'What is this?' Miss Grey asked the class.

No one put up a hand. There was a long silence.

'This,' said Miss Grey, 'is what Charlie's nose will look like when he grows up, if he goes on picking it.'

Humiliation. How it dominates memory. 'What is the worst thing in life for you?' Virginia Woolf once asked T. S. Eliot in the early twenties. It was night-time. They were in a taxi, passing through the damp market gardens of London. 'Humiliation,' Eliot said unhesitatingly. As I call up that first-day scene for Olivia, my second biography, on Virginia Woolf, is due for publication, and I'm struck by her innovative idea of Lives, questioning her father's necessary focus on Lives in their public aspects, as the first editor of the *Dictionary of National Biography*. Looking back over six lives, the passage of one generation, in her masterpiece *The Waves*, she perceives that all our stories of birth, marriage and death aren't true, only the 'moments of humiliation and triumph that come now and then undeniably'. This fits my mother's sense of the unseen, her focus on the inwardness of existence.

To go to school is to switch from my mother's expansive story of suffering and transcendence to narrow rituals of obedience versus disobedience. It's simply a matter of learning the rules. One rule is to put up your hand and say, 'May I leave the room?' if you need the lavatory. Unable to utter these words, I postpone the need so unbearably long during drill that, very quietly, I wet the floor and leave the puddle there, pretending it can't be me. Cowardice adds to my shame.

When we can read for ourselves we devour *The Naughtiest Girl in the School* by Enid Blyton. Here, allegiance to school replaces home, and an obliterated mother appears solely to wave her daughter away. Farewell to nurture through the domestic affections. Whatever the reasons – custom, class, empire (still intact in 1940, when the book came out) – those affections are distanced at an early age, to be replaced by head girls who enforce rules. Elizabeth Allen is a hot-headed girl prone to forget the rules but well up to spelling them out to a new girl, a scorned Mother's-precious-darling, in *The Naughtiest Girl is a Monitor*. Central to this ethos is the disempowering and exclusion of Mother.

At the bottom of a colonised Africa, we're fascinated by school stories from England – that far-away, superior civilisation we look up to and try to copy, so far as our noisy voices and flat vowels will take us. Mrs de Korte employs an elocution teacher who makes us recite with rounded, elongated vowels. Some mothers affect this pseudo-English manner, a sign how posh they want to be.

There are few Jewish children. One called Gilda Myers, with brown eyes and a lovely bloom, is chosen to be the princess in a school production of *The Sleeping Beauty*. She's tearful when she proves just a little too plump for the princess costume and the part goes to a thin, Afrikaans girl called Welien. Of course I long to be the princess, but am cast as the ugly fairy, who has to cackle evilly from the folds of her black cloak. My mother tries to comfort me that it's a more active part than that of the princess who has little more to do than lie back and be kissed. She bestirs herself to make me a wand, and this effort is somehow more effective comfort. Laboriously, she draws its star with a ruler on cardboard, and then carefully cuts it out and covers it with silver paper.

I can't be jealous of Welien because she isn't proud. She and her straight-backed older brother Hendrik say what they mean. Inevitably, they are seen less for themselves, but as Afrikaners whose parents, it's assumed, vote for the party in power. Even before the Nationalists come to power in 1948 and put their policy of apartheid into law, separate groups exist beyond racial divides. School is a microcosm of the white group with its separate sub-groups, divided by class, language and religion. Jewish children stay in an empty classroom during morning prayers, as does the sole Roman Catholic, a rosy child called Linda Prest with straight blonde hair behind her ears. We call her *Padda Kwaak*, Afrikaans for 'a frog croaks', because she has a wide mouth stretched in smiles.

Conformity has always held for me an intriguing otherness, like theatre, shaped as I am by an apart and questioning mother. Can I play this unlikely role, I ask myself en route to school, and later as I approach unlikely roles as wife and mother. Those who confer normality, daughters especially, are dear, not only for what they are in their home selves but also as playmates on the public stage. In this spirit of play, script in hand, I skip down the slope of the playground, unprepared for unscripted scenes.

The elocution teacher runs every side-show at Mrs de Korte's. It's she who casts me as the ugly fairy and burdens my mother with having to produce a costume to her satisfaction. Her next venture is to audition us for a children's sequence in a mannequin parade. This is another of the stories I will pass on to Olivia when she goes to school.

The Mannequin Parade

In Sub B, the second year at Mrs de Korte's school, our speech teacher, Miss Lurie, wanted the six-year-olds to join in a mannequin parade at the Sea Point Town Hall. 'The audition,' she said, 'will be held at Marion's house.'

Now Marion lived in a very grand house and, to tell you the truth, she was a very proud girl who never invited me to play. So when Miss Lurie asked 'Who can't come to the audition?' I, together with Gilda, put up my hand.

'Why can't you come, Gilda?'

'I have Hebrew every afternoon,' said Gilda.

'And why can't you come, Lyndall?' asked Miss Lurie.

'I – don't know,' I faltered.

'What a silly you are,' said Miss Lurie. 'You must come.'

Unwillingly, I made my way there when the day came. Close up, the grandeur looked gloomy. The house stood back from Kloof Road in the shadow of Lion's Head. At the long windows, shutters hung half-closed. In the dark lounge amongst strangers, I was told to look through a blue hoop, then to roll it, chase it, and pretend to slip. Miss Lurie thought up this act. 'It's not hard, is it?' she said. 'See how silly you were.'

When the day came for the parade, I was put into a sweetheart dress, blue, covered with love letters sealed with red hearts. The act went to plan but next day – oh dear – there was a photograph in the gossip section of the *Cape Times*, headed GIRL FALLS IN PARADE. There I was, pictured for all to see, with legs in the air.

During our last year at Mrs de Korte's each seven-year-old has a turn to be head girl or boy. I'm paired with Frank Guthrie, who'd been a wooden soldier in *The Sleeping Beauty*. He'd mastered an eye-catching turn: his body stiff, to attention, would rock back and forth on his toes and heels, more and more violently, until he fell over – still rigid – for the hundred-year sleep.

Head-girl responsibilities are delightfully trivial. Puffed up with temporary importance, I repeat to myself a line from the *Naughtiest Girl* – 'the tall head girl walked up the steps' – as I mount the steps from the playground to Mrs de Korte's stoep to report a nosebleed. Mrs de Korte comes with a brass key to put down the back of the bleeder. I can't see how this can help; it belongs with adults' inexplicable rituals, like sticking Elastoplast behind a child's ears to prevent car-sickness.

My mother takes me to see Alicia Markova in *The Dying Swan* at the Alhambra. At the end the audience is too rapt to clap, not for almost a minute. My mother says, 'Silence is a higher tribute to perfection.' From this moment I want to learn ballet. Unfortunately, my toes won't turn out and my point is poor. Still, I love bending to music at the barre, the beats of the *battements frappés* and *entrechats*, and the rhythms of *grands jêtés*, soaring and turning across the studio. Behind the closed door of the top room I practise the leaps with more abandon. In the same way, I respond to the abandon and decorum of prose that comes down with its feet on the ground. Though I'm no good at ballet it remains as a rhythm in the blood. When I prepare a talk, I pace it with my feet, moving to the rhythms of prose with its leaps and turns.

King's Road Junior School is bigger and stricter than Mrs de Korte's. All the classes are assembled and the head, Miss Goodchild (not a made-up name), tells us to sit cross-legged on the floor.

'Hands on heads. Hands down. Hands on heads. Hands down.'

When we are still, Miss Goodchild calls for Jill Habberley to step forward, and in a solemn voice accuses her of forgetting what sounds like a trivial rule. Then Miss Goodchild, gripping the culprit's arm, whacks Jill Habberley, who looks like a stumbling spider with long limbs around a closed rose mouth.

In those days, every school has its feared teacher. At the age of nine we enter Standard Three (fifth grade), taught by the school's terror, Mrs Thatcher (again, not a made-up name). We sit in our double desks with dipping pens poised above inkwells. In unison we repeat a multiplication table. We are baa-ing, not thinking. At ten each morning a hush falls and all eyes swivel as the door to the classroom opens. A girl called Isabel with a high, polished forehead is carried like a doll to her seat in the front row. Her legs are stiff. Her face is closed against stares. We suppose she comes late because she has to have daily treatments, perhaps for polio, but we don't know because nothing is said. No one ever speaks to her because speaking is not allowed.

Uncle Sydney, who lives in America, has sent me a book called *Seatmates*, and I'm friends with my seatmate Marcia. She says 'Gah!', growling the 'G' as in Afrikaans, with a jerk of the head like play-play English gentlemen who throw back their heads to say 'Pah!' It's irresistible to cheer on Marcia mouthing 'Gah' when Mrs Thatcher turns her back to chalk a sum on the board.

'Who was speaking?' Her fierce ears catch the sound. Reluctantly, I have to own up.

'Don't let me catch you again.'

She turns again to the blackboard and in a lowered, almost inaudible whisper I mouth something to Marcia.

Mrs Thatcher whirls around. 'Go – out – of the room,' her voice stabs. 'No – go – to the Office.'

The Office means Miss Goodchild. My legs take me down the stairs and along the corridor towards the Office, and then they carry me past it to the row of lavatories at the back of the school. I hide there for what seems an age, and then, heart beating, I run away from school.

At the time, my parents are away and I'm staying with the top girl in the class, Jasmine. Her mother says firmly, not unkindly, that I'm to go back to school next day. It's a relief to find Mrs Thatcher says nothing. Not so the children. Nesta, arm in arm with a chum, comes up to where I'm sitting on a bench in the playground.

'Why did you run away from school?'

I lie. 'I felt sick.' It sounds lame.

Once each term we are bussed to the botanical gardens at Kirstenbosch to learn about plants with the curator, Miss Johns.

'Gather round,' says Miss Johns as she examines an indigenous flower in its bed. We crowd about her, and because the flower is so small and the crowd so tight, I edge this way and that in order to peer.

'Did you step on a plant?' Miss Johns's iron hand clamps my arm. Dismayed, I look down and see that I probably did.

'I'll have to give you a paddy whack,' nods Miss Johns archly and slaps my shin, while the girls watch in silence.

'What's your name?'

I force it out.

'Are you Harry's daughter?'

'Yes, Miss Johns.' I'm sorry he's brought into this.

'I know your father,' says Miss Johns, her voice softening, 'and he wouldn't like his daughter to be disobedient.'

This disgrace follows me back to King's Road. Mrs Thatcher, grim of face, says, 'I hear you were disobedient.' It confirms her opinion, and nothing can change it. For years to come, my eyes are shut to Kirstenbosch – until, at seventeen, I went there with Siamon. In a glade, under overhanging trees, we threw pennies in Lady Anne Barnard's pool, and wished.

'What did you wish?' I pressed him, thinking he might want to kiss me.

'I wished for peace of mind,' Siamon said, looking away. Somehow this dispelled the blight of Miss Johns.

Rhoda's room seems a far cry from what goes on at school, yet all the while its books and dramas echo in my mind. Jo March, obliged to keep Aunt March company, shades into my mother's urge to write, blocked by a woman's duty. Sun and Moon, children thrust aside by partying parents in Katherine Mansfield's story, call up yapping voices at Granny's tea parties, jarring to Rhoda's finer feelings. Her own voice, resonant with import, impersonates the monotone of Dr Manette, holed up in the Bastille. And then comes bloodthirsty Madame Defarge, one of the knitting women counting the heads severed by the guillotine: I hear even now the dire 'aaah' of Defarge, as my mother pronounced the name. I've never read *A Tale of Two Cities*. It's a book heard in childhood, not overlaid with an adult response. I lie spotted with measles in my mother's darkened room as emotions rise like a wave: my mother reads right through the day – a marathon read – until she comes to the famous ending: 'It's a far, far better thing . . . ' Far better for a man to give up his life than continue to degrade his body. I'm all for the moral imperative of sacrifice that emanates from my mother as much as from Dickens.

On top of Katherine Mansfield, or sometimes under her, is the Bible. My mother relates the parable of David and Goliath, the simple shepherd boy versus a giant warrior – she is partial to the innocent, the obscure, the weak and pure of heart. But more significant for her than David on the battlefield or David the King, is David the poet whose psalms walk him through 'the valley of the shadow', certain not to be abandoned by his heavenly Father.

Familiar too is the story of Jacob on the road to his destiny as one of the Chosen, who wrestles all night with a divine force. In the morning he limps away, his hip out of joint. His injury is proof that it's not a dream. 'I have seen God face to face,' he claims. Two women, each secluded at home in complete obscurity, venture to make like claims. As day breaks, Emily Dickinson's astonished Wrestler finds that she has actually 'worsted God'. Her spirit is that strong.

My mother's wrestler is less of a winner. There's 'no Jacob's dawn, limping triumphant'. The sign from on high is rather like a seizure, an encounter so fraught it nearly wrecks the wrestler. During the course of the night, 'the desperate soul is nearly torn from its socket'. Come dawn, and it's not over. 'Starved for light, in abbadon we grope at noon . . .'

I see now that there's no given word for the dislocation of her being in the wasteland that follows the seizure. 'Abba' is Hebrew for 'father', so 'abbadon' suggests abandon by a divine Father. It's fear, not the actuality of abandon. For in the end the wrestler does survive by holding on to Psalm XXIII:

> ... *Turn*
> *on the edge of death and walk on the tightrope psalm*
> *steadfast to the end: 'surely goodness*
> *and mercy shall dwell'*
> *till the clayhouse body knows*
> *the Inrush of the Spirit*
> *and the fountaining of love.*

As a child I can't fathom what she's saying beyond an unspeakable horror I'm reluctant to know. Clearer to me is her tenacity, and I'm somewhat relieved when she moves on to love. And of course I'm glad that she's making me into a person who, she says, 'will one day understand'.

So it happens that while my mother scribbles in her wire-bound notebook, I become a watcher of her chrysalis. Rhoda elevates this role of watcher, through her feeling for Dorothy Wordsworth, who watched and often prompted the creative fount of her brother. Wordsworth catches 'gleams of past existence' in his sister's eyes. Years later, as a biographer, this will put me in sympathy with others who watched at the side of writers and seers: Emily Hale, who watched T. S. Eliot, and waited for him; and 'Fenimore' (great-niece to James Fenimore Cooper), who watched Henry James; and Charlotte Brontë, watching her sister Emily, who was herself a watcher of the night, awaiting the 'wandering airs' at her window – reminding me how Rhoda each night opens her window to the roar from the ocean's throat.

Lives I will watch years later turn on the inner life of that room, its moral character, its sufferings and resilience, above all the 'fountaining' of a writer's voice.

*

Rhoda after her marriage, with her three bachelor brothers.
Left to right: Hubert, Sydney and Basil

Rhoda brightens when Wordsworth calls Dorothy his 'dear, dear sister'. In her late twenties, when her friends are unavailable, she's missing her brothers, especially Basil.

As a doctor in the army during the war, Basil has been posted to Walvis Bay in the former German colony of South West Africa. After the First World War the colony was taken over as a South African mandate (with red stripes on maps, not as entirely red as fully British colonies). The German inhabitants of SWA are so pro-Nazi and the anti-Semitism of South African troops so blatant that Basil, usually unperturbed, finds it disturbing to be there.

Once, in the officers' mess, they ask him to leave so that they can joke about Jews without of the constraint of his presence. Another time, he's summoned by a German woman to examine her sick boy. No sooner does Basil enter the house than he walks slap into a poster of Hitler. The boy, shivering with malaria, leaps out of bed and kisses the doctor's hand – unaware that he's kissing a Jew.

After the war, Basil joins his brothers, Sydney and Hubert, at Edgars, the family's chain of clothing stores. Basil had intended to move on to specialist medical training, which meant going to England or America, but Sydney asked him to postpone this because help was needed with the mail-order side of Edgars. Basil began travelling to small towns around Southern Africa, and when there were sufficient customers the Presses would open new branches. In time there were hundreds, and Basil never went back to medicine. His sister lamented this often; she felt he had the caring nature of a born doctor.

The three brothers settle on a farm called Evermore in Morningside, now swallowed up by Johannesburg but then on the outskirts where it's still country. In 1946 my mother decides on a visit. It's a two-day journey by steam train, and at one stage a second steam engine puffs up behind the train to push it to six thousand feet above sea level. I'm given a Little Golden

Book to read on my own, the story of the Three Little Pigs and the Big Bad Wolf who says, 'I'll huff and I'll puff and I'll blow your house down.' Pip clutches his own Little Golden Book, *Tootle*.

The train stops at Matjiesfontein in the Karoo. My mother recalls that Olive Schreiner lived here. Rising from this bare landscape, as isolated as Klaver, came her feminist *Dreams*. In 1891 she sent them to London. Reprinted twenty times, and translated into eight languages, they sold eighty thousand copies. Lady Constance Lytton read aloud one of the *Dreams* to fasting suffragettes in Holloway Prison. My mother writes a poem for Olive Schreiner; it's about the longing to write in a landscape where the distant horizon stands to attention.

Lenie, who accompanies us because no white woman can manage without a servant, alights from the 'coloured' coach, to see if help is needed. The train has barely stopped before our restless father is racing along the platform, reaching up to other carriages to shake hands with travellers who listen in to his broadcasts. I'm scared he'll be left behind, and in fact the engine steams up and belches tremendous hoots before Harry, sportingly, leaps onto the last carriage as it leaves the platform to wind its way around the koppies of the Karoo.

Towards evening, a rather tired engine is rolling slowly through the long grass of the Highveld. The sun, which had been white-hot at its zenith, is now a red ball on the horizon. We jerk the wooden shutters so that they fall into their bottom slot, and put our heads out of the windows to sniff the acrid smoke wafting back from the engine's funnel, rub the occasional bit of grit out of our eyes and turn our heads to the carriages behind us in the curving tail of the train. Behind the coloureds in second class is the sole, packed third class carriage for 'natives', who sleep on bare ledges, not on bunks with fresh bedding made up for the night.

My mother points out how 'each tree has a shadow like a wing outstretched'. The swiftly fading light 'silvers the auburn grass'. Then she's scribbling 'High Veld Time Exposure' in her notebook.

> . . . *The veld to velvet glows;*
> *Dark moles the anthills seem*
> *And bushes have a gentle look.*
> *In the sunsucked grass*
> *Africans stand*
> *With legs loose-lagged*
> *Talking slow . . .*

At Evermore two thickly grown hillocks promise secret places. To the right is a tennis court where our uncles entertain. A Zulu got up in white with a tasselled red sash serves drinks to visitors reclining under their hats after a game. Fenced off at the bottom of the garden are horses, cows, hens and bales of straw. Granny Annie, presiding in the home of her three bachelor sons, orders a male cook to boil new-laid eggs 'for the children's supper'. Here, in the interior, there's more vigilance against infection; here, our great-great-grandfather, fresh from Europe, unprepared for what was alien in Africa, soon died of dysentery. He was forty-five. Malaria is still rife, and we are put to sleep under mosquito nets hanging from hooks.

My mother doesn't figure in my memory of Evermore. Was she re-absorbed into her family? Certainly, she resisted a mercenary Johannesburg in a poem, 'The Great City of Goli' (with an epigraph from a Zulu song: 'Over the banks of the Vaal lies the Great City of Goli [Gold]'), with its 'costly portals' and 'backdoor rapes'. Dominating the skyline, mine dumps testify to the exploitation of black miners who are paid a pittance, housed in barracks and separated for years from their

Granny Annie in Johannesburg with her younger sons
Hubert (left) and Sydney Press

rural families: 'Lords of the Rand sphinx-idols lie / The gold dumps white in a black sky.'

It may seem strange that, until the age of thirty-one, Rhoda doesn't ask what her illness is. In 1948, while Harry is away at the Olympic Games in London, she has 'a bad attack', her phrase for a full-on seizure. Afterwards she again consults doctors who continue to prescribe powders she tries not to take because these doctors, like the doctors she'd seen in London, treat her as an hysteric who brings illness on herself. But this time she resolves to articulate her suspicion that there's something more to know. She puts this to her brother, the only doctor she can trust.

My Dear Basil,

I'm writing to ask you to come down [from Johannesburg] during the next long weekend. Besides the pleasure of seeing you again, I urgently wish to discuss with you matters concerning my health.

While you are away I always determine to speak to you when next you come down & always fail to do so while you are here. Recently I had another of my attacks. For many years now I've striven for health of spirit by trying to strengthen my character, to purify my thoughts, to perfect my life. I have forged precious weapons wherewith I continually fight off attacks[,] which are especially valuable in conquering the ensuing depression & fears after an attack. But I am beginning to fear that I cannot under all circumstances prevent an attack. I seem to have wasted months, even years fighting this illness. I long to be a free normal human being at last.

As I've imagined & expected the worst for long periods of my life nothing you know or fear can terrify me & I think as an intelligent person & at my time of life, I've a right to know all that is within your power to tell me of my illness. Only the truth can help me . . .

Much love from
Rhoda

Basil does come, and he breaks it to her that she has the severe kind of epilepsy known as grand mal. How he puts it I don't know, yet at last she understands that her illness is physiological. It's a huge relief. For Basil's words release her from the obligation to control her illness through acts of will. From then on she accepts the necessity for daily and nightly doses of anti-convulsant pills, Epanutin and barbiturate, even though they dull her imagination. At last she can get up and go out with a degree of confidence.

Four years later, freed from attacks, she makes up her mind to leave her refuge.

8

'Lapp Heights'

On 10 June 1952 Rhoda leaves home, bound for Finland. Why Finland? If anything were simple in her intentions, the answer should be the Olympic Games, where her husband will offici-ate in the swimming. But Rhoda has no eye to any competitive event. For her, the tug of Finland is its proximity to Lithuania. Guided by her dream life, her imagination calls up 'Chagallian villages', her father's memories and the luftmensch aloft in northern skies. To go to Finland is to reconnect with her 'father-root'. Her dream is not only fantastical; it's allegoric in the way she assigns people to moral compartments: a poetic father-root to be claimed; a mundane South African mother, well intentioned but alien.

Rhoda is thirty-five years old, with two children, aged ten and eight. We will remain with our grandmother, Annie, who's hap-pily down-to-earth. We three visit the well-appointed cabin on board the Holland-Afrika liner, the *Klipfontein*. When my father travels alone he cuts corners, but first-class comfort is considered necessary for Rhoda's better health, and her brothers would expect no less. The cabin is full of farewell bouquets from friends, and the orphanage has sent a basket of fruit for the long voyage. The siren blasts a warning of departure and we tread carefully down the ridges of the gangplank, turning to wave to our parents on deck.

I'm relieved to see our mother elated, and ease into Granny's hands. Unstoppably, she surges forward in the main thoroughfare of Adderley Street, holding up the traffic with the point of her sunshade. She loves to shop, and we spend hours matching a ribbon to furbish her newest hat. In the shoe department at Stuttafords we choose warm winter slippers in preparation for a holiday up country. Schools shut for three weeks in July, and Granny is taking us to Vredendal, four stations north of Klaver. Throughout the night the train stops at sidings, lanterns swing, '*Maak gou, Meneer*' drifts by the windows, footsteps quicken and milk cans clank. At dawn, an arid landscape of bush unrolls in shafts of sunlight, and a rather sleepy engine puffs and subsides as the train's long tail winds across the veld.

Granny has no time to look at the veld because she's rummaging in suitcases. Her fuss leaves me free to dream my way into books; rolled in her puffy pink eiderdown, I join far-away Canadian children in *Rainbow Valley*. It's one of my mother's childhood favourites, an old hardback with the inviting smell of thick, rough-edged pages and printer's ink, acquired for the orphanage. Strictly speaking, I have no right to it, but no one objects. Part of that library's appeal is its smallness; the books are selected to mend a child's heart and invigorate courage. In the gravel outside Eisenberg's Hotel on the corner of the wide main street of Vredendal I play hopscotch with a girl called Hereen van Zyl. Her English vocabulary is small, my Afrikaans likewise, but the game is all, and we understand each other better by the day.

Then Granny spoils it. She sends something from her stylish wardrobe to Hereen's mother. When I go with Hereen to her house, I find Mevrou van Zyl furious.

'Tell your grandmother I'm not in need of cast-offs!' she says, and shuts the door against my open mouth.

I see now what my mother means about her mother's shaming ways.

Meanwhile, the *Klipfontein* is sailing on into the northern hemisphere. Rhoda's deckchair companion turns out to be Laurens van der Post, with whom she can share her feeling for the *vlaktes*, the untrammelled spaces of her early childhood. En route to Stockholm a poem, 'Midnight at Malmö', rises as her train streaks through the night. This hurtling speed is strange, like taking off into a fairy tale.

Swedes appear 'glassy', unlike the 'simple friendliness' aboard a Finnish boat plying between Stockholm and Helsinki. Her impression is coloured by Sweden's neutrality during the Holocaust, in contrast to Finland's protection of its minute Jewish population. For Marshal Mannerheim refused to hand Jews over to the Nazis, even though, in 1941, Finland entered the war on the German side – a consequence of Finland's struggles with Russia. It was an unprecedented situation where Germans found themselves encamped, one Saturday, near Jewish soldiers in a field synagogue.

Rhoda's letters home invite us to travel with a semi-invalid as she wakes to a new life out in the great world. The decks are packed with comers from every country. They huddle in sleeping bags, exposing children's 'carved eyebrows and lids like pointed buds'. A man lies with 'a water-lily hand in his gloved one'.

I can't go to bed, Rhoda thinks. She moves from group to group, talking, a little touch of nearness in the night, and crossing paths with children 'sleepwalking' in red woollen caps.

Above this knot of peace hangs 'a single fringed star'. Throbbing, the boat slides past dark islands 'asleep on the ocean'. Rhoda's knees are beginning to freeze.

They stay in a white wooden manor on a lake. On the opposite side lives the composer Sibelius. The building itself is a bit decrepit, but it's well run by staff in national dress. There's an interpreter, an elderly Russian-French intellectual, who is half-Jewish and calls Rhoda 'dearest', and whom Rhoda suspects is deeply corrupt. She wears grand, ancient clothes and is fond of the bottle, like the madam of a brothel, and in fact there are 'goings on' in the manor.

Rhoda steps out in navy organza and a silver-grey stole to a party in a semi-circular restaurant on a more distant lake. She's animated between Harry and a tanned South African water-polo player, Solly Yach. Both have participated in the Maccabiah Games and know almost everyone at this largely Israeli party. Rhoda ventures to stumble through a few Hebrew phrases. Her

gameness is welcome; an American judge kisses her hands. She
and Harry drive back 'as dawn was almost breaking into silvern
lakes in the dark foliage of the sky', and walk up an avenue 'of
honey-scented lime trees' towards the manor.

During the swimming finals, my father is broadcasting for the
BBC and other Anglophone stations when, suddenly, he spots
that the grandstand opposite is swaying. It's overloaded with
about four hundred visitors, and might collapse at any moment.
Stopping his running commentary in mid-flow, he addresses the
crowd through the microphone. 'The stand is unstable. Please
follow instructions. Sit still. Stay calm. Top row, come down.'
He talks them down, one row at a time. This is Harry in his
element, with a quick eye and ready to act.

One night Rhoda and Harry go down a long white jetty to
a sauna. They stand in the steam and beat each other with birch
twigs, as an extra tonic. Three times, as instructed, they sweat
up their bodies and then, each time, dive into the lake.

'You feel as good as after a bathe at Muizenberg,' Rhoda
decides, 'only much cleaner.'

It's half-past ten, but scarcely dark. Rimming this scene of
silver air and water are dark clumps of 'porcupine earth'. On
closer inspection these turn out to be 'tree-dark islands like children's heads asleep'. As she looks out over the lake, there rises
in her mind a half-formed prayer to share Finland with someone.

While others go daily to the Games, she goes to the
Ateneum, the national art museum, in a square with linden trees
in the centre of the city. One Wednesday in late July, the guide
is an art critic, Sirkka Anttila. Her long black hair is drawn back
in a casual bun, baring high cheekbones, and her slanting black
eyes snap and flash as she points to soulful paintings, punctuated
by 'Hey ... hey ... ' when she draws back from a conclusion.
Rhoda warms to Finland's best-known woman painter, Helene

Schjerfbeck, an invalid who withdrew into seclusion in the provinces. Her self-portrait of 1915 bares a face pared down to intense inwardness. She has the unwavering gaze of an observer, similar to the gaze of Katherine Mansfield when she's fine-drawn and alone, arms folded over her tubercular chest, in a photograph my mother has on her desk.

A viewer amongst the visiting party asks why a sculptor has made a woman's legs absurdly thick. Sirkka hears behind her 'a small, small voice' explaining – 'so marvellous, intelligent', she records that night in her diary – the deliberate disproportions of modernist art.

Slowly, she turns a hundred and eighty degrees to see who this is. It's a woman of her own age, mid-thirties, with dark hair, in thick glasses with pale-blue rims around attentive blue eyes. After the viewing Rhoda asks for Sirkka's address at the very moment that Sirkka asks for hers. Sirkka lives in one room, teaching art in a high school, reviewing exhibitions and editing art books.

She feels, she remarks to Rhoda, 'rich each flash of time when there is a moment to glance up from work'. Flash. She knows. Their eyes lock.

When they meet for lunch the next day Sirkka plunges into the kind of inward utterance Rhoda has ventured only in poems.

Rhoda shows Sirkka two poems on Finland that she's written. Sirkka seizes them to translate into Finnish. I think Rhoda wrote 'Sallinen – Finland' overnight because the first of its two stanzas responds to one of the museum's paintings by Tyko Sallinen, *April Evening*. It's the rough-hewn landscape of the north:

> *Patient under the wind lies land*
> *Stripped to the rocks.*

One bony tree spreads a jointed hand.
Since Creation this sky knows this land,
This land this sky.
Loose clouds above, knit rocks below,
Only the blizzard between.

This pre-human land takes the observer close to Creation, and the second stanza re-explores this proximity through a seascape where sky, rocks and sea give and receive 'Familiarly / No human voice divides them'.

Two days later, on 26 July, Sirkka writes the following letter to Rhoda:

> My dear, dear Near-One,
>   I began to translate your poem ... I'm out of wits being touched so deeply by the pure strength, perfectly the stern ... Dear You, it is after all a surprising present to get you thus, although from the first flash of the intuitive contact with you I know what you are. It is amazing in you the silent ascetic strength, clear & pure – spontaneously sure as ever a archaic soil. Impossible to express myself in English. I hope I do it better in Finnish – in my article.

Sirkka will include 'Sallinen – Finland' in an article on foreigners at the gallery, which *Finlandia Pictorial* magazine is to publish, illustrated by the painting. She singles out 'Rhoda Stella Press from Cape Town' as a visitor whose feeling for Finnish art and nature 'gave birth to a group of sensitive poems. In their rhythm and words she has captured the mystic spirit of the desolate back woods of the north.'

Sirkka's family, Rhoda hears, comes from Karelia, a setting of white birch trees on the fought-over border with the Soviet

← Self-portrait: Helena Schjerfbeck, the greatest of Finnish women artists, as she saw herself in 1915. Many consider her the best of modern Finnish artists. She created her subtle style while an invalid, lonely and withdrawn into seclusion in the countryside.
→April Evening: In T. K. Sallinen's works, the gray colors of Finland's barren and rocky land reflect the rugged rapture of northern nature. With his primitive strength and closeness to nature, Sallinen is the most noted artist among Finnish expressionists.

the combination of these qualities is born the mystical twilight, the feeling of the destiny of the northlands, which is revealed so well in Wäinö Aaltonen's «Maid in Black Granite» and in the work of expressionists such as T. K. Sallinen, Alvar Cawén, and Marcus Collin. In young Aimo Kanerva many saw a guarantee that the qualities that make Finnish art what it is still are inexhaustible.

D. Los Baños, a teacher from Hawaii, was struck by the intensity of Finnish works, even those in which the grayness of lichen and peatbogs predominate.

«Strange,» he said, «that these artists surrounded by winter and darkness do not feel the need for brilliant colors and light.»

«Yet,» he added, «it is just that which shows how close they are to nature itself.» He said Finnish artists seem to gain strength from harsh surroundings in which other artists would be lost.

Many visitors ranked the monumental works of Juho Rissanen and the intimate and symbolic works of Hugo Simberg among the top treasures of Finnish art.

Italians often compared Rissanen's works to frescoes of their own country. Rissanen also got the vote of J. Methuen, a Rhodesian architect, who was asked to name the greatest Finnish artist after having viewed the entire collection.

J. K. Weckl, a Vienna art critic, rushed out of the Atheneum after viewing the works of Simberg. The exper-

SALLINEN – FINLAND

Patient under the wind lies land
Stripped to the rocks.
One bony tree spreads a jointed hand.
Since Creation this sky knows this land,
Loose clouds above, knit rocks below,
Only the blizzard between.
— — —
Grey green sea
Relaxes on rocks.
Sky lowers a pale mustard mist.
Wind whips a flare of white.
Sky rocks sea
Each give and receive
Familiarly.
No human voice divides them.

By *Rhoda Stella Press*

Rhoda's poem is published, fittingly, on the same page as two paintings she particularly admired in Helsinki's Ateneum

Union. This is a region of folk craft and the oral tales collected in the national epic, the *Kalevala*. In 1939–40 the Red Army had invaded Karelia: the brief Winter War. Sirkka, then an art student aged twenty, had swum by night across a lake, behind the Russian lines, to retrieve – of all things – three painted spindles as objects of Finnish folk art. She went to 'steal' is the way she puts it, laughing triumphantly.

Rhoda's part is to talk of the apartheid regime, and she dashes out to find Sirkka a copy of *Cry, the Beloved Country*.

Sirkka tells Rhoda that her real destination is the far north – her poem has already marked it out for her own. Lapland will meet her need; it will transform her; it's her destiny to go.

She hands Rhoda her boots.

'Be clear, be open my Rhoda,' she urges. 'My strength is yours, Rhoda, you, who have the transparent and human eyes.'

So Rhoda postpones her departure. 'A tremendous power of urgency to go to Lapland' seems to be taking her there. To do this in the past, to travel to a far-off place on her own, would have seemed 'insuperable' to the semi-invalid she's been. Now, she tells herself, 'If one wishes to be an observer, one must be alone.'

She boards an overnight train to Rovaniemi, seven hundred kilometres north of Helsinki, and then a bus takes her to the outpost of an arctic wilderness more than three hundred kilometres farther north. The terminus is Muonio on Finland's western border with Sweden. From there she will enter the lonely fells of Pallastunturi in the Pallas-Yllästunturi national park. On 8 August she looks back on this journey.

Lapland freed me from the last of my prisons. The 10 hours with Finns and Lapps in the bus going to Muonio ... ended in a burst of laughter ... At a kiosk on the roadside I am deciding with a Swiss girl whether to take a taxi to Pallastunturi – Suddenly I hear a rumble – our bus has started off. But my luggage! It's on the bus careering down the road – back to Rovaniemi. 'My luggage!' I run, shouting. There is a man on a motorcycle outside the kiosk. A Finnish woman mutters swiftly to him. She tells me to get on the pillion behind him. 'But what of my coat?' She takes it, a tall American my hat, and a British girl my book of Scandinavian poetry. Away I fly. Hair streaming, clutching the shoulders of an unknown man. I have never even seen his face. I don't know where my legs are, and I don't seem to care about them. I am fine, loving it – and laughing, but laughing!

When we reached the bus & got my luggage I . . . emptied my purse of small coins into the reluctant palm of the 'motorcycle man'. He phoned for a taxi but before mine could arrive, another turned up – & inside I am astonished to see – my coat, my hat, and my book of poems! The Finnish woman had sent this taxi . . . Back at the kiosk they laughed at my 'Charlie Chaplin technique'. I waited with them for the bus to Pallastunturi. At a quarter to eleven we climbed among the bare blue hills – never, except in pre-human vision, have I known a blue like that. In summer there is no night over those glowing coal-blue fells but now the horizon was ringed with pink fires.

Early next morning she climbs Pallas fell. After about two and a half hours she reaches the wooden tower at the summit, from where she looks out on 'blue hills streaked with silver lakes'. It's like 'the round top of the world', a place close enough to Creation to see 'God's shadow'.

Harry follows her. He arrives that evening and climbs Pallas fell until three in the morning. Up there, more than a month past midsummer, he sees the sun set on one side and rise on the other within an hour. So it is that this gregarious sport joins, for a space, Rhoda's lone pilgrimage. He finds her alight with a resolve to remain in Europe, and here, at Pallastunturi, Harry is persuaded to agree. For Rhoda invites him to lend himself to what she sees now as her future. It's a proposal of sorts, a passionate sequel to the legal business of getting married. What she offers her husband at this moment is the chance to bond with her real self.

For the rest, I don't know exactly, but can guess. She's been imprisoned since the age of seventeen, she would have said, and now Lapland is conferring on her the blessing of recovery. She must carry recovery through with a further lease of life. To do this she must go to London and nourish her mind and poetry with a year of higher education. This is the basis of a pact with her husband: the Pact of Pallastunturi, we might say.

Needless perhaps to say is that in 1952 a pact of this sort is unheard of for an obscure housewife and mother, with no profession, no visible talent.

Sirkka's farewell gift is a book called *Voices of Finland*; opening it, Sirkka intones lines from the *Kalevala*, and its pulsing rhythm takes over their bus to the docks. Finns listen with grave attention.

Thirty years later, Rhoda will affirm: 'Finland was my soul's window through which there fell on me exquisite blessings.'

9

Free in London

As her train passes through Germany, Rhoda averts her eyes. In 1952, Germany is still 'the poisoned stomach' of a Europe that degenerated into the Holocaust. Happiness returns when her eyes open to works of art. In Florence, Giotto and Filippo Lippi, she finds, 'lift me out of the decay that is Europe into the purity of their vision'.

She drafts a letter to Sirkka, who will understand that though she has to cope on her own, 'loneliness is what I have chosen'.

Sirkka commends her breakout. 'You are a lonely one too, so different & so perfectly like me.'

How miraculously 'our two souls leapt together', Rhoda replies. It was 'one of those strange things that happen once or twice in a lifetime'.

Harry, who has been in Spain, joins her for a day in Rome, and then, on 30 August, flies home to us. Pip and I are leaping about at the gate to welcome him.

Rhoda is now really alone. Her stagnation for so many years has not accustomed her to plan ahead in practical ways. What exactly will she do in London? Until she gets there it's a dream: in part the colonial dream of a great civilisation across the sea, in part the dream of lone writers who long for guidance.

Uneasy about money, dependent on a husband whose optimistic investments often prove shaky, she roughs it in Rome and Paris, where she sleeps one night in a bathroom. She lingers too long in Paris, entranced by art, and reaches London 'dog-tired' at six in the evening of 9 September.

That night, at 250 Elgin Avenue in Maida Vale, she finds herself in one of those unwanted rooms that Reception can foist on a woman travelling on her own. It's at the back on the third floor: small, with dirty bits of carpet, stained walls and mice.

There are two letters from home: one from her husband and the other from Monica. Her friend's advice is to stay no more than two months, and return for the school holidays in December.

There's no need for a mother to organise school holidays, nor is Rhoda one to do it. Her illness meant that we'd never depended on her physical attendance. Yet it's clear from Monica's letter that within three days of our father's return to Cape Town he is talking over his children's deprivations with Rhoda's most influential friend, more than ready to concur.

Monica may not know that Rhoda has never been the kind of mother who packs her children's days with educational outings. Monica herself is the epitome of the selfless maternal woman who finds complete fulfilment in tending her babies. She carries no shade of regret for other gifts – for learning and games – nature bestowed on her as a girl. This shadowless maternity, and the force of it despite the mildness, is shaped by the absence of Monica's own mother, Rose, throughout Monica's childhood and that of her sister Zelda.

According to my mother, no one knew exactly how Rose (born in 1889) came to disappear. Rumour had it that this mother was 'mental' and had been sent away overseas to a British asylum, which was only possible because the sisters' father was wealthy. Rose never emerged, and her daughters never saw her again. My mother remarked that Isabella Shaw, wife of the novelist Thackeray, had suffered a similar fate after the birth of her second daughter. My mother would speak darkly of those wasted and unreachable lives, and – though she may not have said as much – I conceived them as victims of medical practice who shut away young mothers who could not perform as mothers. When Rhoda came to know Monica at the age of nine there was a substitute for a mother in the form of 'Nurse'. The large house on Belvedere Avenue, opposite the Reservoir, was dark with the gloom of Monica's father, aged forty-five, who sat eating in his braces, and behind him, the brooding presence of Nurse Eppie Howes. She may have served her employer's sexual needs, so my mother will hint when I'm older. As girls, both Rhoda and Lilian sensed something awry in that home with Nurse as dominant figure. Small, forbidding, Nurse Howes vetted who might or might not visit. Rhoda and Lilian detested her, but dared not show it.

So behind Monica's mildness was a desire to fill that vacant maternal space. In 1952, when Monica spells out the duties of motherhood, Rhoda calls this 'gentle' advice, but Monica's tone is firm, risking (she articulates the risk) intrusion. Her firmness is surprising, because neither Monica nor anyone at home asked if we missed our mother. If they had, I could have assured them that we felt cocooned. There's Lenie dabbing icing (flavoured with orange juice and grated rind) on a Lenie-cake, and Granny who allows me to choose a red sundress – my mother would think it garish – for the sake of its elasticised bodice. And there's an outer layer of security provided by our father.

As always, I walk to school, about half an hour up Kloof Road, and then cut across the 'coloured' area of Tramway

Road, to the slope of King's Road, sheering steeply downwards towards the Main Road with its trams. Often, King's Road girls in brown uniforms and panama hats stop to stare at a lamed tram, while its grim-faced driver manoeuvres a long implement to fish for a lost feeler from the top of the tram and re-attach it to the line overhead.

Every Saturday morning, as always, I take the High Level Road bus to a studio in town, carrying ballet shoes, folded inwards with soles on the outside. Uncle Sydney sends me one of the new black leotards from America, which schoolgirl conformity forbids me to wear.

'Harry tells me you spoke about sending the children over to England,' Monica writes. 'Well, Rhoda, as a very old friend I think it is a rather hare-brained idea. Uprooting children of their age really does not do them any good, and they are too young to benefit from a stay in England.'

How can motherhood not come first? Five weeks earlier, Monica has given birth to a third boy, who is proving a champion at the breast. And there is Lilian, who also has given birth to a third child, the longed-for girl to be a companion on the farm. Monica has taken Lilian and the baby into her home, for Lilian, she says in her mild, caring voice, is 'het up'. Lilian herself is matter-of-fact when she speaks of her husband. 'Bertie is busy with water-boring and putting in pumps.' The silence around this statement resonates with marital loyalty in the face of the farmer's incomprehension.

'I can't write to you with my usual buoyancy. I think I must be suffering from that period of deep depression that sometimes sets in after childbirth,' Lilian confides to Rhoda. 'At night, when one's thoughts are so wild, I think of you and a calmness comes over me when I realise that you have conquered that turmoil.'

Can it be, I wonder now, that my mother was less of an

oddity than she appeared? Was she, after all, not far off from other women who entered into a dark night of depletion?

Into this maternal scene at Monica's, with yards of hand-washed nappies flapping as they dry in the wind, steps our father. He's dressed in his after-office shorts, and his muscled calves flash down the steps to Bayhead. His forehead, touched by a slanting ray of sun, is creased, for it's disconcerting to come back to a wifeless home. How did it happen that he gave way in Pallastunturi?

Far from solitary Lapp heights, local talk is closing around him: a gallivanting wife, a broken home, neglected children. For a divorce lawyer, these are common narratives. The raw meat of the courtroom obliterates the fountaining inner life Rhoda will attempt to release in London. Wives don't go off to be poets abroad; they are taken along by husbands to enjoy a tour. How is he to explain?

Unlike Lilian, who has transformed herself into a farmer's wife, Rhoda has shut the door on her husband's concerns. More than anyone knows, she has lived unhusbanded, not letting go the landscape of childhood. Her husband can rely on her attentions to his family, to servants and to the household, as well as the occasional favour of an appearance at a swimming gala, to present the cups, but beyond this, she does not pretend to enter into Harry's life, and of course illness has excused her. All along, though, she has made the divergence of their minds and purposes abundantly plain, and he knows that however confident he feels on radio or when he blows his whistle at the poolside, he cannot engage the wife he looks up to and loves in his exuberant way.

As a father, he likes to squeeze: 'Oochy-coochy-coo' he says, clasping me to him with three breathless hugs. He runs his rough cheek over mine and sometimes over my back, and though it scrapes on tender skin, that's his way of showing affection.

How far my mother yields something of her self, I can't say. They never quarrel. I assume that they are too far apart to strike that sort of spark. Yet until September 1952 she's been there, not fully present but physically in place. Suddenly she's not, and it occurs to him that she may have left in some more permanent way neither has foreseen. A whole year on his own stretches out; he wonders if she will meet another man more fitted to her tastes. This is what his family and others hint. What might Rhoda's friends think of her disappearance from the scene?

It's uncommon for him to feel at a loss, and being a man of action he doesn't waste time brooding. He's here at Bayhead to talk over his abandonment with his wife's closest friend, and not to put too fine a point on it, he's here to co-opt her influence. Monica, if anyone, can reel Rhoda in. As biddable wife, as gentle-voiced mother, Monica speaks for the womanhood of 1952 with the appeal of maternal intelligence.

So it is that Monica posted her letter on 3 September to await Rhoda's arrival in London. Don't overrate a university education, she counsels. Neither Nadine Gordimer nor Doris Lessing has a degree. It's irrelevant for a writer. What Rhoda needs is not to study overseas, but rather to exercise the discipline to work regularly at what she does.

'Your family is so thrilled by your new zest, they are prepared to indulge you to the utmost,' Monica says, 'even to a long stay away from Cape Town.'

But what does a long stay mean? Monica concurs with Rhoda's husband that December must be the limit. 'I have a feeling that by then you will want to be with the children.'

When I look at these letters from Rhoda's maternal friends, particularly Monica and Ren (who agrees with Monica), a question of jealousy occurs to me. These are reading women; they are very intelligent; and yet they disapprove of a woman who puts her head outside the home, except to perform what their society sees as acts of charity like the orphanage library or Ren's dance lessons for motherless girls. In a provincial town in the fifties, it's peculiar for a mother to stay away for the sake of a 'great opportunity'. As it happens, I feel no need of their protection. I was a child enjoying a more carefree life with father and grandmother, relieved that my troubled mother was finding a way to be happy.

Alongside Monica's letter is Harry's, listing problems at home. His mother-in-law, shaking her head over her daughter's hands-off domestic management, is empowered by Rhoda's absence. Lenie is put out by Granny's interference in the kitchen, while Granny herself is put out by children who ha-ha at her raised forefinger.

'It's true Mom does not understand children at all,' Rhoda replies, projecting her uneasiness with her mother onto me. '*I* know how she must be reacting.' In truth, I'm the cause of

Rhoda (left) was dependent on her mother (centre), whose domestic management jarred her. On the right is a rabbi's wife, Mrs Kiwelowitz, who was Basil's mother-in-law

the trouble, for I take advantage of my mother's absence to tease Granny.

'You're giving me aggravation,' Granny protests, but so calmly that I annoy her all the more.

One day while I'm bent over the bathroom basin, holding a facecloth over my eyes while she washes my hair, she tells me about menstruation. Gleefully, I follow at Granny's heels, muttering 'drip, drip, drip', until she's cross.

My father duly reports this 'bathroom incident', and my mother bats it back as a matter of no great moment. A spell of 'grannydom', she asserts, won't do the children any harm.

Harry's letters don't survive, but the replies register a barrage of household complaints: Granny's friction with Pip over piano practice and reverberations of the bathroom incident. Nothing appears to deflect Rhoda's intention to stay in London; she deals with complaints one by one. Her mother should stop supervising Pip's practice because he might lose his love of music. Then, too, her mother should stop exhausting herself furbishing up the house and bothering about the children's clothes. A happy atmosphere is all that children need. Patiently, she explains that if the children were ill she would return at once, but kitchen and piano squabbles are not going to rush her back. It's expensive to cross the sea, and an effort to establish herself in London – not to be thrown up lightly.

'Naturally today & tomorrow will be difficult days,' she goes on, 'not knowing what will happen or I if shall be able to choose the correct path to follow.' She reminds her husband of his agreement. 'It's good of you to fulfil the pact we made at Pallastunturi. I know how difficult the next few months will be for you but I feel what I am doing is Right however difficult it proves. Even if this time does not bear fruit, it is still Right for me to do this. It is not easy for me either. I think I shall need some food parcels and warm pyjamas. It is very cold already.'

That day she trundles in buses across London to visit five universities. Wherever she goes, it's too late. Courses are already full.

A different sort of difficulty arises from her decision not to stay with Auntie Minnie or near other members of her family in Hampstead. This, she finds, has been misreported as a wish to have nothing to do with them. She does what she can to correct the mistake. Her aunt is, as ever, a hospitable darling, and there are three dinners at Auntie Minnie's during her first week in London and a visit to her cousin Rita in Buckinghamshire.

There's a worse misreading of her intentions. At lunch with Harry's cousins, Greta Brown from Manchester and her brother Benny, Rhoda fizzes with her burgeoning sense of freedom. Benny, a physician whom she's consulted from time to time, declares that he's never seen her looking better, yet he's strangely cool. Afterwards, Rhoda hears that Mrs Brown's schoolgirl daughter Laura does not want Rhoda to visit, 'because she's not a nice person, and won't go back to her family'.

'I thought I was amongst *friends*,' Rhoda reflects, astonished that Harry's cousin can have spoken in such a way to her daughter. However unworldly Rhoda may be, and entirely lacking in malice, she does recognise the danger of gossip.

'Please Harry,' she asks, 'don't discuss me with everybody & be very reserved . . . about my absence because in a small place all sorts of false ideas start circulating in no time. Merely tell people the simple facts: after 10 years at Home with the children I'm taking advantage of being overseas and having a little extra holiday.'

It's politic, she finds, to call it a holiday. A decade or more earlier, Auntie Betsie had left her children with Granny, her eldest sister, for five months while she toured Europe with her husband. Their youngest daughter, Garda, was miserable to be left alone in the dark when Granny shut the door on her night fears. To this day Garda remembers lying on the floor next to a crack of light coming from under that door. A letter she wrote to her parents, asking them to come back, was intercepted. No one asked Auntie Betsie to cut the tour short on account of a child, because holidays abroad were highly prized.

While Rhoda is in London, Ren takes a holiday in Madeira where she performs with 'unRen-ish' abandon before an all-male crowd. Her account of this scene to Rhoda presents another face of fifties womanhood. In an outdoor bar her husband Sonny, squat, beaming, takes out his ukulele and belts out a song. Once the drinkers join in he orchestrates a rollicking scene like a Hollywood musical, like Marilyn Monroe strumming a ukulele as she advances her hips down the aisle of the train. Ren, lifted onto a table, does an African dance, then an undulating Spanish one with alluring glances over her shoulder. What makes this virtuous is that her glance turns repeatedly to her 'adoring husband' who's masterminding the sway of her body.

Dancing on a tabletop, holidaying, mothering: all are approved in 1952. But for a mother to stay abroad with a serious purpose of her own, for her to speak earnestly of poetry and long-term study, is quite another thing: it puts my mother in a suspect position.

Reading these letters as a daughter and a writer, and a mother myself, knowing full well how much she gave of herself as a mother and how much she needed to write, I feel for her situation. She conducted herself with admirable rationality when people back home forced on her a conflict between aspiration and children, opportunity and marital duty, London and Cape Town. On the one side there was Sirkka, calling her out as 'my sister in fate', emboldening her to unbury herself. 'My strength is yours, Rhoda.' On the other side: Monica, who would draw a mother back to the fold. And behind Monica stands our father the lawyer who relies on Monica to make a better case than he can devise.

The Rhoda of the past would have acted on Monica's advice,

but this is a different Rhoda, whose hunger is such that she must feast now – not vicariously, like colonials, like Monica re-warming the events of *John O'London's Weekly* at a distance of six thousand miles – but here, at first hand, bathed in the abundance of London, 'an oasis in the middle of my life'.

The oasis turns out to be lectures on contemporary poetry, philosophy and Shakespeare at the City Literary Institute in Goldsmith's Street (now Stukeley Street), in the theatre district of Drury Lane. Its purpose is to offer a second chance to pupils in their thirties and forties, and the fee charged by the London County Council for a whole term is all of one pound, seventeen shillings and sixpence.

After failing to convince Rhoda how badly she's needed at home, my father simply demands her return. It comes as a bombshell. On 24 September, after only two weeks in London, Rhoda gives way. She books a passage on the *Jagersfontein*, due to sail on 19 December and reach Cape Town by 2 or 3 January. She has just three months to be in London.

'Harry,' she pleads, 'please bear my absence patiently. After all I had to be father & mother on all your trips away from home including England and Israel, during one of which the children and myself were continuously ill.'

For a mother to claim an equal right for herself in 1952 is unheard of. It's twenty years too early. Rhoda tries to assure her husband that she's not taking on anything too demanding, and yet her enthusiasm breaks out – together with what is bound to gall him, her separate tastes, compounded by minimising the household issues he's put forward.

> I have only been to one lecture and found it most stimulat-ing – unlike anything I could find in South Africa. I am not doing any courses. Only four evenings a week I go to these discussion-lectures at which I have an opportunity to meet

people with the same interests as my own . . . Now that I am here I must not waste time. This is my opportunity . . . It would be silly to drop everything & rush home unless of course there is a serious reason to do so. I have been ill and stay-at-home for so many years that I would not like to have to cancel my plans unless it is necessary.

At this point the publication of her poem 'Finland' in the *Cape Times* plays into her hands. Here would seem some proof that her sense of herself as a poet may be justified. But Harry has been taken aback to find 'Rhoda Press' at the bottom of the poem.

Why not her married name, he asks.

'Whatever poetry is in me comes from the Press side,' she insists.

Monica is thrilled to see 'Finland' in print. She perceives an improvement on Rhoda's earlier poems, some of which might be publishable if she can bring herself to revise them. If she resolves to shut her door to visitors (it's usual for people to drop in), she might clear three hours for herself each morning.

Monica offers an idea that might console her friend for leaving London: why doesn't Rhoda approach one of *John O'London*'s poets and reviewers, Richard Church, for a one-off consultation – 'on a business basis of course' – on how to improve her poems.

Instead, Rhoda joins a craft of verse class at the City Lit. The first assignment is a poem on Charlie Chaplin, and she discovers that she can, if required, turn her hand to humour:

> *Crazy cooing eyes, a mimouthed smirk,*
> *Nidnodding missus, coquettish shoulder jerk*

before the little tramp vagabonds over the last hill.

The class goes on from year to year. Its members are all aspiring practitioners, discussing one another's poems. Rhoda makes friends with Edith Roseveare – Roseveare, as she always calls her – who has listened 'with pointed ears' to Edith Sitwell's 'quixotic eloquence' in a performance of *Façade* at the Festival Hall. She describes how Sitwell, in a flowing white mantle lined with black, strode boldly about the stage, taking a 'long breath' to deliver each of her lines. To Roseveare, seated far above 'with the five-shilling intellectual crowd', Sitwell's face had been a blur but her voice, riding Walton's music, reached them. This is the iconic woman poet of the day. Though Roseveare applauds this 'splendid old trout', she herself cultivates a cooler voice: 'Distrust the clouds. Turn your back on the view / From the ornamental tower of your hopes ... '

Roseveare's distrust of the blue haze of dreamscapes is bracing. Keep your eyes on the ruts and the traffic signals, Roseveare warns. 'Will nothing break you of sucking your dreams / Like sweets?' There are other things to observe, like 'the loud hard street' outside the City Lit. Stop, she orders in her no-flummery, English voice. Stop scanning the great horizons and unattainable peaks.

There's a reservation on Rhoda's part. Roseveare, she discovers, has German antecedents, and she repeats this to me after her return, as though she's entered into a surprising, almost forbidden relationship. Roseveare, she gives me to understand, is more contained and ironic, alien in a way Sirkka, the sister of the lit-up soul, is not – and, by extension, Finland is not. It escapes her notice – or she allows it to do so – that in the second phase of the war Finland did *not* join the Allies. In that post-war decade there are many, like Rhoda, who refuse contact with Germans as well as German goods, feeling that anything German is tainted with the stench of the gas ovens. At the same time as Rhoda nurses a prejudice against Roseveare, the two will correspond for years to come.

A male classmate observes Rhoda's 'almost biblical charm' as she tiptoes into the room ten minutes late. What 'fascinates' him (as he teases in a set of couplets, written out for her in an educated hand) is 'something in her face / Of ancient, semitic grace / What centuries of suffering lie / Covered by that velvet eye!' In her, a woman of the Bible lives once more, coming through the door with 'an invisible amphora on her head' – ten minutes late.

I recognise the lateness. It's hard to organise herself. The pills she has to take fog her in trivial ways: she'll forget where she's left her handkerchief or put down her glasses. Before leaving, she will rummage distractedly through her bag, muttering 'I'm im*poss*ible.'

Discussions go on after class in the café at the institute. One of the lecturers is John Heath-Stubbs, whose verse is in a book she owns. News is passed around about the Poetry Fellowship, run by another lecturer, J. W. Reynolds, a small man with a 'sickle smile' and a 'big, resolute mind'. His aim is to 'bring together in the spirit of fellowship all students at the Institute who are interested in poetry'. Happily, fellowship is what Rhoda finds at meetings and talks. 'Is there a new poetic drama?' is the topic on 18 October. Ten days later she attends a reading of poems on poets and poetry, including Richard Church on Wordsworth, Siegfried Sassoon's 'To an Eighteenth Century Poet' and Gerard Manley Hopkins' 'To R.B.'. The only poem by a woman is 'Poetry' by Marianne Moore.

After much searching, Rhoda settles in a mansion block near where she stayed in Elgin Avenue. It's a relief to be in a clean room overlooking a stretch of garden with trees and lawn behind this ground-floor flat. Her room has a Persian rug over a fitted carpet, reading lamp, desk, armchair, eiderdown and even flowers. There is an ample shelf for her books, a shelf in the kitchen cupboard and the bottom half of the fridge. All this for three guineas a week (the same as she'd paid for the squalid room near by) in a flat belonging to a refugee from Germany, Mrs Mannerheim, whose interests are art, music and literature.

'I don't see how you will survive going out to restaurants in all weathers,' Mrs Mannerheim says, eyeing this lodger who looks in need of nourishment. Might cooked lunches (for four-and-six or five shillings, considerably less than a restaurant) be welcome, as well as breakfasts? Yes, they would. Rhoda feels no need to own that she's never cooked a meal in her life.

For her breakfast, Mrs Mannerheim orders 'special milk' that is a quarter cream. Arriving back late from the City Lit, Rhoda finds her landlady ironing the undies Rhoda has washed in the bathroom they share. Rhoda decides that the way this woman has taken to her and goes on 'spoiling' her is 'of the same strange calibre of the magical things that happened to me in Finland and Lapland. I was "led" here.'

Afterwards, when she's back at home, my mother will act out a comic scene when her 'nudist' landlady opens the door to receive a basket with gefilte fish from Auntie Minnie's driver, the respectable Edward, startled into an eyes-front, glassy stare. How can I not believe in this nudist? I see her through the haze of a South African summer, little knowing how relentlessly damp England is, how people can't wait to put on their woollies. The point, though, gets through: how my mother's bohemian drama, playing off Maida Vale against Hampstead propriety, underpins the pleasure she took in independence.

In fact, the place is, and ever was, comfortably middle class: a row of dignified red-brick blocks in a tree-lined street. When they were built in 1897 it was a largely Jewish area, near to the Spanish and Portuguese Synagogue, the headquarters of the Sephardi community in Britain.

Since rationing is still in place, tighter in fact than during the war (one egg a week, one and a half ounces of cheese, meat limited to about 1/9d), Granny posts off parcels of supplements: tins of Silver Leaf peas, stewing steak, baked beans, soup, peaches, pineapple and, somehow, butter and eggs. In the fifties, flats are unheated, but kind Mrs Mannerheim moves her own heater into Rhoda's room when she's due back.

This is a make-do but culturally vibrant London. One Sunday evening, 16 November, Edith Sitwell recites 'The Shadow of Cain' together with Dylan Thomas, a cataclysmic atom-bomb poem, to a musical setting by Humphrey Searle played by the London Symphony Orchestra and described by *The Times* as 'shattering noise, dead silence and instrumental monotone or held chords'. Emlyn Williams performs as Dickens; Claire Bloom, with her black hair and pointed chin, is an 'exquisite' Juliet; and Alec Guinness has the lead in a comedy, *Under the Sycamore*. Mrs Mannerheim takes Rhoda to a preview of an Epstein exhibition at the Tate; Rhoda returns next day to a greater delight in Blake; she sits in the institute café with members of the poetry class and is quickened when they applaud a poem she submits, anonymously and trembling, to a workshop.

It must be 'Sing Heart', for that poem (as well as 'Charlie Chaplin') is included in a City Lit anthology for 1951–3. Like many of Rhoda's poems, it's about utterance: the struggle to articulate the dark night of the soul. This big subject, central to the lives of Jeremiah and Jesus, makes utterance daunting, particularly for a woman in an orthodox tradition that reserved the higher reaches of the devotional life for men.

'Sing Heart' takes us into the terror of 'a dark pit', the biblical scene of spiritual trial. A parallel trial from her own life is to cross an abyss, based on the childhood scene when her brothers dared her to cross the one-track railway bridge above the

Olifants River. In 'Sing Heart' the crossing is made on an untried, spider-like thread 'spun from the entrails'. But unlike the unending ordeal in other of her poems, and unlike the female avatar of Jacob wrestling to no good with the angel, here, in the finale, comes an exulting release, couched in the seascape of the Cape:

> Sing heart
> of the Sea
> that bursts from sunrise
> with a rush of foam vision white,
> (O silverflitting bees
> Sunmantling the seas)
> Sing heart.
>
> Sing joy-shot heart
> Dune-high
> Catching the wind in my throat
> I wave the veil of the sky.

After years of writing surreptitiously and alone, it's heady to be in this great city where others care for poetry as she does. What she used to term 'attacks' are now no more than 'flaps'. They happen, but she can 'manage 'em'. Not for years has she been so well as in this chilly, rainy autumn. In the parks, skeleton trees wade in evening mist, 'serene silk of sky and water'. In the noisy Strand she sits 'dream-lidded' among packed and grubby tables in a crowded café. A band plays and, in a poem, 'Café Music', music 'spreads a space'. This space is Europe, she tells herself – a Europe distilled as architecture of a grandeur inconceivable in Africa – and she muses 'how far I've come / from tunnelling underground / to this world's peak alone . . .'

Throughout the autumn of 1952, Rhoda feels nourished by

all the arts, with poetry at the centre of her life, as it was meant
to be. The real issue is about what is central to a woman's life.
Her poetry group is 'a great opportunity', she repeats. Though
Monica hears these words, she can't hear their import. Why do
you keep saying this, Monica asks. You can go overseas again in
a few years.

However plainly Rhoda makes her case, she's unable to pen-
etrate the mindset of time and place. She cannot communicate
the urgency to her husband and mother and the like-minded
people behind them, including Ren, who signal a simple message: think of your children. She's closer to arguing with
Monica than she's ever come, diverting her protest through the
ready-dug channel of exasperation with her mother. 'May I
point out that it is not my absence, it is *what I am doing* she disapproves of.'

Rhoda blames her mother for her husband's opposition. She
can hear her mother's voice all through his letters. 'You must
realise,' she warns him, 'Mom understands me and my purposes
even less than she does the children. She simply has no idea
whatsoever what my life's about.'

Since Rhoda is easily moved to anxiety over obligations to
others and any signal of displeasure, I imagine my father's surprise to find her so resolute. I suspect he's more alarmed by this
composed character – this changed wife – than he can admit,
even to himself. She's detached from the perspective of Cape
Town, not rebelliously but with a courteous dutifulness that is
actually more challenging.

'When I return I shall devote myself to the rest of the children's holiday,' she promises. 'As for ourselves, we have fitted
our lives together for the past twelve years in the face of illness
and disparity of interests, and will, I hope, with the help of God,
and the exercise of our best qualities, adjust ourselves in the
Future.'

It's one thing to look up to the wife you possess as a superior being; quite another to find that wife exercising her superiority in this distant way. Since Harry is 'woebegone', Rhoda hastens to say that all she wants is to prove she's 'no longer a cripple' and 'to water the seed that has lain for so many years in drought-stricken earth'. As always, her train of thought turns back to her own drama. The comedy of the woebegone husband – in line with her friends' humorous accommodation to oppositeness of 'the opposite sex' – does not look into a possibility of something more disturbing: a widening of the divide already between them.

Each letter reminds her husband to send ten pounds to an American artist in Amsterdam, Mike Pedulke, from whom she's acquired an etching called *The Prophet*. He's yet another stranger for whom she felt affinity. Back in July, when she and Harry were travelling together, he had wanted to give her this work for her birthday, but in the end she has to pay the artist herself. Is the non-appearance of the ten pounds mere carelessness on Harry's part? Is it tightfistedness? Can it be that the artist reciprocated the warmth which Rhoda had felt for his work and a husband had felt left out? Or may it be a signal of his displeasure? It's common enough to be displeased with those we block. Harry feels uneasy, if not guilty, at going back on the Pact of Pallastunturi; all the more reason then to take a tough line. He stops writing.

Fourteen days before Rhoda's ship is due to sail she makes a last plea that her London life should not be 'thrown away'.

... As in Finland my pangs grow greater as the time draws near for me to leave the rich full life I have made here. This time however there is an equal urge towards you and the children. At times I fiercely regret feebly relinquishing (during the first trying two weeks in London) our original

plans forged at Pallastunturi that you should bring the
children over for a year. But as soon as you slipped back
into Cape Town's conforming garment you were aided and
abetted in your desire to have me back by parochial hands
raised in horror at such a 'new' idea . . .

My Verse Class cannot believe that I am leaving just at
this critical juncture when someone is undertaking to
publish a poetry magazine which will be fed by our class.
We all met in a Pub the other evening to discuss this new
and thrilling development. And both my lecturers have
expressed extreme regret at losing me and my poetry. One
said: 'We just won't let you go.' And another – 'I'd like to
sabotage your ship!' Quite another lecturer has invited our
class to spend Christmas at his house where he has
arranged (between parties) some Poetry Lectures by
famous people. In January I am also missing a University
Residential Weekend on Poetry held at a lovely old Manor
House on the Downs.

It is not easy to throw away the Cup towards which I
have been fumbling in the dark from earliest childhood.
Because I am so happy I know at last that this is my life-
blood. Is there perhaps still a chance of your flying over
here with the children? <u>Please answer at once.</u>

Eddie* was here for tea (and to fetch his groceries)
yesterday. He was surprised to find how frugally I live. I
live on less than half of what he does per week . . . My
landlady took me to 'Claridges' for lunch the other day for
a treat and I sat right next to the Duchess of Kent's
daughter who was with her governess, dressed in a shabby
school jersey. We had a fine time and then I went on to a

---

* Harry's feckless youngest brother, who depended on him, and perhaps others, for
handouts.

French film which made me laugh and weep together, then to the British Museum and on to my Lectures in the evening. I also saw the opera 'Figaro' and was charmed, charmed . . . On Saturday afternoon I am going with my Theatre Club to 'Porgy and Bess', and then on to our Poetry Society in the evening . . . If I must return on the 19th there is scarcely time. I have a sort of suffocated feeling at the moment.

As it happens, at this very moment, millions of Londoners are feeling suffocated physically, by the yellow-brown smog spreading across the city. Coal is rationed, but the government has given a go-ahead to small lumps of inferior, peculiarly filthy coal. Chimneys pour polluted smoke into the air, thickening the smog. A performance of *La Traviata* is halted because the figures on stage are barely visible. Spectral figures, heads down, cover their mouths with scarves as they struggle home through the murk. The environmental disaster lasts five days, from 5 to 9 December, with deaths rising to four thousand, a number comparable to the cholera epidemic of 1866 and the Spanish flu of 1918.

Is my mother too absorbed in her private drama to notice? Pressure and silence are tugging her away at the moment when her life-blood has started to flow. As I read her plea to my father, I can't help thinking how like her it was to ignore what's happening. And yet, all the while she's speaking, I remember my mother's excitement over poetry, art and theatre. Was there, I wonder, a heightening of the arts that was concurrent with the physical gloom, in some sense called out by it?

Sirkka comforts her friend. 'I am not too sad that you must leave your valuable loneliness in London so soon.' Fertilisation, she says, will suffice, for Rhoda to 'develop and create' by herself.

Once more, Sirkka sends Rhoda on her way. 'My boots' –

lent to her for walking in Lapland – 'are always there for you, Rhoda. Know that I am smiling with secret triumphant happiness all the time you are trotting around in them.'

I've turned eleven by the time my mother comes back. During her six-month absence, the mental space she'd occupied has been filled with try-outs of normality. It has been easy to lay down the freight of my mother's alertness. Courtesy of Granny and my father, daily doings have filled out, untrammelled by insights: the automatism of long division in Standard Four (sixth grade), games of snap and Monopoly, and the commotions Granny sets up – starched napkins, polished cake forks, a spread of triangular cucumber sandwiches, soft cheesecake and sticky meringues – when her friends came for tea. Her friends, these brides of 1914, have sweet-pet names like Girlie and Toffee, and they are sweet in the way they say 'shame', the South-African endearment for babies, little girls, puppies and kittens; or '*Ag*, shame' in commiseration when Granny fusses over a missing teaspoon. Little is required as I hang around the edges of Granny's teas; it's enough to be her granddaughter in a freshly ironed dress, hair neatly parted on the side and combed around Granny's finger into sausage curls, as though I were as sweet as they.

My mother deplored the way aspiring parents loaded children with extra lessons. For some schoolmates, afternoons are so packed with music, ballet and elocution that little time is left to read and dream. As a child, my mother had not enjoyed her piano lessons; she resolved to spare her children if they weren't talented. My brother is; I'm not. All the same, I was alight when Granny, seated on the piano stool one autumn evening while my mother was away, taught me to read music so that I can look at the sheet and finger the opening notes of 'The Blue Danube'.

On weekends my father took me to the Union Swimming

Club at the Long Street Baths. You were given a pink card, folded over, and when you opened the two cardboard sides there were the names of the worthies of the club, including my father. As a favour to him, patient old Mr Mitchell taught me to breathe out bubbles in the water. At King's Road the ten- and eleven-year-olds exchanged brown lace-ups for white tackies before we ran on to the netball court. Blonde Miss Eales, feet apart and bouncing lightly on her toes, coached us for a match against Ellerton, the junior school in the neighbouring suburb of Green Point.

'When I blow my whistle, I want you to run as fast as you can towards the circle,' she said, as though this were of the utmost importance.

I loved this instruction as I turned with the ball at my shoulder in the centre of the court. It wasn't only sport; it was the first efflorescence of a lifelong love affair with normality. And so, it's a routinely occupied daughter, less dreamy, less watchful, who awaits, quite matter-of-factly, her mother's return.

'Loneliness is what I have chosen,' our mother said.
Our father looks after Pip and me while she's away

10

Mother to Daughter

A healthy mother with a spring in her step descends the gang-plank to embrace her children and our father. He is beaming with triumph to have brought her back, to his way of thinking, in record time. Excitedly, she turns to draw forward two unknown young women coming ashore at her heels.

On the voyage home in the Dutch liner, the *Jagersfontein*, Rhoda has befriended Dorrie and Astrid, sisters who appear to be on their own. With a distant father and no mother, they are all-in-all to each other. Rhoda tells us how she came upon them in the ship's library. They were conversing in French, and it was all about books.

Speaking with ready aplomb, they confirm the delight of this encounter and enthuse over Rhoda's readiness to read (in translation) their favourite French authors, Colette and de Beauvoir and the tales of Balzac and de Maupassant. For young women still in their teens, they have an astonishing intellectual confidence and an almost voluble flow of words. They enunciate each English word with the perfection of cosmopolitans, rarely seen in Cape Town at the time. Mainly sporting and sailing people visit, or naval officers bound for the British base at Simonstown. After the ship docks, my mother adopts Dorrie and Astrid, as if she were a kind of older sister.

As a girl of their age, my mother's hair had fallen into ringlets, and it had been her habit to wind my hair into similar curls – even though ringlets look old-fashioned and silly surrounding a face marked like mine. How tactfully Dorrie alters that in front of the bathroom mirror, alternately brushing and pulling my hair straight back from the forehead; 'Like a Swiss girl,' she says, banishing absurdity. Dorrie, who has been to finishing school in Paris, is elegant, unlike anyone I've seen in South Africa where stylishness often seems contrived – a studied imitation of 'overseas'. 'Overseas ... overseas' resonates in our uncertain colonial world.

My mother brings back an aura of belonging in a London circle – no longer the outsider she had been during her invalid years. Her participation over there, across the ocean, comes through obliquely in comic scenes: the motorcycle chase in Lapland with Rhoda clinging to the back of a stranger whose face she hadn't seen, and the bohemian eccentricity of a nudist in London opening her door to Auntie Minnie's driver. All this sounds fantastical and far away. But Dorrie and Astrid are here, an authentic sample of overseas, chosen, as it were, by my mother to bring home to us. They laugh a lot in their vibrantly alert manner, amused at our ways, like sophisticated older sisters a girl can look up to. Being with them is like an introduction to cultivated, foreign forms of life I've known only vaguely and at a distance.

Contact with my mother reignites over two new books from England: *A Dream of Sadlers Wells* and *Veronica at the Wells* by Lorna Hill. Veronica is an orphan with a talent for ballet, but as the *Dream* opens she's forced to leave her classes in London, as well as the comfy Cockney landlady, Mrs Crapper, who has looked after her. She's on a train to Northumberland to live with county relations she's never met. Apprehensive and displaced, she confides her longing to be a dancer to a stranger on the train, a humorous boy called Sebastian, who confides, in turn, his dream to be a conductor. Their secret dedication and dread of obstructive provincialism reclaim me for my mother's narrative. Normality subsides to the status of diversion, and once more the outsider holds sway.

Lying on my back in the dark, I'm ready for one of her talks after she switches off my light. Sometimes she tells me things in the palm of my hand, like the drama of the French Revolution: she pictures the rage of the women marching on Versailles to demand bread; the oblivion of Marie Antoinette, asking why they don't eat cake – a curling question in my palm; the uprightness of the queen's bearing when she stands in a tumbrel on her way to the guillotine; and the knitting women – a sinister tap, tap on my palm – placidly occupied as heads fall into a basket. Then there's Sarah, the wife of Abraham, eavesdropping in her tent – my mother closes my palm around her Sarah-finger – when an angel announces to her husband that she will bear a child. And Sarah, barren and ageing, laughs in disbelief. Women long gone laugh, speak, feel, unlike history at school narrowed to rulers, colonies and wars, the fighters of the Great Trek, surprised by the *impis* of the Zulu king Dingaan at the battle of Blood River, when the river ran red.

'Marriage is the proper ground for men and women to come together,' my mother is saying. 'Otherwise you degrade the body. Men are always ready, but they despise girls who offer themselves.'

I think of my father's divorcées with raised cocktails, who flirt gamely as he buzzes from group to group at sports parties. Though my mother is no longer an invalid, she does not join him for these events and they resume their separate ways. Perhaps because they lived in different milieux, an exception stands out in my memory: an evening when they went out as a couple to a ball. Dressed, our father in black tie and our mother in silver-grey scalloped tiers from her slender waist and pearl-drop earrings, like an exquisite doll, they appeared before Pip and me to show themselves off before leaving. We were entranced by this image, like a film about a romantic pair about to waltz away into the mist.

She has hastened back – my mother adds – to tell me that, hallowed by marriage, 'intercourse is beautiful'.

Until now I've trusted what my mother says as coming from the soul of truth. For the first time, I don't quite believe her. The words are flat; they call up no scene. Then too it seems unlikely for a mother to travel from the northern to the southern hemisphere in order to spell this out.

Though I don't ask, she wants to explain. Her haste has been to counteract Granny, who has usurped a mother's role and provoked laughter over the serious facts of life. Once my mother reclaims me, the female body is not to be demeaned with hilarity. Her tone forbids it. Though I'm aware how rude I'd been, and how annoying, I let well-meaning Granny take the blame. Sex now takes a back seat; we've shifted to familiar territory: the scarred ground between Rhoda and her mother. I listen with the solemnity her concern invites.

What's definitely unbeautiful is the prospect of becoming 'unwell' each month. Joking had served to dismiss this fact of life; taking it in, I foresee mishaps: blood seeping onto a dress. Others will find out. Nice girls don't speak about the body. We are adept at keeping beach towels tucked under our arms as we step into a bather. Am I about to be different again, and embarrassed? My newly acquired normality fades before the prospect of bodily change.

A few months after my mother's return, I do start to be 'unwell'.

I show my mother the stains. Is this what Granny told me about?

'So soon,' my mother sighs.

She'd started at thirteen – the better age, she intimates. Her sigh carries a vibration of reproach, as though I'm not like her after all. My body is too ready, too forward by two whole years. I'm wailing at the wrongness of it. In Standard Five, the last year of junior school, I'm still officially a child. I dread going to school with an unaccustomed bulk between my legs; they stiffen with potential embarrassment in gym and netball. Those lessons become a test of secrecy, for no girl, bar one, ever admits this happens. I remember the only exception, some years later in high school, when a girl called Pam will rise from her desk after a long Latin class and hint at the sensation – unexpectedly pleasurable – of a swelling flow. There's an instant of complicity as I smile back.

Otherwise the only acknowledgement appears in American magazines like *Mademoiselle*, commercials for 'feminine fresh-ness' nudging girl-consumers to be worried enough to persuade mothers to buy a particular brand of sanitary napkin. Mothers bought a supply for daughters; it was unthinkable, then, for a girl to ask for herself over the counter at the chemist.

An added embarrassment is daily swimming, since my mother believes females are too 'unwell' for that during the first three days of a period. Awkwardly, I summon a lie to my lips – 'I have a cold' – and detect suspicion in the eye of Jasmine, the cleverest girl in the class.

To prove what a child I still am, I join a chase after Valerie, who has the biggest breasts in King's Road Junior School. We are after her to 'feel if she's wearing a bra', and she's made to flee into the bushes at the bottom of the sloping playground, below the netball court. I race after her with the others, thankful that my breasts don't yet merit attention.

Dorrie's sister Astrid is only fifteen, and my mother persuades her to finish school. She's sent to my mother's old school, Good Hope Seminary, where a year later I follow. At assembly the incoming twelve-year-olds in Standard Six file into the front row of the school hall. We are singing the school song, 'Between the mountain and the sea / Our alma mater stands ... *constantia et virtute*'.

The principal, Miss Tyfield, stands gravely on the stage, like a small hawk in a black academic gown sliding back from her shoulders. My mother has told me that Miss Tyfield is uncommonly clever and has published a set book for schools called *The Living Language*. I'm agog, looking back over my shoulder, to see Astrid, with straight hair and a strong, intelligent face, standing on the balcony amongst other full-breasted girls in the top class, 10A, who have the privilege of Miss Tyfield as teacher.

Next day, Miss Tyfield enters our classroom along an outdoor passage to the boarding school. As she pushes open the door a gust of the south-easter roars and blows out her gown like a shadow behind her. Twenty-five girls, some menstruating for the first time and dazed with afternoon heat, wake up from daydreams and shuffle to their feet. A scripture lesson is in progress and Miss Tyfield walks up and down the aisles inspecting notebooks. She stoops to peer at my drawing of Jacob's wedding night when the couple is left together in a tent. I'd pasted over Leah a removable striped flap for the veil covering the bride's face; opened, it reveals an ugly girl with a reddish, bulbous nose and thick eyelids. Miss Tyfield chortles as she lifts the flap. It isn't meant to amuse, but one could never explain.

*

In consultation with an architect, Dorrie helps Rhoda build and furnish a room of her own, the sunroom, on top of our garage, with rough-textured 'kaffir-sheeting' curtains and bookshelves constructed from bricks and planks – a novel idea then. Two divans at right angles, forming a seating corner, are covered with striped, goat-hair fabric made by Africans who use natural dyes.

Dorrie, who likes simplicity, accomplishes this with astonishing assurance for a young woman of nineteen, venting her neighing laugh, head back, showing all her handsome teeth. Quite soon Dorrie marries the architect, Sam Abramson. I'm disappointed because he's shorter than tall, lithe Dorrie, and not handsome.

'Not a romantic choice,' I say to my mother, thinking of the Scarlet Pimpernel.

She disagrees. 'Better a good man who's interesting.' She takes a poor view of handsome men who drink too much and gad about. Privately I note that my father is handsome and gads about – though not a drinker.

As Sirkka predicted, Rhoda is not thwarted by leaving London. Sirkka's translations into Finnish and the unexpected acceptance of her poems by fellow poets in London initiate a fertile period when her return to her sea-girt landscape extends the breakthrough mood of 'Sing Heart'. As David the Psalmist lifts up his eyes unto the hills from whence cometh his help, Rhoda looks to the sea, and not only for help in healing; her beat lends itself to the tug of eternity in the ebb and rise of the waves.

> *Ocean throat, well of peace,*
> *Draw me back like a wave*
> *Into your being's bliss*
> *My sky-blue childhood.*

Draw me back
From the seething edge of teeth,
The roaring that feeds
On the soul's food,
Into the deep heart of sleep
Home of my healing.

Crowned I will rise, and unfurl
Over the curve of the earth
My white sea wings, with songs
I will arise – with praise –
And hold the earth firm in my embrace.

A double glass door opens from the sunroom, down a spiral stair into the garden, and around the balustrade Rhoda plants honeysuckle to bring back the scent trailing a visionary moment in her youth. The glass door is her 'prayer door', where she stands absolutely still at night before bed. Her fingers spread as her spirit swells out like waves that reach into a hot, blue sky, and then stay there – stilling that swell into permanence

as mountain-waves
lifted to blue fire,
static forever
in a gesture of desire.

Affirmed from afar by letters from Sirkka, Roseveare and her circle in London who assure her she's still 'one of us', Rhoda longs to find some kind of public task, a counter to all those years of enforced seclusion.

In the course of 1953, as Rhoda remakes her life back home, a new friendship ripens with an Israeli Hebrew teacher called

Cille. She's a short woman with hair clipped in no particular style. Like other professional women of her generation she makes no play of femininity, though unlike her local counterparts, who depend on servants, she's a hands-on homemaker. Born in Germany, she has an intellectual energy that galvanises the women around her who are readers of Olive Schreiner's letters and Marie Bashkirtseff's diary, and have not concerned themselves with masculine opinion short of Shakespeare, Chekhov and other classics. Cille is up on the latest heavyweight controversies in biblical scholarship. Her small eyes are keen behind her glasses, focused fully on her listener, and from her wide, plushy mouth comes a flutelike voice. Her lips are mobile as she flutes in her instructive manner. It's a charismatic manner because it's so direct, so certain in her opinion and also so convincing as she holds your gaze, even a child's. Although my mother's friends are mothers above all, none sees me as Cille does, in her teacherly way. She's not concerned with dreaming. What she perceives is some reflection of herself, a more purposeful character who shouldn't be encouraged to dream her life away, but should think of work to do.

Not long ago, Cille married an engineer called Albie – an appropriate name, I think, because there's something a bit albino in his appearance, a fragile skin overlaid by unhealthy patches of sunburn. He's patient, faintly humorous, puffing a large pipe in the corner of his mouth. His air of refraining from comment is too mild to be critical. Like Dorrie's Sam, this is the type of good Jewish husband – the kind, family man – whom my mother never fails to commend.

Cille's verve is a lesson to plain or ugly women who fear to be left single, my mother says. 'If you don't think about looks, others won't think about looks.'

It's indirect advice to a daughter who's not pretty. One of my dreams is to be transformed when I grow up, so that I

might be worthy of romance. My model of manhood is a discerning hero, Mr Darcy or Mr Rochester, who can fall in love
with an intelligent woman even if she's not a beauty. Their historical distance helps my dreams. The current heroes of the
beach, my older cousins Gerald and Peter, often stay with us
for the summer at Kilve, on Wherry Road in Muizenberg,
around the corner from Sun Blest, where we used to stay
during my mother's blighted years. Peter and Gerald never
forget to thank Auntie Rhoda for breakfast, but they've hardly
downed their toast before they sling beach towels around their
necks and push off to the Snake Pit. This is a triangle of hot
sand between the pavilion and the bathing boxes where
teenagers slither side by side, oiling their bodies and eyeing
one another. Heavy-shouldered swimmers, talking about times
to my father, seem even more remote: they never look at a girl
who isn't a 'doll'.

I see Cille through my mother's eyes, a plain woman with
the wisdom to make the most of the tame man who comes her
way. In any case, that's the model for women in the fifties: a
man who returns from an office in the evening to find an
orderly home. In a small, Lakeside flat Cille takes pleasure in
home-making. While my mother was abroad, Cille nearly died
giving birth to a son, but she brushes this aside as nothing
beside the love that fills her for this vulnerable creature. Her joy
gives my mother pause. Can Cille's radiance reach back to marital contentment?

My mother confides one of those startlingly intimate facts she
sometimes relays to me in my sister capacity. The fact is this: Cille
had her hymen surgically removed, with the practical forethought
of a mature virgin who wants to enjoy her wedding night.
Unwittingly, my mother is revealing that a first sexual experience
is unlikely to be enjoyed – or it may be much worse. I mull over
this for a long time, along with a question too intimate to ask:

how does a bride, if she has her period, convey this to a bridegroom? What words would she use?

Another startling confidence from my mother is a question about frequency. How often should a couple make love? This question concerned her enough to consult a doctor who gave it on his highest authority, as it were, that once a week should satisfy a man. It happens that this particular doctor is a womaniser not known for his restraint, yet my mother, though aware of this fact, chose to exercise the peculiarly deferential mindset women of her generation cultivated for male doctors. Though my mother is usually reticent, she doesn't hesitate to proclaim this once-a-week ruling not only to me, but to other women, as a kind of defiance of husbands who expect too much of their wives. It justifies a wife who holds her husband off. The private issue is barely veiled, and I don't much want to hear it.

What I don't know is that my father consulted Basil's wife, Naomi, on how to stimulate a wife's desire. According to Naomi, he preferred to complain rather than hear what she could tell him. A twenties manual of *Ideal Marriage* laid it down that a wife 'must be *taught*, not only how to behave in coitus, but above all, how and what to feel'. A wife must adapt to a model a husband offers: an array of positions. When, as a curious teen, I discover this manual at the back of my mother's cupboard, it's disappointingly mechanical, full of tricky diagrams. Meanwhile, Pip reports something I'd also rather not hear: he's spied condoms in our father's suitcase. Lilian thought the satisfactions he took on his travels didn't matter. So Lilian said when I brought this up in 2004. She sided with Harry, and said that Rhoda should have surrendered more, and lent herself to her husband's concerns. 'Harry longed for her to come with him to swimming galas.' I too feel for him because he was hurt by the detached reserve of a wife he loved.

*

Cille is filled with initiatives animating to the dutiful housewives
of Cape Town. She's a born teacher who brings pupils on, and
she has a proposal for Rhoda: if she will produce a story every
fortnight, Cille will undertake to produce a story as well. They
will then discuss their work – an attempt to restore the stimulus Rhoda enjoyed in London. One of Rhoda's stories, 'If Only
I Can Say "Peep"', is a comic monologue of a young Jewish
mother – her age, accent and fairly recent immigration suggest
a Holocaust survivor – in the next bed to mine when I'm in a
nursing home to have my tonsils out. This survivor is about to
undergo a dangerous operation, and all she wants, she tells my
mother, is to wake afterwards. To say one word, 'peep', is all she
asks. In the event, her resilient voice cuts out with shocking
abruptness. At Cille's urging, Rhoda sends this to the *Jewish
Chronicle*, which publishes it, accompanied by an author photograph.

My mother reads me 'Early Spring', a daughter and mother
story. Emily, about my age, has a small-minded mother, preoccupied with appearance.

In the final scene, the gong goes for dinner and Emily goes
into her mother's room:

> *Before the mirror her mother was fixing a Spanish comb into her coil
> of hair ... Emily nuzzled her head against her corseted stomach:
> 'Mommy ... ' she lisped.*
>
> *But her mother told her to stop being a baby. 'What you look
> like!' she exclaimed. And she told nurse to tidy her up for supper at
> once. She wouldn't have Emily going around neglected.*

She's like the bustling mothers around us. One day, when
we girls are mothers, will we grow impervious in turn to our
daughters' tastes and feelings? I am lucky to have a mother
who's not like that. I go with her to the City Hall for a

An author photograph was published with
'If Only I Can Say "Peep"'

performance of *La Traviata* by the Eoan Group, a 'coloured'
company. She writes to Sirkka, 'I have always shared books
with my children but now for the first time, I have tasted the
pleasure of sharing concerts and ballet with Lyndall – and to
one who has no sister, who is an island in an alien but affectionate family, what a surprise, what a delight, to discover in
one's own child the close companion one has learned to lack.
The ballet has never seemed so enchanted with such a youth-
fresh dreamer beside me.'

At twelve, I'm allowed to read the stories she's turning out.
One is about a young man who is dying in hospital. To give
me this story is a gesture more intimate than maternal hugs.
For it reveals, as my mother must know it will, why her loss

before I was born had a painful twist to it, when the young man turns towards the night nurse who tends him and away from his girl. Recalling the fractured, imperfect days with Lou, she thought 'Now you would have loved me.' Our closeness is based on her writing and suffering. I'm proud to be her chosen reader.

My mother's 'blessed years' last from the age of thirty-six to thirty-nine, 1953 to 1956. When, later, I approach Emily Dickinson's extraordinary fertility over the years 1859 to 1863, my mother's *anni mirabiles* will come back to me. Both women with thin, delicate bodies speak of an almost annihilating 'Bolt'. Both know the horror of a soul wrenched from the body and put back askew. Yet I'm not thinking of sickness as such, rather the way both use and transform sickness as part of a visionary life: 'My Loss by sickness – Was it Loss', Emily Dickinson asks, or was it 'Ethereal Gain'? My mother has a similar compulsion to tell her unmentionable secret (what Dickinson tantalisingly calls 'it'), but where Dickinson tells it 'slant', through metaphor, my mother tells it as a transforming episode in a lifelong allegorical journey – the traditional journey through the wilderness that originates in Exodus and is re-enacted in the life of Jesus Christ, in the grail quests of the Middle Ages, in Dante, in *Pilgrim's Progress*, and in the poets Herbert, Hopkins and Eliot. My mother's metaphor comes repeatedly from an actual scene: the abyss into which a child can plummet as she edges, terrified, along the narrow track over the Olifants River.

On the second night of Passover in late March 1955 my mother has a full-on 'Bolt'. Next morning she relates the events of that night. 'Avalanches of mental horror' descended on her as she lay asleep in the sunroom. It's six years since the last attack, and she'd come to believe herself safe from all but minor

The railway track over the Olifants River became
an imaginary scene of moral trial

flaps – so much so that she had neglected to take her bedtime
pills. That's one way of seeing it. What she actually says is that,
at Cille's during the Passover Seder, she felt her 'emptiness', neither a poet nor a person with work to do.

A second Bolt hits her the next night, and again, 'like shrap-
nel stuns / plunges to precipice edge'. A poem in three stanzas,
which she types and hands me to read, takes me with her into
this horror, stage by stage. At first there's no bridge; then, from
her entrails, she spins once more 'prayer's tightrope walk /
Slippery as panic'. Walk, she repeats to herself, 'with rod and
staff / through the death-edged psalm'.

Precarious after the attack, she plays a game with Pip that
evening, hoping to soothe herself. Then she turns on her side
and feels about to faint. It's warded off by holding, again, as in
a vice, to Psalm XXIII. Never, it seems to her, has she come so
near to the Shepherd who restoreth the soul. She holds to the

words, she says, 'with the intensity of deathbed prayer'. And this time something different happens, recorded on a torn scrap of paper. '*The aftermath of this attack seemed different because of the "Presence" I sensed near my glass prayer door as the soul was restored to the body.*' Instead of the usual miasma, she's pierced by three waves of 'Light'. The first enters her body; the second fills her body from end to end; and the third takes her into a Dickinson-dash on the frontier of consciousness, beyond what words can record.

My father, woken by her groans, came into the room, she recalls, and she thinks he must have sensed her state of grace without knowing it, for he said to her, 'Never have I loved you more than at this moment.'

A day or two later my father, mother, Pip and I are walking on the pipe-track at the back of Table Mountain, a high-up but level path along a series of peaks called the Twelve Apostles. It's late summer turning to autumn, when sunlight strikes the *fynbos* in gold shafts. Rhoda lingers behind, looking up at the still peaks looming above the ocean that is and was from the beginning, and there, at that moment, it seems as though a 'visionwhite fountain of Love' rushes upwards from her head.

Early that April an Israeli called Nahum Levin arrives in Cape Town. He's director of the Educational and Cultural Department in Jerusalem, and his mission is to forward study of the Hebrew language in the wider world.

It's seven years since the Declaration of the State of Israel in May 1948, and ever since, the country has called for the Return to a homeland for survivors of the Holocaust. At the same time, it's more than a refuge; it's a dream of recreating the Promised Land in Exodus, at source a dream rising out of a book, and part of the appeal of this dream lies in recovering the language of the Bible as living speech. Jews who may be thriving in countries like America, Canada, England and South Africa are invited to recast themselves as exiles – exiled two thousand years ago from the land of the Bible. After the displaced persons camps, in the wake of the war, the 'ingathering of the exiles' carries an immense imaginative charge, fortified by the even stronger tug of a socialist utopia. In the fifties Israel's political elite (including the first Prime Minister, David Ben-Gurion) comes from communal farms, the kibbutzim, committed to an ethical code of selflessness. This opens up a compelling biographical drama for the young and especially for young women: to turn our backs on a materialistic society based on 'getting and spending' and to shun its model of 'dolled-up and dependent femininity'. Mr Levin delivers a summation of this at the anniversary of independence celebration.

What is he *not* saying? This is a question for after years. It's not a question my mother and her friends ask in 1955. What they aren't told is that certain people are denied entry to Israel: returning Arabs with Palestinian passports; gentile wives of Jews; and their uncircumcised sons. This policy will relent to the latter two categories: wives can enter if they convert, and their sons if they submit to circumcision.

That May, when Mr Levin delivers another address, my mother is caught in a press photo, in the forefront of the listeners, beside Cille. She wears a round hat on her crisp, brown curls. How much is she taking in? For Levin, whose English is limited, is speaking in Yiddish, a language unknown to Rhoda.

Love shapes a life, Levin insists. Two kisses had quickened him. The first kiss had been high-minded: the metaphorical kiss of *shechinah* or enlightenment, an understanding of Jewish history, which had led him to the Promised Land. In 1922, as a young man, he had gone on *Aliyah*, gone 'up' to settle in what was then Palestine under the British Mandate. He appeals to his listeners to commit themselves to this redemptive journey and ensure that the next generation will follow. The other had been a farewell kiss from his mother in the Soviet Union, the sacrifice of 'a true Jewish mother' who expected, he says, never to see her son again.

What is a true mother? As a mother myself, looking back, I'm not too sure, except that a mother is bound to go wrong one way or another. That's what my generation of guilty mothers, the women's lib generation, will say ruefully to one another when our children question our determination to work outside the home. How can I judge Mr Levin's mother, two generations before mine, and far off amidst the Persian architecture of Bukhara? What did such a woman say to herself? Did she sacrifice maternal closeness for the sake of her son, as he declares a true mother would? Or was there some consolation in an offspring who would be in a position to rescue members of the family? Call it prudence, call it calculation, when my turn comes to go my mother (and others in apartheid South Africa) will be explicit about the obligation to go away as insurance against an unsafe future for loved ones who remain at home.

There's a photo of Mr Levin, one hand neatly in his pocket held in place by a thumb, the other palm open towards his mouth as though it were a microphone. Children should have twelve hours of Hebrew a week, he is saying. Mothers should encourage them to go, when they take off to settle in the homeland. Expatriation will be hard – the climate, he concedes, will be enervating – yet this is the path to a rooted and genuine self, the only safe way into their future.

'It may be that this is difficult for the child, but it is best to let her go the hard way to happiness.'

Rhoda's chin is lifted towards the speaker, eyes keen yet half-covered by their lids as she enters this dream. Her rapt gaze can't

Rhoda (with hat) and friend Cille behind her take in the message
of Mr Levin, May 1955

be a response to words, which she can't translate. What she's responding to is rather the look and tone of a messenger, who appears to have walked out of the Bible, beckoning her to a further transformation.

11

At the Crossroad

In the mid-to-late fifties my mother changed, changed permanently, and with it, our tie. What I didn't know then was that my mother, at thirty-eight, was 'in love' with Levin, 'an elderly man of fifty-four'. So she confides to Sirkka. Only two other people know about Rhoda and Levin: one is Levin's friend and emissary, the Israeli Hebrew teacher Cille, twinkling, enthusing, who brings them together and acts as go-between for two people who lack a common language; the other is Harry, my father, as my mother will tell me years later, after he died. Even then she spoke in her tight, secrets voice – 'I can't tell you ... ' – and I continued to know too little until I came upon their letters amongst Rhoda's papers. And even then, what they say to each other feels far off, like voices coming from the Bible.

How is it that a man I saw only three times, and hardly to know, could – through his tie with my dreaming mother – mould my life? The first sighting happened on 13 December 1956, when I spotted a distinguished, white-haired man head and shoulders above a crowd. This was in HaYarkon Street, parallel to the seafront in Tel Aviv. I was leaving the Gat Rimon Hotel and he was making his way towards it.

That's him, I thought.

Not that my mother had said much, but I was used to significant silences, and understood in a casual way – I had just turned fifteen – that we were here for him. We'd landed only the night before.

The second and third times I saw him, during a year abroad in 1959, were longer and somehow less memorable. In March 1959 I called on him in Jerusalem – at my mother's insistence. I was seventeen, newly arrived, this time on my own, and too miserable to feel anything but a reluctant sense of duty. He lived in Jabotinsky Street (named after the Irgun militant whose terrorists blew up the King David Hotel during the British Mandate). It was a quiet area, with flats of pink-grey stone, near the Prime Minister's residence.

Mr Levin had the weary air of a man who's recovering too slowly from an operation. He intended to return to work as Director of the World Hebrew Union; his aim, he said, was 'to build a lasting edifice to the Hebrew language'.

His wife was short of delighted to see me, and why indeed should she welcome someone's daughter come to tire her husband? In those days, eleven years after the state was declared, the first question of every newcomer was 'Have you come to stay?' The only acceptable answer was yes, and I couldn't say yes because all I wanted was to fly back home. In minimal Hebrew, I stumbled through evasions, not meeting his eye.

Afterwards he wrote to my mother, 'Your daughter's visit made me very happy, because she has a spark of your soul in hers.' He tells her what she would wish to hear, for I had no sense of being 'seen' and nor, to be honest, did I try to answer my mother's need by 'seeing' him.

To me, he didn't look like a lover, more a foreign admirer, to whom my mother referred in a deliberate way as a 'friend'. I did understand that Mr Levin, with his grave, reserved, rather aloof face, was a very special friend and, as a high-minded educator, fitted my mother's cast of mind, but I made little of it since she was given to Meetings with strangers. In case this sounds peculiar, which of course in a way it was, it's fair to add that in the late forties and fifties friendships did seem 'predestined'. That's Muriel Spark's word for the manner of friendship then. It wasn't a matter of liking or not, she said; even if liking fell away, the friendship went on.

Even so, my mother meant something more momentous. She adopted 'Meeting' from the philosopher Martin Buber, who says, 'all real living is meeting'.

It's an April night when Rhoda meets this stranger at Cille's new house in Golf Links Estate in Plumstead. (Cille sheds her light from this unlikely spot, a suburban housing development.) A mild night in early autumn. The window is open. Through it, Rhoda hears strains of Mozart as she leaves, walking down the path to wait for her lift at the gate. And as she steps into deepening shadow the stranger follows and says, 'Why are you so beautiful to me?'

'Well, you see I am blessed.'

Since 1952 Rhoda has had signs of the grace bestowed on her as 'God's child'. The stranger's awareness of this secret self and the drama of their exchange come like 'a bolt of confirmation' that she's singled out for some purpose. Levin is a 'messenger'; his coming carries the authority of 'annunciation'. Afterwards, she aligns it with the destiny Isaac confers on Jacob when he grants him his blessing. It troubles her not at all to reconfigure the Patriarchs' drama, reserved for father and son, as a scene where a chosen woman can be centre stage.

In the Bible, the chosen are re-named. Accordingly, Rhoda

brings out her identity as Tsviah, the gazelle. That's how she signs her letters to Levin, while he calls her 'my sister, my bride' from the Song of Songs.

During the remaining weeks of his stay Levin and Rhoda meet seven times. When he's taken to visit the orphanage Rhoda diverts the tour to the backroom library, and there points to the shelf of Judaica, wanting him to know her as a reader digging into these books in his field.

At Cape Point, where the currents of the icy Atlantic and warmer Indian Ocean meet, they commit themselves to an all-time bond. Levin speaks of 'the two oceans which witnessed the covenant that was made between us forever'. His eye casts back into pre-history; he's not seeing Rhoda's sea, the seething element where I watch her frolic and run out, radiant, dripping, unfastening her cap. He uses the biblical word, *brit*, the Covenant the Lord enters into with humankind after the Deluge.* Bonded to an old-new People embodied in Levin (who declares he is hers '*ve'ad olam*', for all eternity) she is swept by a purpose to her existence for which she has prayed.

Her first step along Levin's route, while he's still in town, is to attend a debate on a recent law to ban secular marriage, proposed in the Knesset. Her protest is published a week later in the *Jewish Chronicle*, drawing on the Bible to pose her argument against what we now call fundamentalism. 'Are we to sow . . . the vision of the Prophet or the Scribe?'

This catches the eye of a women's charitable organisation. The Bnoth Zion, the Daughters of Zion, whose focus is on nurseries and vocational training, resolve to try out one of Levin's recommendations: a study group for women. My

---

* *Brit* is also the word for male circumcision, signalling the maleness of the Covenant made with Abraham.

mother is invited to run it and accepts with alacrity, though in the past she's had no part in communal activity. Harry, Pip and I are proud of her move into the public eye. She's keen to start with the prophets.

After Levin leaves, his many letters to Rhoda never mention his wife or son. I notice something else missing: his home address. My mother's replies are sent to a post office box in Jerusalem. Levin's Hebrew is graceful, and accessible in Cille's translations, yet in a curious way it's distant, the language of a luftmensch who has dreamt himself into an ancient frame of mind where men, with souls in the making, are on easy terms with their Maker. The language of my mother is indeed 'turned' to her Maker, yet she's planted on the earth, and she speaks (as do her favourite Bible tales) from within the net of family ties.

Reading these letters now, I'm puzzled by my inability to know Levin through the written word. Why is he so unknowable? And then it occurs to me: all his letters are the same. An oddly unvarying voice comes from a stratosphere of eternal love, too elevated to notice who my mother is and what she's like at home. In fact, home, the whole edifice of domestic existence with a mother at the centre, does not appear to exist.

It does not surprise me to discover that Levin's mother, that 'true Jewish mother' kissing him goodbye for ever, settled in America. She preferred America to being near her son. Whether she migrated before or after Levin's pictured scene of maternal sacrifice doesn't matter; he floats too high to know her.

Was Levin like a guru, drawing my impressionable mother into a tie that can eventually distance family if they don't yield to where his master-dream is taking her? Can Levin, in fact, be that most dangerous kind of enemy who sees himself as God's instrument? For the correspondent Levin reflects is not the person I know as a daughter; to him my mother exists as a pure and beautiful soul – no more. Nor does he lend his attention to the study and work she takes up as his devotee, which she mentions sparingly.

'I too – although I have not spoken to you of this – have Work to do.'

Only the capital letter indicates how crucial Work is to her, how excited she is at the prospect of teaching. There are no capital letters in Hebrew. In translation* this would have vanished for a man who is anyway too far off to see, as her family do, how carefully she prepares her classes, how they absorb her and how mystical poems have shaped her, above all Emily Brontë declaring if suns and universes ceased to be, 'Every Existence would exist in thee'.

Like Emily Brontë baking bread and Emily Dickinson kneeling on a rug as she digs her garden, Rhoda's visionary existence does not detach her from domestic life. A month after Levin's departure she writes humorously of our school holidays in Knysna, a rainy town on the Indian Ocean favoured by British expats:

> We are living on a lonely island in the midst of a silver-finned lagoon which flows between cliff-heads into the furling waves of the sea. At first it seemed inhabited only by Colonels and 'she-Colonels' but as I expected, these walking-sticks soon grew human and these umbrellas unfolded! Indeed I am already heart-to-heart with one of the she-Colonels, a salty old darling.

I remember that the she-Colonel thought me odd, at thirteen, to be carrying around a volume of Wordsworth. In the inviting bookshop, well placed next to the tearoom in

---

* Levin translates Rhoda's letters in English, while he writes to her in Hebrew.

Stuttafords department store in the centre of town, where mothers treat daughters to anchovy toast, my mother had encouraged me to use book tokens for my birthday to buy this volume of poems. She thinks one should buy books for life.

How much Wordsworth I read, if any, I can't now recall, but imprinted on memory is a childbirth scene I come upon in another book my mother recommended on the strength of my childhood fascination for the French Revolution: a biography of Marie Antoinette by Stefan Zweig. I'm appalled by her wedding night at fourteen, only a year older than I, put into bed with a clumsy bridegroom, the future Louis XVI. But far worse was giving birth in public, before the assembled nobility at Versailles. The girl had to keep up appearances in the midst of birth pains while onlookers chatted and sipped champagne. This is what stays with me from that biography: a girl exposed and fainting from her effort to preserve decorum.

I plead with my mother to let me join a Good Hope classmate on holiday with her mother at the Wilderness, the honeymoon resort, not far from Knysna. Scampering along a corridor we glimpse, through an open door, the bedding rolled back, and I wonder how it is for the pretty blonde bride with a husband who looks like he's made to kick a rugby ball. At thirteen I have no hope of real life outside the books in which I live.

Later that year, spring comes 'in puffs of morning air'. Enclosed in a letter of 5 September is a flower from the mountain where, Rhoda tells Levin, 'I drove my daughter yesterday. All day we lay among the daisies which have snowed over Signal Hill – sleeping, eating, reading good (and writing bad!) poetry, while the sea below shone motionless as the sky.'

My mother is so awakened by teaching the Book that in February 1956 she embarks on three years of university study

with a view to reading the Hebrew Bible in the original language. In February–March 1956, in a drafted report to Levin,
she marks the date when the Bible venture takes over her life.

> *I seem to have come to the crossroads between my writing life and*
> *a life of service – between my creative and my missionary self . . .*
> *Unknowingly, you have been the apostle of the missionary in me,*
> *and during the past year this side has taken precedence over me –*
> *who ever since I could read have struggled to express myself in*
> *writing.*

I'm shaken to come upon this dilemma because it shows how
consciously my mother surrendered her very self, as if Jane Eyre
were to surrender to the missionary St John Rivers and subdue
herself to his call.

So it happened that my mother remade herself to fit a cause.
Not that she hadn't always cared for that cause, but until Levin
came into her life her sensitive feelers led her. The combined
call of Cille and Levin broke into Rhoda's poetry life, broke
with a somewhat insensitive force, carrying a vein of oblivion
amidst the appeal of personal claims. Promoting their language,
they did not pause to consider what English meant to Rhoda
as a writer. Patriots both, they did not question their claims.

This alters her. No longer an obscure watcher of obscure
drama, she's planted on a public highway where great oaks can't
be uprooted.

At times my mother sweeps me along; at other times I argue.
When she praises the virtuous woman of the Bible, whose price
is above rubies, I squirm for my sex. Price. Rubies. How can
my mother endorse that estimate?

At night, when she's splashed her face – slap, slap, drip; slap,
slap, drip – she reverts to her old self. She'll look up from the

basin, wet and fresh. In her powder blue, tucked Barbizon nightie, washed clean of make-up, she's seen at her best in bed, where she lies, propped on pillows, wrapped in silence, reading. Moonflowers, long, creamy funnels in the Finnish vase on the bedside table, send out their scent at night.

I sit on her bed, as she'd once sat on mine, and she talks in the old way with all her feelers waving. Why, I wonder, has she relegated discrimination to the margins of her daytime life: the kind of judgement she can still relish in Jane Austen ('A lucky contraction of the brow had rescued Mrs Ferrars' face from the disgrace of insipidity by giving it the strong character of pride and ill-nature'). According to her revised moral grounds, it's wrong to speak ill of anyone.

I prod her newly anodyne comments about individuals, and question her retreat from judgement. What does she really think of the headmaster of an unruly afternoon school for plodding through the Hebrew of the Bible as a set of grammatical issues? (The headmaster has renamed me Leah – that weak-eyed, unwanted bride. Leah is stupid at Hebrew, crawling from letter to letter, unable to see a word as a whole.)

And what does my mother think of Uncle Eddie, my father's sponging brother who fancies himself a singer? But my mother will not be drawn.

That's a way of putting it, not very satisfactory. I should perhaps say that grace gives her access to universal love. Yet I don't want her to rise above the way she's shaped me as her companion. Nor do I want her to surrender her judgement to the claims of a community. To my gaping teenage gaze, she seems to disappear into consensus and close the door.

Rhoda plans to take me with her to Israel after her end-of-year examinations in November 1956. A reunion with Levin is 'intended to strengthen and renew us in our separate lives'.

What she hopes for most is a renewal of grace, which she fears to have lost. I see that this is bound up with a fear of putting herself in a culpable position with a married man. At just that time, the Suez Crisis starts. As she hesitates about going, she reverts to being ill. This adds to the ordeal of sitting her exam in the vast Jameson Hall of the university. Everyone around her bending over their papers is about nineteen. She is thirty-nine, in an era before mature students. Perhaps she should wear puffed sleeves to disguise her age, she jokes. As a precaution (her illness is not disclosed), she asks for a glass of water, not to sip but to splash her face if needed. Under these circumstances it's a feat to get a first, though in her deprecating way she dismisses it as 'baby Hebrew'.

My mother has sent me to the Movement, as it's called, a youth group of idealistic intellectuals, and I'm agog about the alternative it offers to a girl who's what the fifties call 'a social misfit'. My face is still wall-to-wall freckles, hardly improved by adolescent spots. Relieved from the false cheer of a wallflower at parties, I take to folk dancing and socialism. The aim of the Movement is to send people to Israel, and my mother's plan plays into my wish to show willing and gain credibility. Though she's plainly ill, I press her to go. We fly to Tel Aviv on 11 December 1956.

Her reunion with Levin takes place the night after we arrive. It appears a coincidence that a dashing South African, serving in the elite Nahal division of the Israeli army, asks me to come with him that very night to a Sephardi wedding. Since I've never had a date, I take this to be the miracle of Israel. I see only now that this date was orchestrated by my mother with the help of a former Good Hope schoolfriend called Isabella, who ran a South African club. Isabella's thin, square mouth is all smiles as she greets us and introduces Barry, the soldier, as soon as we

The first morning in Tel Aviv, December 1956

arrive. Although my mother needs me as her travelling companion, it's essential to have me out of the way when Levin arrives.

It's when Barry collects me at the door of the Gat Rimon Hotel that I catch that glimpse of Levin coming like a comet through the crowd. My eyes turn back to Barry who is affable, ready to please, a familiar manner of men at home, yet in this foreign scene feels protective. He lifts me above the milling wedding guests to see the bridegroom circle the bride seven times. My body zings to the touch of his hands around my waist. The firmness of his hold is reassuringly casual.

Barry does not ask me out again. Did I do something wrong?

I change from stovepipe slacks and a sweater to a pleated skirt, socks and lace-ups. It consoles me to be a schoolgirl after all, as plain as plain can be. In the same kind of clothes, a straight grey skirt with a pink thread and a pink buttoned-up jersey, I fly to Athens. My unworldly mother waves me off, unconcerned about a girl barely fifteen travelling alone, and perhaps my prim clothes protect me, for nothing happens to jar my innocence. I jaunt off to climb the Acropolis, and late at night catch a plane crossing Africa. This Greek plane is not in great shape. At dawn next morning we are grounded at one of the stops, Nairobi. Feeling rather grown-up to be coping in Kenya, I lunch out-doors alongside matronly colonials – who enquire, as well they might, about a lone schoolgirl – at a British club in town, and then there's another plane to Johannesburg, and the puffing, two-day train across the Karoo to Cape Town, in time for the new school year.

January 1957. Miss Tyfield, her academic gown slipping back off her narrow shoulders, enters the Standard Nine classroom. I open my mother's copy of *Wuthering Heights* – illustrated with haunting woodcuts – and meet the ghost of Catherine Earnshaw putting her hand through the window; we meet the untamed Heathcliff who's calling to her; and we revel in the dream of deathless love.

'Their affinity,' Miss Tyfield explains to nice girls who loll on Clifton Beach, angling for a date. She writes 'affinity' on the blackboard. Meanwhile, my mother is staying on, meeting Levin from time to time, eventually in his stronghold, Jerusalem. There's a gap here. What happened with Levin? Was she 'crowned' after all on 'the throne of Jerusalem'? That's how she speaks, secrets furled in allegory. All I know is that, after two months away, she flies home. She comes back in a bad way.

*

It's the old illness, shuddering, it seems to her, on the brink of insanity.

A poem, 'Undine', written a month after Rhoda's return and sent to Levin, makes it clear that a relationship between a 'sea-bride' and a dreaming man is bound to go awry because embodiment, much as the sea-bride longs for it, proves impossible. It's a poem haunted by loss, as an opportunity ebbs away.

Levin misreads the poem. Instead of seeing the elegiac gesture of a sea-bride retreating towards her own element, Levin reads what he expects and wants the poem to be: an affirmation of 'the eternity of our love'. His reply comes in the same rather monotonously elevated tone. A more alert lover, reading 'Undine', might have realised how delicately ready she was to be embodied, but the grace for this – the grace he was to confer – did not come.

For this, she blames only herself. 'There was no excuse for going,' she mutters. 'I have no excuse.'

While she resists further invitations from Levin to join him in England and America, she continues to pursue the nationalist dream. Rhoda is not alone in living more fully in this dreamland than in the place where we actually are.

Assorted Israelis – the teachers and *shlihot* recommended by Nahum Levin in the memorandum he left behind – descend on South Africa during the later fifties.

These men have been through the military; they are forceful; their speech comes in brief bursts. Movement girls are taught a form of self-defence with sticks, called *kepap*. When Yoav Tibon, the *shaliah,* rushes at me with a lifted stick I quail. Unless I hold up my stick crossways to block his, he'll see I'm a coward. Yoav's wife keeps in the background, confined to household tasks. I wouldn't wish to be in her place.

Yoav has a solution for everyone: to settle on kibbutz. It's the best life. To make this choice takes a special resolve, he warns, daring us to take the risk. By risk, Yoav means that students should drop their professional training. Yoav's words come out as imperatives without nuance. 'Burn your bridges.' 'Crystallise your aims.' His foreignness, not so much his accent as this unblinking directness, is unnerving. Can you take it, this manner seems to ask, can you nerve yourself to leave home for ever? Have you the courage to make a choice, right now, at sixteen or twenty, that will determine the rest of your life? What we enthusiastically call indoctrination has the appeal of a challenge. Will we defy parents' expectations that we'll live the same bourgeois lives?

It's almost disappointing when my mother dissipates this challenge because she ardently favours emigration to the Promised Land – wants it as much if not more than I. Sharing this national dream, as I'd shared her solitary dreams, I think little of the divide to come, and welcome too blithely the test it presents.

12

Dividing Dreams

As school ends, I go out with the jokey student, Siamon, the night when I blurt out what has never been said aloud before. To utter the taboo word for my mother's illness feels more sudden and reckless than to have declared how much I like him. At sixteen I'd seen his green eyes light up when he spoke or smiled. For the last six months I'd thought of him in tandem with Movement dreams. My disclosure, binding him to my secret, and his serious response, lasts till three in the morning,

while I swing back and forth on our gate. Far from the romantic fantasies I've let loose in the course of the crush, here is sense
and understanding.

Siamon comes from the dairy-farming region of the west
coast, where his father, a rabbi, who'd died some years before,
had served a scattered community. Siamon's first language was
Afrikaans, until he went to boarding school at the age of fifteen.
His speech sounds blunt to my ear, infused with Afrikaans
phrases, like the language of other up-country folk when they
speak English. There's a directness to Afrikaans, an energy in the
breath behind its consonants, that had appealed to my mother
from her early days amidst Afrikaners at Klaver, and I pick up
this appeal.

My mother takes me shopping to fit me out with clothes for
settling in Israel. During the last year at school I've been saying
that I want to go, and my mother supports me. In truth, she's
more active than I when it comes to specific plans. It's increasingly unthinkable to let down my schoolmate and fellow
member of the Movement, Jasmine, who's going too. We are to
learn Hebrew; then work on a kibbutz; then join an American
programme over the summer at the Hebrew University; and
then take the Hebrew entrance examination for the university
later in the year.

What incentive there was fades in January 1959 after I 'go
steady' with Siamon, six weeks before Jasmine and I are due to
depart. He's at the start of the fourth year at medical school, the
first hands-on year in the hospital, and like most Movement students he hasn't succumbed to Yoav's urging to drop out. Kissing
for hours on the rocks with the Atlantic breakers pounding about
us, I don't think about leaving. It's my mother who dictates my
letter of application to the organiser of the American programme. It's she who packs my suitcase. It's filled with modish

shortie pyjamas, wool sweaters, sensible shoes and a jar of Nescafé (unobtainable where I'm going), 'To equip you,' my mother says, 'for the future.'

What it means for her to send her daughter away, perhaps for good, she confides to Sirkka. 'For me it would be a happiness to continue my burgeoning friendship with her in close companionship. Nevertheless if she wins a way into the Hebrew University or takes root in the soil of Israel that too will be a joy to me.'

She commends my 'contribution to family life'. Her words convey a tone of ending, as though I'm leaving with the finality of her father leaving home. The linking narrative of Jewish history, a subject she now teaches alongside the Bible, is an obligatory migration from one country to another.

As she packs neatly in folds of tissue paper, her voice advises me to be patient with the hurdles ahead. I hardly hear, much less imagine any hurdles because I'm dreaming about the sweet sorrow of parting from Siamon.

'I'm looking forward to a sad love affair,' I tell him, and it isn't wholly a joke. Nothing in my experience so far can match up to the romantic drama of my mother's youth: the loss of Lou. The sadness impresses me as all the more poignant since she doesn't speak of it. All I know are hints and guesses from her hospital story. I'd page through her photograph albums of the thirties, wondering which young man he was.

My sadness explodes on the night of 18 February after the train pulls out of the station. That night I can't sleep, and at four in the morning leave the compartment to get a drink of water at the end of the swaying corridor. Only I am awake, I and the train, rushing together through the darkness. The low bush of the veld stretches to an infinity of solitude. The rhythm of the wheels, soothing on previous journeys, seems (I write to Siamon) 'like the "deliberate speed" of God's footsteps in "The Hound of Heaven", driving me against my will along a certain path'.

International flights leave from Johannesburg, and at this first stop en route Jasmine and I are to stay at Evermore, where Basil continues to live with his sculptor wife Naomi, another of my mother's sisters. Almost the last words of advice from my mother were a reminder to be 'cheerful and helpful' with her family 'who are helping you with their affection'.

I sense uncomfortably that she's intimating something about gratitude, and see now that she was trying to tell me – not too bluntly – that my venture abroad, and all she'd bought to equip it, depended indirectly on the largesse of my uncles. In other words she, not my father, is funding all this. It's not something my father would have pushed, he who had given up study abroad because he took a frugal – we might say, short-sighted – view of education. I leave replete with gifts, scented bath powder and coloured soaps, and with pats on the back for doing the right thing.

Everyone we know talks up the approved narrative: a latter-day exodus from our own Egypt, the decadent luxury of wealthy whites who thrive off the backs of impoverished blacks, often migrants parted from their own families, in apartheid South Africa. Entering into the Promised Land is to be a kind of moral cure.

I want to pause at take-off to hear once more a phrase my mother repeats: I am, she says, 'an extension' of herself. This may be a truism of universal motherhood and daughterhood, yet given the glowing eye of my mother's narrative and my tie to her imagination I'm about to experience a new birth. At this moment my life is energised and reprogrammed by my mother to enact and fulfil the Return. Her weekly letters over the next year will attempt to reset the programme when, at a distance, I deviate. At issue between us is her denial that I'm to enter an alien environment. It's an article of faith that the Holy Land will not be alien.

My mother embraces Israelis as 'bone of my bone', and speaks not of 'them' but of 'we'. The same identification prevails in the Movement. Neither they nor my dreamy mother has prepared me for predators on the prowl. Within hours of landing at Lydda airport, I allow myself to be picked up by an Iraqi. I think it's fine because he's Jewish and will see, as boys at home can, that I'm a nice girl, unavailable for casual romps. In fact, I'm keen to cross the colour bar in a country where races are not divided by law.

The Iraqi offers to fetch me that very night to see the sights of Natanya, a sleepy seaside town north of Tel Aviv, and a bus ride away from the suburban straggle ('pretty villages', my mother had imagined) where we have come to learn Hebrew at an ulpan. I think this grown-up man is giving me the welcome with open arms all newcomers are said to receive. In his taxi, parked in the woods, I fight him off and wrench open the door of his car. Bellows of obscenity – without understanding much Hebrew, I do know his language is vile – reach my ears as I flee through the trees, uncertain what direction to take. Next day in the dining room at the hostel an English girl, the head-girl type with a fair plait down her back and fresh from

Roedean School, makes an audible aside. It's about girls who go out with taxi drivers.

What happened is too humiliating to mention, certainly not in letters home. They would think me stupidly naive to bring this on myself.

Ulpan Akiva is run by Shulamit Katznelson, whom my mother fancies a friend. There's no sign of friendship beyond a courtesy cup of coffee in her house. She does not trouble herself unduly about individuals. We belong with the flotsam: displaced Romanians with whom, at first, I share a room; sturdy Polish housewives who live locally and have been here long enough to grasp the language; and gallant single women who need suitable husbands – sadly, there's no one suitable on the present course.

I admire a Lebanese girl called Vered, aged about nineteen, who has left her mother in Beirut and come via Cyprus because the border between Israel and the Lebanon is closed: no phone connection, no postal service. Cut off in this way, Vered speaks of her mother with mature concern, adores her, yet is too promising to linger in the Lebanon – Vered also plans to learn the language and go on to the Hebrew University.

As we sit in one another's rooms, stirring our precious Nescafé with sugar to make a rim of foam, we joke that middle-aged Shulamit is out to find her man, and it comes as no surprise that she does later marry a twenty-something Argentinian.

Holding herself apart amidst her divans and Arab tat, the directress appears now and then in the communal dining room to talk up the Return. Her rousing speeches are disconcertingly close to those of my mother.

'However tumultuous & bewildering the existence of the everyday,' my mother writes, 'be awake to the realisation that you are participating in this ingathering of the Exiles and this unfolding in history of a Divine plan which the prophets have envisioned. I did not expect you to find this easy.'

I can't take this in for two reasons. One is that it doesn't take long to notice the hostile apartness of Arab inhabitants whose past has to be obliterated by the ideology of the Return. At the same time the ideology of the new state compels immigrants to surrender their children to remaking according to the hardy, pioneering model shaped by school and army.

It comes to my ears that some time earlier Levin, then close to the centre of power as Director for the Cutural Absorption of Immigrants, had been involved in an incident that almost brought down Ben Gurion's government. The 'Magic Carpet' migration of a million Yemenites took place in 1951. Crowded in immigrant camps called Ma'abarot, the Yemenites protested against the removal of their children to secular schools. This policy, masterminded by Levin, had enforced a divide from parents, who'd brought their past with them. Levin's 'nation-building' generation had believed they were justified in doing whatever it took to compel adaptation to the model they themselves represented.

The other reason I can't take in my mother's dream of the land the prophets envisioned is that I'm not in the place she thinks. A fantasist myself, as adept as she at being somewhere else, I dream my way back, the train rolling into the station and Siamon on the platform, his varsity blazer slung over a shoulder – even though he too, a stalwart of the Movement, wants me to adapt. At the same time he lets me say what I feel, and that freedom to admit what would be inadmissible to everyone else proves a lifeline. The letters I write to him all the time (for when I'm not putting pen to paper, I'm saving up details and running up the scale of emotion) hold the kernel of a different life.

One of my first assignments, in March 1959, is to visit Nahum Levin in Jerusalem and deliver a book from my mother. She has alerted him that I will bring what she has pored over, 'sharing (in imagination) certain poems and pictures, as I do share all loveliness & all harmony with you my dear brother being ... In this book I visit you.'

I'm to report on Mr Levin, but though my mother is waiting to hear, I neglect to write. Meanwhile, four letters arrive from her, questioning my silence.

Jasmine's mother, she tells me, has word of our 'dream-weekend' in Jerusalem. When her friends enquire, my mother has to have recourse to what Jasmine's mother relays every time she phones my mother to proclaim 'fabulous' news from her daughter.

In fact, Jasmine is almost as miserable as I, and in one way worse off: she's detaching from her Movement boyfriend, and my backward longings hold up her ultimately successful effort to keep the future in sight.

My mother wants details. Testing if our sisterhood will prevail on her to hear the truth – how far will she draw in her feelers? – I make bold to offer the unheated dorm in winter, the glee of a matronly Romanian as she tries on my clothes, and idling men with oiled hair who eye up girls when we get off the bus in Natanya.

This is the wrong script. Any gesturing towards lacklustre reality reflects badly on the non-dreamer. As it is, I refrain from confessing more serious non-dreams: the rudeness of men in military uniform shoving other hitch-hikers out of their way as they clamber onto a passing truck; their talk that doesn't lend itself to other points of view; and a close-up of an Israeli woman at home, the wife of Jasmine's uncle. His wife's existence seems bounded by washing nappies and sterilising bottles. Motherhood, it appears, turns a woman into an *ozeret*.

I know in advance that *ozeret* will displease my mother – displease her with me. It's hard now to convey the disgrace of these observations, as much as if a Christian daughter were to cast a cold eye on Bethlehem, or a Muslim daughter on Mecca.

'Being catapulted suddenly from a luxurious life has darkened your vision of things,' my mother decides. 'I am troubled that this inevitable "desert journey" should be associated in your mind with Israel. On the other hand for a mature being who has fought through to wholeness, Israel could become in retrospect the country of your growth.'

'Luxurious' stings. The mirror my mother holds up reflects a spoilt girl who can't put up with minor privations. Yet physical conditions are not really the problem, and her further conclusion that I crave a 'millionaire' existence comes as a puzzling reproach.

My mother enjoys her dream of how she'd manage: how, if she were 'allowed' to be here herself, she'd live 'in a little room' with a few books and nibble on blintzes in a modest dairy restaurant. This is unlike her usual life.

For the Sabbath dinner on Friday nights, my mother orders flowers to be delivered; gladioli come arranged stiffly in a bowl. She adds more graceful flowers from the garden: a silver vase of fragrant sweet peas and small posies of pansies with their upturned faces. Three courses – gefilte fish, soup and casserole – are prepared by Lenie, and a light cake, a variety of *melktert*, comes out of the oven when Lenie serves tea later in the evening. It's unthinkable for my mother to do all this herself. But I turn out to be unfit in other ways. My mother asks me to put a shoulder to the communal effort of making where I am a better place. I have to own that my unwillingness precedes any good reason, and has to do with the habit of living through dreams: my dream-narrative carries me back homewards. Divested of my mother's eye for the red lacquer beak of a bird, her ear for a baboon's 'bacchanalian cries', her decided tastes in literature, in fact, divested of my mother I hardly exist: 'a very ordinary girl', my diary admits.

In this stagnant place, I'm dormant. Nothing contradicts my sense of failure, an embarrassment to my mother and a burden to Jasmine. Dead days, alleviated by reading *Cry, the Beloved Country* and Alan Paton's later novel, which I like even more, *Too Late the Phalarope*, about a forbidden love affair between a black and a white. I curl up in the unwanted tomorrows of a mediocre boarding school. We will hibernate here.

In June my mother relents. This is occasioned by a German refugee, Miss Hirschberg, one of Cille's friends whom my mother wished me to visit. A retired teacher of great charm and empathy, she draws out my impressions.

I blurt out how crude boys appear; how lacking in self-respect to stare fixedly at girls passing in the street. 'Revolting!'

'It's the fault of poverty,' she explains. 'Parents here are in such a hurry to earn money that they cannot waste time on contemplation and learning.'

She takes my hand and closes her other hand over it – oh, the balm of affection – and then shakes her head. 'Seventeen is too young to start a new life alone. One is still too unsettled within oneself and the home atmosphere is too necessary.'

Unexpectedly, I receive a letter from my mother in a softened voice. Miss Hirschberg, it seems, has intervened in my favour, soothing my mother's disappointment.

'My dear, your own feelings and yours alone, must decide your future course,' she says. 'And whatever you decide will make me happy.'

Even so, I don't dare crawl home at once, as I long to do. Even Siamon warns that I wouldn't be able to hold up my head. The only face-saving plan is to stay out the year.

*

My mother visits in August. By this time, after a spell on kibbutz, I've joined a group of friendly Americans who have come to Jerusalem for their Junior year abroad. As my mother and I stroll about the ultra-orthodox quarter of Mea Shearim and the Bezalel Art Gallery, she tells me that Nahum Levin is ill. When she leaves in early September her last words are a request: 'Please go and see him for me.' So I see him for the third and last time, and have to write that he has a resurgence of cancer. Rhoda confides to Sirkka alone that things are going wrong in her home, 'as must happen when the roof-tree is innerly, secretly on the verge of collapse'.

In December, she writes him what she knows will be her last letter. 'I have been walking in your footsteps – far, far behind you, but in your footsteps . . .* I am speaking of your message in my classes and also in public talks. I wanted to be a writer, but since your coming I struck out on a new path.'

Levin dies on 16 December. I cable my mother. I know she expects it, and nothing further is said.

I'm staying for the first university term in Jerusalem, running until January 1960. In a preliminary English test in practical criticism (a test of analysis with the name of the author withheld), it's luck to find a poem by Emily Dickinson, one I've read with my mother: 'A Bird came down the Walk – '. I unroll my feathers like her bird whose flight 'rowed him softer Home – '. But now the Hebrew entrance exam looms, and I warn my mother I'm not up to it.

'I must confess that I shall be disappointed if you don't pass your Hebrew exam,' she replies. 'After all it is the only subject you have really studied this year, and has now become the "practical purpose" of your stay.'

* No omission.

I fail. My mother refrains from further comment.

Since I'm no longer eligible for the Hebrew University, my return is now definite. The prospect of our renewed companionship makes my mother miss me more. She doesn't say this; it's what Siamon relays after they discuss my failure. He too does not express disappointment; instead he spells out what he wants from me, 'an open, sympathetic mind and an eager will to learn'. Then he adds, 'if you have the ready mind I shall try and instil the eagerness (if that is not presumptuous on my part) and we shall look for certainty in this crazy mixed-up world together'.

Siamon's rational intelligence provided an influential complement to my mother as dreamer

These attainable aims come as relief from my mother's unful-filled dream. Here is someone not given to dreaming – not in my mother's intense way – who is opening up a different kind of possibility if I will lend myself to his idea. I respect his intel-lectual confidence and, through our letters (three a week), have come to see how understanding he is.

Siamon's offer of learning in place of dreaming is not meant to supplant my mother. He assures me of her wish to have me back, yet there's a changing sense of home, centred less on my mother and more on a mentor of sorts. It's not that I can turn from her poetic ways with words, but having tested the heat of ideology I crave a cooler climate. Mine is a mother who put ideology before a relationship, while Siamon has done the reverse. His move to limit damage opens the gate to a shift of allegiance.

13

The Way Down

All the while I was abroad, the dream that kept me going had been a variation on the return of the native. Back home, it's not quite the same. My mother, more successfully than I, had detached herself: her friendships, her groups, her recuperative bathes and walks along the sea had closed over my departure. It's incomprehensible to her that the daughter who returns remains unmoved by the privilege of living in the Promised Land, reclaimed by the people of the Book. While there, my longing to speak the truth, as I saw it, was blocked by her conclusion: a girl who didn't take to this storied place must be misguided. Safely home, I give way to an impulse to try out truth once more.

On the first Friday night, at a dinner with a white cloth, candles and *kiddush* in the garden, my mother's many relations, on holiday at the Cape, sit up expectantly when I'm asked to say a few words about my experience. Aware of the risk, I state what's wrong: the militarisation; the know-all bark; the eyes-front walk of students released from the army. If I'm specific

enough and others listen, will my mother hear? No. Her face tenses with dismay at such a daughter.

When I register for the first-year English course, my mother decides to do the same. We are to be a mother–and–daughter duo for the three years of English at the University of Cape Town, and in sharing daily occupations I feel embraced by her once more, once more her helper.

She scoffs at herself as her daughter's dependant: 'I follow her into classrooms,' she tells her own followers. I drive us in Cherry, her Morris Minor, to the campus perched on the slope of the mountain. English is her natural subject, bliss after the challenge of Hebrew.

'I am happy to be in touch with poetry again,' she writes to Roseveare in London. Emily Dickinson, she suggests, would be a fertile subject for the City Lit poetry group.

In the early sixties, T. S. Eliot is the greatest living poet. A few years before, he'd addressed an audience of twelve thousand on the subject of literary criticism, in a football stadium in Minnesota. The media quote his dicta from on high.

Eliot's most celebrated dictum proclaims the idea of a poet's impersonality. Yet my mother perceives that the poems are not so impersonal as they appear. She convinces me that the poet's first marriage to nervy, distraught Vivienne bore on his private waste land. The Eliots' letters, still buried in archives at this point, will later bear out my mother's intuition.

For us two, lectures are futile, groping in obscure corners. Only through my mother can I escape the current mode of reading Eliot as a hunt for the sources of the literary allusions that stud the poems' surface – as though Eliot wrote poems to provide sport for academics.

No lecturer, no critic apart from my mother, appears to offer a coherent reading. Instead of a career divided between the sophisticated satirist, who suddenly, in 1927, turns pious, she sees a single trajectory of what Eliot himself termed 'the sequence that culminates in faith'. She spells out the alternatives of 'the way up', the poet's ephemeral moments of vision, and 'the way down', the dark night of the soul – a psychic ordeal designed to reshape the imperfect self as a vessel the divine spirit might fill.

Shared reading, especially Eliot, brings my mother and me close again. As in childhood, our relationship thrives on books – to my benefit. For her, there's the 'warm soil' of a daughter's companionship. On campus, she tells Sirkka, 'I no long walk by myself and wave my wild tail but live pleasantly in the warm company of L & her friends.' She's 'surprised & pleased' that I attend her Bible class for students.

While I'm relieved to fly again under the wing of her independent mind, I'm also aware of a new responsibility to protect her from feeling lost amongst the vast number of students who sign up for English. I'm never unaware how a dispirited mood can jump the barriers to an attack. If she's precarious in the morning before we leave or jittery over an essay, I worry. I try to help in practical ways like finding the recommended books and driving her car. She's a tense driver, and if her pills fog her she's vague and forgetful.

So I'm relieved in another way when it's time to dash off to Monica Wilson's lectures in social anthropology and Dr Davenport's lectures on South African history, courses chosen because they don't derive from 'overseas'. I delight in their focus on home ground, the implied anti-colonial stance that here, in our local setting, is something to find out, untwisting the bigoted version of colonisation that school texts had imposed.

In the Cape school-leaving examinations I had a poor C for English. That grade determines my tutorial group, and my marks for essays stick in the average B range while my mother gets a well-deserved A for an essay on the moral comedy of Jane Austen. I try repeatedly to drop English in favour of subjects where there's hope of doing better, but then miss literature so much that I switch back. This decision to stay with the subject I love invariably feels right.

Siamon still means to emigrate. So long as I remained in Israel, he'd steadied a lifeline to me – no tugs – but my mother's report of an exchange with him carries a discomforting challenge. When she discussed the local elections with Siamon, he remarked that he'd voted 'for the first and last time'.

'Why last?'

'Because by the next election, I'll be gone.'

I'm not unaware of what lies ahead, and it may contribute to a nightmare: it starts with a familiar scene. I'm coming out of the sea with Siamon, but the situation has reverted to what it was when I left home the year before: it's that I'm to stay abroad, and return only on visits. In my dream it's the first visit, and I'm due to return to Israel that night. It feels like a return to death-in-life. As this hits me, I wake with relief to find it's only a dream.

Not for me, then, that testing narrative, the migration story that's linked with the oldest poetry of the West, the *Odyssey* and the *Aeneid*. On paper, I'm awed by the staying power of Aeneas, who has carried his father on his back, and whose ship still carries the household objects that tell him who he was. I'm gripped, vicariously, by the dream that compels him, that moment when the gods instruct him to sail on, promising *imperium* without end. But what touches me is decidedly not the heroic story with its horrors of fight and bloodshed. It's the melancholy prospect of a stranger in the strange land.

By day, that prospect dissipates. One evening when my mother is washing her face – the time of day we talk most freely – I confide to her that Siamon found me reading a woman's magazine and made it clear he was less than impressed.

My mother has never opened a woman's magazine in her life, which is one reason she's free of the beauty myth and 'must have' mentality. She admires Siamon's mind, and he sometimes accompanies her to lectures by visiting scholars.

I'm adept at reading my mother's furrowed face. She doesn't think I'm brainy enough for him, and fears he may drop me, especially if I don't fit in with his plans.

In the silence that follows, I think: she's too pure to consider physical attraction, and reassure myself that kissing in the shadow of the vine on our stoep and lying between the sand dunes on a deserted Macassar Beach will sustain the tie.

My grandmother, less tactful than my mother, warns me outright that Siamon could take 'the best years of your life, then leave you'. Granny reflects the opinion of the wider family that, given my looks and lack of allure, it's surprising there should be a boyfriend at all.

My own explanation lies in Siamon's alacrity when it comes to helping others: my concern over my mother was the kind of thing to engage him, and medical issues would engage him even more. His previous girlfriend had diabetes. I'm not saying he chose her on that basis – she's pretty and gentle – but, shall we say, her condition did not deter him.

I don't refuse Siamon's plans; nor, privately, do I concur. My mother, though, assumes I'll come to accept this future, which is of course her own dream. When she tells Sirkka how glad she is to have me again her 'friend and companion', she adds, 'It may not be for long.'

Three years after my aborted attempt to emigrate, Siamon and I decide to marry. In the run-up to the wedding my mother and I quarrel. As part of a community, she wants the traditional kind of wedding where bride and groom become a focus for a re-affirmation of community bonds. It's not that she differs from me in wanting a small wedding; it's that she's granting priority to what others want. There are to be myriad guests whom we barely know.

'The wedding is not for you. It's for your parents.' My mother makes this explicit.

Am I to be an outsider at my own wedding?

Yes, I am. I break it to my mother I might not want to go through with this. For once, I have no wish to please her.

As tension mounts Siamon says matter-of-factly, 'The wedding doesn't matter.' It's the marriage that does, he means, and that makes sense. I'm still put out that he doesn't side with me in defying what's expected of us. Where he appears calm, maturely considerate of parents' wishes, I appear a tiresome rebel. Resentfully, I give in.

When the wedding day arrives, my mother, alert to women's experience, knows how an obedient daughter – and even more, a less obedient one – comes to be that unreal construct, the bride, fixed in the artifice of communal rite.

'Think that you are marrying Siamon Gordon,' my mother reminds me before walking down the aisle as she adjusts my wedding dress and puffs up my breasts to fill its contour. I've recently lost weight and am caked with unaccustomed make-up to cover an outbreak of pimples – the result of ill-advised facials with products that stung the skin.

And then, there's a band singing about a sweetheart called Tammy, and to the strains of 'Daisy, Daisy' a dessert trolley is pulled into the dinner by a tinsel bicycle-made-for-two. On it are mounted a stuffed man and woman. To do my mother justice, her eyes meet mine, appalled by the community's keen-to-please caterer, Krafchik of course, who has sprung this surprise. When people shake our hands they say this spectacle

Greeting my mother's friend Zelda at our wedding.
Siamon is behind, on left

has been the highlight of the wedding. It's the first and last time we set eyes on a lot of our wedding guests.

'You are a lucky, *lucky* girl,' are my mother's parting words. I am indeed lucky, but wish she wouldn't say it with solemn emphasis, as though I may not be sufficiently thankful.

My resistance will not be forgotten. Twenty-five years later, when we are living in Oxford with two daughters, my mother phones from Cape Town.

'Are you happily married?' she asks in a stricken voice. This is Rhoda's way: she's given to sudden compunction.

During the political upheaval of the year we marry, 1963, when Mandela and his underground comrades are caught and tried, and the country seems on course to perdition, our plan – common to our generation – is to leave. After the Rivonia Trial, with Mandela starting his imprisonment on Robben Island, there's no place for the likes of us in South Africa. Many Afrikaners tolerate other whites only as participants in a racial segregation invading every corner, from separate entrances to the post office to seats on buses.

In the meantime, until I finish my course, Siamon and I live at 22 Lisdale, on the rocks at Sea Point, with Robben Island in sight. My mother's walks pass Lisdale. She wants to press the buzzer, then refrains, she says.

'This is absurd,' I assure her from the heart.

'A couple needs to be alone,' she insists, quite unnecessarily to my mind. We'd both love to see her, but she's resolved not to be a possessive mother and I can't budge this act of renunciation.

On a balcony over the ocean with Lion's Head looming behind, I read *Middlemarch* for the first time. The high-minded Dorothea, a St Theresa of the Midlands, is said to like 'giving up'. Here is a woman's life in a provincial town, which constrains her aspirations and reflects them in small mirrors. Dorothea idealises scholarly Mr Casaubon as her superior tutor, much as my mother has idealised Mr Levin. Craving higher education, they defer to educated men. And then, like Dorothea, my mother finds 'work-in-the-world': the agency to give to others in the modest sphere open to her.

Siamon too reads *Middlemarch*, and pronounces it the greatest English novel. He's taken with the doctor, Lydgate, who, back in 1829, dreams of discovering the 'primitive tissue', which he rightly assumes underlies and connects the different organs of the body, with its powers of renewal and repair. This is a historical version of Siamon's own ambition to move into experimental pathology, and it's not lost on him that Dr Lydgate is thwarted in the end by a fantasy of doing his research, undisturbed, in a provincial backwater.

If you grow up in Cape Town, where sunlit mountains rise steeply out of the sea, you can never be anything but a creature of that place. Ours, though, is a generation who see '*net blankes*' ('whites only') on benches along the sea and know that we have to live elsewhere. People like us who are still here are either waiting to leave or casting themselves into what appears a futile Struggle against an entrenched regime.

Our immediate plan is to spend a year in London en route to New York, where Siamon has a post lined up at the Rockefeller University for two or so years with a view to gaining research experience in a laboratory. His hope is to become a scientist worthy of the Weizmann Institute in Israel. I'm excited at the prospect of a new life in an England never seen but imagined through books. And it's a comfort to go with Siamon.

He has an unpaid attachment to the Wright-Fleming Institute at St Mary's Hospital, where Alexander Fleming first observed the penicillin-producing fungus. I find work in the library of the Royal Society of Medicine. It's a grand building on the corner of Henrietta Place and Wimpole Street – not far

At UCT, outside Jameson Hall after graduation, with Yasmin Behardien.
On left, behind, is Granny Annie (in hat)

from the fashionable doctors of Harley Street – in the West End.
The salary is £750 a year, enough for us to rent an attic with a
chilly bathroom down a few stairs at ten pounds a week, the
going rate in 1964. The attic is at 31 Netherhall Gardens in
Hampstead, not far from Auntie Minnie.

My mother predicted rightly what a comfort Auntie Minnie
will be when we come to London, and how charming I'll find
the quiet voices and considerate manners of her English relations. I'm delighted with them and with the kindness of Auntie
Minnie's welcome. At the time of our departure my mother is
reliving her heady time in London twelve years earlier. The
City Lit, having played the starring role in my mother's history,
beckons: I join an evening ballet class. In 1964 Fonteyn and
Nureyev's partnership is at its height. We sit in the highest
gallery of the Royal Opera House and I hang so far over the rail

to take in Nureyev's leaps in *Le Corsaire* that Siamon laughs and
has to hold my ankles. In summer we travel to Finland to stay
with my mother's soul-sister, Sirkka.

My love of books and my mother's wartime role as orphanage librarian has encouraged me to work in a library.
Unfortunately, medical books turn out to be in a foreign language. My daily job is to shelve and file. We librarians have no
contact with members of the society, and at lunchtime eat our
sandwiches in the basement. Every afternoon the hours creep
at their petty pace. After eight months I sign up for typing lessons three evenings a week.

When I mention this, the eyes of the Assistant Librarian
gleam. Next day she offers an opportunity for useful practice.

From then on, I'm in the office to help Beryl, the secretary
to the society. She's very nice, as they say in England: a mild,
middle-aged woman with dark hair sculpted round the head in
an off-the-face fifties style. Beryl has the comfy femininity I'm
drawn to in my grandmother. Chat with Beryl, starting and
trailing off and picking up again at intervals throughout the day,
has the cosiness of knitting needles going click, click in an even
rhythm. No jolts of surprise; no confessions; no demands; no
tests of competence. Beryl seems unbothered by my slow fin-
gering of the typewriter.

Am I to go on lying low in this bath of warm water? I think
of Eliot in his office at Lloyd's Bank in the City during his first
years in London: he did this job for the sake of the poetry he
wrote after hours, and yet he didn't dislike it. If anything, he
welcomed the peacefulness of sitting there, adding up figures.
I prefer Beryl to a senior librarian, Norma, on the watch for
shortcuts to the labyrinthine routines she's laid down. Her cold-
eyed questions are designed to trip up a subordinate. Aren't I
fortunate to be paid to practise typing in pleasant company?

I look over a letter of recommendation from the head of the

To the left is J. M. Coetzee, who did some lecturing, and
on the right a fellow student, Itamar Avin, at a party in
Professor Howarth's garden, December 1963

English Department in Cape Town, Professor Howarth (whose
yellowed lecture notes make an appearance in J. M. Coetzee's
Youth). He'd thought me diligent enough to assist a scholar, and
the idea is appealing. I want to be that kind of woman: a helper.
I'd liked the role of helper to a writing mother. Now, turning
the pages of the *New Statesman*, I come upon an advertisement
from Benjamin Waife in New York, who wants a research assistant (who can type) for a book on confessions. He agrees to pay
me the same salary as the library, though calculated on an
hourly basis. I resign from the library, say goodbye to Beryl and
turn to the lives of St Augustine and Rousseau.

*

As planned we move to New York a few months later, in April 1965. I meet Mr Waife, who turns out to be an affable journalist for Jewish papers, writing as Ben-Zion Goldberg, and his wife turns out to be the youngest daughter of the Yiddish writer Sholem Aleichem. She smiles gently as she brings tea and toast while her husband and I review the situation.

He's satisfied, he says, with my writing, but can't afford to pay a New York salary. This is why, he tells me proudly, he'd conceived the idea of a cheap researcher in England. If I go on as before he might let me collaborate on his next book. Might I collaborate on the present book, I'm emboldened to ask. No, is the answer, because he already has a contract. I consult my father as well as a New York lawyer, Victor Frankel, and am not surprised to be advised against an oral promise. Their warning is reinforced by a sense that Mr Waife is losing interest in the present book, and in fact it never appears. Then, when I tell him I can't go on, he pays half of what's due for ten weeks' work on Nietzsche, saying we must share the loss.

We find an apartment overlooking the Hudson River at 417 Riverside Drive, a block from Columbia University on the teeming Upper West Side. As a wife, I've come in tow to America without much thinking about it. When my mother travelled she approached a foreign country through its writers, and so accordingly I apply for a graduate programme in American studies at Columbia. It's a blind step because I've never encountered American literature, apart from T. S. Eliot, some poems by Emily Dickinson and an extract from *Tom Sawyer* in a children's anthology. When I visit the chair of the department, Lewis Leary, in his office on the top floor of Philosophy Hall he is reassuring and the seminar, run by Professor Hovde, a Thoreau scholar, is everything an ill-prepared newcomer could wish: friendly and stimulating.

I'm puzzled by the absence of Dickinson in the official guide to the nineteenth century, *Eight American Authors*. All eight are men. A Texan in the seminar explains that this is a literature of men without women until you come to Pilar in *For Whom the Bell Tolls*, 'and she's a man'. The focus is on Thoreau's solitude at Walden Pond; Ishmael with his savage bed-mate Queequeg; Huck with an escaped slave, Jim, floating down the Mississippi on Huck's raft; and the Deerslayer with his red brother Chingachgook tracking through the woods of the frontier. A typical exam question is 'Discuss the renegade from civilization.' I drink this in, entranced by a self-reliant freedom to escape a contaminating society. My first report is on Thoreau's influential essay 'Civil Disobedience', written in prison when he was jailed for refusing to pay a tax that could be used to fund an indefensible war.

In the free period before our seminar I have coffee and muffins with two women who are classmates. Sometimes it's dark-haired, insightful Pearl, at other times blonde, vivacious Louise with a stylish silver bangle on her arm. Louise has come straight from Sarah Lawrence, an advanced college for women, and reminds me, I tell my mother, 'of the American girls in *The Little Locksmith*: strongly intelligent, fresh, groomed, beautiful'.

It's demanding to make up the primary reading the others have done at school and college. 'I am always behind,' I write to my mother, 'but it is so much better than the dread "emptiness." I could never stretch out the "woman's role" to fill my entire life.'

I'm four months pregnant and so far haven't ventured to see a doctor. In England I'd picked up a manual, Grantly Dick-Read's *Childbirth without Fear: The Principles and Practice of Natural Childbirth*, and am converted to its promise that a woman can exercise control over her body. This matters all the more to me having witnessed my mother's involuntary loss of control. An obstetrician at New York Hospital waves this away impatiently. What's customary, he explains, is to tie down a woman's hands 'to keep a sterile field', and fathers aren't allowed to be present 'because they get in the way'. A second obstetrician says the same, while Siamon, who delivered ten babies while he was a medical student, warns me that 'natural' childbirth is a misnomer. 'What's "natural" is for women to die,' he tells me dryly, and tries to wake me up to the reality of labour pains. I don't of course want to hear this, and think he's siding with his profession against more innovative and humane forms of practice. He agrees to 'go along' with what I want to believe, and I find a Belgian doctor at the French Hospital who's prepared to go along too.

Natural childbirth prepares a woman to banish pain and fear by taking a positive attitude. This doesn't happen. The doctor is kind, but dead-eyed orderlies wheel me, panting, into a public lift where the Marie Antoinette nightmare – birth in public – becomes a reality. In the middle of an agonising contraction, as the orderlies dump me like a sack of potatoes on the delivery table, I hear my cry of pain – can this be me, giving way – and then it has to be a forceps delivery after all. My lovely baby is born but I feel a failure, and relive that moment of losing control. Handbooks say that women forget, but it's impossible to wipe out this scene.

Towards the end of 1965 a line in a letter to my mother and grandmother mentions depression: 'Although Anna is now three months, I haven't yet recovered.' My obstetrician wants me to see another doctor, but I hope to improve by going home to South Africa. We are due for a visit during the end-of-year vacation, and Siamon ventures to warn my mother that the depression is serious. 'Our friends and contacts here are quite ignorant of this, and to a certain extent surround us with an illusory idyllic vision which ignores reality. There is probably no one bar yourself that we can turn to for understanding.'

Back where I'd thought to belong, my weight gain, bitten nails and uncontained offensiveness do not go down well. At the end of the visit I travel alone with Anna on the return journey through Johannesburg. There, I'm shaken to hear a rumour of my family's opinion that I'm fat and spoilt. It's not said unkindly; it's a fact I should know.

Fat. Spoilt. I'm not. Yes, I am. For don't I have what women want: a lovely baby?

I look into this mirror on the long flight back to New York, and once there, go under. There's some relief in going under: no more struggle. At St Luke's, a hospital near by on Amsterdam Avenue, a woman doctor training to be a psychiatrist listens carefully, and makes a provisional diagnosis of post-partum depression. Nothing is said about my mother's post-partum crisis, because epilepsy is perceived as her overriding illness. I open Dr Spock's best-selling handbook on mothers and babies, and stare at the flip phrase 'baby blues'. This guru of anything goes has not a clue what's going on. I turn to my mother, who's been in dark places; she will understand, I think.

She says she does regret not talking when we were together, and assures me that what I'd heard was misreported. But she thinks it wrong to dwell on hurtful words rather than how benevolent her family has always been.

Why does this response come as a blow? What she says is not unexpected. She has always put family feeling first and expects me, as an extension of herself, not to indulge a disruptive state of mind. Her insistence that I suppress what happened for the sake of harmony comes as confirmation that she will not defend me. The blow is this confirmation that I matter less to her than others do. She evades a conflict of loyalties by stressing gratitude as the appropriate emotion. Yet, since my mother herself experienced a breakdown after childbirth, I'd continued to hope she'd lean my way. That hope is gone.

Early in March 1966 I'm admitted to Clark 8, the locked psychiatric ward on the eighth floor of St Luke's. My mother now comes from South Africa to look after Anna. I'm sceptical about psychotherapy, like my mother who has a different answer.

'Abraham, Isaac and Jacob are continually tested and tried,' my mother says, 'and through these trials they are taught how to live. God speaks to them in what befalls them, and what befalls them has the power to teach and transform them.'

She wishes to save me as she had saved herself, by turning to her Maker. For her, this accompanies visitations – she is 'never alone'. I, though, am alone in a mental enclosure, and no one, least of all myself, can spring the door. I'm shut off from everyone who upholds that all-time norm that a wife follows her husband, whose career must take precedence, even if it means moving to another country. I want to go home, but the people on whom I depend are bent on migration. I'm trapped in their narrative, real to them, unreal to me, with no prospect of escape. The less they see the falsity of expatriation, the more I deteriorate.

In Clark 8, this is the way I think: adaptation, even transformation, is a biological necessity, yet don't creatures do this at a cost? Does the caterpillar blowing back and forth in its chrysalis, metamorphosing into a thing of the air, not regret its home in the earth that kept it warm? In human terms, is it not false to mouth the politically correct mantra of our contemporaries – 'I never want to see South Africa again' – as they take on the colouring of other people? How is it that everyone I know is managing to become something else? Why do I lack the resilience to do this thing – turn my back on the landscape that made me? My mother says, 'Geography doesn't matter.' She means it won't matter if you open yourself to your Maker. I look up to her faith, but cannot elevate myself in that manner and become that sort of extension of what she is. As a creature of the earth I'm a failure who couldn't even carry through natural childbirth. Nor, having made this move, can I go home. There's no way out.

A cold-eyed man I shall call Dr Kay is brought in to replace the trainee whose empathy had opened a channel of communication. Instinct warns me off Dr Kay the moment we meet. I refuse to see him for three days. But institutional rules insist that the apparent caprice of a mental patient can't be allowed: he's the one assigned, and if I want to remain in St Luke's no one but Dr Kay will be allowed to take the case. My protest is an embarrassment to all concerned, and Siamon, as a doctor himself, thinks Dr Kay entitled to the courtesy of allowing him to practise his profession.

Dr Kay conducts interviews from the safe hollow of his citadel, and from there he diagnoses a hopeless case. I test him once by saying that someone distasteful had got inside me: metaphorically it has some truth, but a flare in his eye tells me he's thick enough to take this literally. Earnestly, he probes the likelihood of delusions. After that I have no respect for him as a doctor, though the continued need for St Luke's means that I have to accept him.

The nurses are distant, keeping to themselves in their glass office, but the inmates are kind to one another and this makes Clark 8 a refuge of sorts. At first it's relieving to be on neutral ground.

After I've been in hospital for eight weeks, Dr Kay urges a new plan, a long-term asylum. To avoid this, there's a trial week back in the apartment, from 8 to 16 May.

Two days in, my mother reports to my father, who has asked for details: 'I find I am on duty from eight in the morning till 10 at night. Nonetheless love makes all burdens light, and I am continually upheld & sustained, as I have been from the beginning. There is a 20% chance that she might have to go back into Hospital, but although she has had a tough time for the past 30 hours she is putting up a good fight controlling the deep depression. This is the real progress in my opinion, that she does not give way as she did, but realises that she has to endure, and control herself or worse will follow.' 'Control' is my mother's watchword. She imagines me better when I'm 'considerate' and 'affectionate', and advises against 'letting go'. If I do let go, she warns, 'worse' can happen. What is 'worse'? The Terrible Sonnets of the Jesuit poet Gerard Manley Hopkins, which my mother and I had studied together, claim there's no finite superlative to the comparative 'worse': 'No worst, there is none.'

The more I subscribe to civil conduct, the more untrue living appears. Under layers of obligatory lies, the divide from my mother widens. Undoubtedly, she is generous in coming to New York, leaving her classes and her ethics course at university, taking on domestic responsibilities she's never done, and not least in her care for little Anna. There's a maternal ardour, unreleased with us, her children who were born to a semi-invalid. Now she's on all fours hunting a lost earring. Has the baby swallowed it? Anna laughs at such antics. Her Gran adores her and is never too ill to pick her up. Yet these offerings and sacrifices don't touch me because she believes women must follow husbands. It's too self-evident to be aired. I'm up against the fact that I must stay in New York. But more divisive is the fact that she had impressed on me, as a child, the nightmare of doctors who had judged morally, had judged her illness as her failure to control herself. I had felt shoulder to shoulder with her outrage. And yet, now, it's abundantly plain that she reads my illness as something that shouldn't have happened – a loss of self-control.

She delays this letter home, hoping to report improvement. In Riverside Park, where she continues her letter on Sunday morning, I'm heavily drugged after six days of depression, while Siamon looks after Anna. 'I shed a tear for both of them. We thought everything was coming right but this past week at home has put L back. She wants to return to hospital.'

Back at St Luke's the depression lifts a little, but Dr Kay repeats his plan for the long-term 'home'. He allows me out the following weekend so that I, together with Siamon and my mother, can view the home in western Massachusetts; we are expected to be impressed with its landscaped grounds and we meet an inmate. I don't find this place has anything to do with me, and actually feel rather better. We stay that night in a charming inn in Northampton, and next day I'm well enough to join my class tour of Edith Wharton's home, The Mount, and the towns in the Berkshires where Hawthorne and Melville lived and wrote in the early 1850s. My spirits lift in the company of intelligent classmates, and bathe in the bracing truths of literature – even fantasy must be 'true to the human heart', Hawthorne insists in his preface to *The House of the Seven Gables*. Melville, writing to Hawthorne from Pittsfield in April 1851, commends him for his 'NO! in thunder . . . For all men who say *yes*, lie.' Melville's certainty brings a measure of relief. So does his character Bartleby, with his passive resistance to the hollow-heartedness of commerce. And so does Hester Prynne's self-reliance as social outcast. In their company, with books, I'm not alone. For here is what Emerson calls the integrity of a private mind.

My letter to Granny on 26 May says something simple and true: I'm homesick and have far to go to get over it. This is a sane letter. Could the determination of Dr Kay to push me into an asylum for the long-term insane have been a defence against his inability to communicate, reinforced perhaps by my resistance to him? What I couldn't articulate then, but see now, is a conservative, who moves to lock away the rebellious element in mental disturbance. If he detected as yet unnamed women's issues (wanting a life of the mind, wanting a life outside of domesticity, wanting equal partnership) latent in me in 1966, he was bound to outlaw a state of mind rising against the status quo. Only a guess, of course, but Dr Kay certainly tried to persuade Siamon to institutionalise me. As such Dr Kay was a danger, masked as benign doctor.

My resistance was merely instinctive; it takes Virginia Woolf to see through an authority figure, as she does in her portrait of the 'obscurely evil' Dr Bradshaw in *Mrs Dalloway*. He's based, in part at least, on one of her consultants, the distinguished Sir Henry Head, who had sent another patient, Henry James, 'down into hell'.

Dr Kay asks me to see him immediately after we return from the Berkshires, and once I enter the shadow of this wooden fortress, the threat of the asylum begins to erode the incipient cure of our excursion into the world of literature, those congenial nineteenth-century Americans. If I feel cut off in New York, an asylum in western Massachusetts will be more cut off. It's a fate I can't bear to contemplate, but the rationale is plain enough. If I don't recover soon at St Luke's, this is the alternative on offer. The alternative that isn't on offer is what I want, but can't voice: to return to the roar of the breakers on the rocks and the gulls overhead beating their wings against the wind.

I'm 'frightened', my mother reports to my father. The conditions are indeed frightening, for if I'm 'sent away' it has to be for a long time – might it be for ever? The policy of this institution is to review a case only once a year.

My mother is a different matter. Here is a sensitive being, alert to doctors' shortcomings and sceptical, on principle, of psychiatric diagnosis. If horror of life is not a symptom of derangement but a fair judgement, then an obvious course – tested in her own experience – is to follow a narrative that culminates in faith. So, as well as feeling I should stay in New York with my husband, she believes in the well-tried path, based on Exodus, where there is always a dark period of trial, whether in a desert, or pit, or prison, or a slough of despond or illness, followed by the divine light.

I do comprehend that my unwillingness to follow this course, to see it in either of her ways, is the cause of the divide growing between mother and daughter. Up to a point I understand the inflexibility of the social norm to which my mother was forced to yield when she resigned her 'great opportunity' in London in 1952, but I'm put out to find her siding with the laws of conformity when it comes to her daughter. Decades on, having read my mother's love letters, I now see how much the influence of Levin gave her a missionary purpose. At the time, the priority she grants to that remains incomprehensible in view of the mother she'd been, and I continue to struggle with the longing for home versus the route – migration – that seems to have been prescribed for me and Siamon. In 1959 I'd coped with migration by imagining a future return; now in 1966 there's no future beyond New York, except the continued possibility of migrating to Israel.

That possibility will remain active, supported by my mother, until Siamon visits the Weizmann Institute in 1967 and the offhand manner of his interview dims that hope; he nearly faints in the heat when he leaves. So America is to be our home for now.

Knowing I can't stay indefinitely at St Luke's, I decide to leave before being discharged. By leaving, my mother reports to my father, 'she's burnt her bridges'. She means that there's now no alternative to a stark either/or: either adapt or else be sent away. My mother herself is valiant, and doesn't complain how hard it is for her to be with me every hour of the day. Nor, from the other side of our divide, is it easy to live every hour with a mother's poor opinion, unvoiced though apparent in pats on the back for trying to put a lid on disruptive thoughts; that is, not complaining.

What a woman of my mother's generation deplores as complaining will surface four years later as a political movement, Women's Liberation: a full-throated public refusal to subordinate women's lives to those of men. The divide between mother and daughter looks like an isolated case of mental illness in 1966, but I believe that illness has everything to do with women's role and non-communication between a mother who'd worked out a way to conform to the norms of her society and a daughter who's awakening to an obsolete gender code, and refuses.

Time has proved my mother right about South Africa: I see now we couldn't go back. There was the evil of apartheid so that, if you were there, you were participating, whether you wished to or not. For me to abandon migration (to New York or Israel or wherever it might be) never, so far as I know, occurred to her, and without her backing I could not go home. There seemed no solution – my mind circled the same hopeless track. Cut off from the light on the waves, the salt wind, the big sky, to me the towers of New York look like prison bars.

One Friday night in August she takes me to dine with a South African doctor, Renée Abt, who had attended my mother's student class on the Bible. Unable to cope with prayers and conversation at table, I lie in a darkened bedroom in a kind of stupor. Even to raise a limb feels futile. Kind Renée gives me a game of Scrabble to take back to the apartment. 'To pass the time,' she suggests.

Siamon has recently been accepted for the doctoral programme at Rockefeller University, one of the first foreign
students amongst the hundred or so best science graduates in
the US. To have spent the last eighteen months in this place is
to understand how much he has to learn, and this course makes
it more feasible to switch from medicine to a research career.
The programme, with a generous stipend, will extend our stay
in New York by five years, well beyond my one-year master's
programme at Columbia.

All these tomorrows stretch endlessly ahead. A 'confidential'
letter from my mother to my father and brother admits how bad
things are, and asks them to say nothing to anyone in Israel.
Why Israel? It can only be because that's where she expects me
to go. My father, in his neat, legal hand, underlines in red what
he wants to remember, and nowhere else does he underline so
thickly – his red pencil moves back and forth. This is serious:
it has to do with his daughter's reputation. The prohibition does
not extend to talk in our home town, because I'm not to live
there again.

Back at St Luke's, in a hospital wrap, I lie on the stretched white
sheet with the passivity of a vegetable on a kitchen table. The
vegetable will be made to have a fit. At the time I make no connection between my mother's epilepsy and this artificially
induced fit. Dr Udall, bending over me to administer an injec-
tion, says, 'Just a pin-stick.' A wave rushes over my head.

The first four treatments are administered while I'm an in-
patient in August. There's some improvement, but it doesn't last
beyond a week. As an outpatient, from late August into early
September, I have a second course of six treatments. Afterwards,
it jars to be fetched by my mother, who appears detached. For
her to perform this duty is to accept what's done by authorities
in white coats. Pushing Anna, aged one, in the stroller, she

walks us the short distance from Amsterdam Avenue across Broadway, because in the aftermath of the jolt I may not remember my way to Riverside Drive.

These treatments are on alternate days. After each one I'm low and then improve somewhat by the second night, just before the time comes for another shock. This hardly seems useful. So what next?

After Siamon leaves for work one morning, I catch a bus at 114th Street that will carry me down Broadway; then wait for a cross-town bus at the Lincoln Center. I feel reckless, courting the relief of what my mother has warned against: giving way. I'm about to do something that I've not done before, and that other wives don't do – all those wives of Rockefeller scientists who, it appears, exist to give themselves to their husbands' meteoric careers.

I mean to surprise Siamon at work. Instinct tells me to meet him where he really is. I have to meet a man in the setting of a world-class lab, preparing to complete his leap from village school into the scientific stratosphere.

So long as I continue to accept the help of an end-of-day husband who comes home to change the baby and haul her diapers to the machines in the basement of our apartment block, I can't speak from where I actually am, at the far end of a widening distance that has opened between us. Siamon's considerate acts – too matter-of-fact to care for my mother's praise – prop up the home front, but the side effect is to close off feeling. Practical needs fill the hours, in the manner of people who don't address the ways they've diverged. A surface civility has silenced outrage at my mother's solidarity with Siamon. This life has nothing to do with me. Nothing, that is, beyond the helper role ingrained since earliest childhood.

In the cut-off cavern of my mind, I'm incredulous over the

compliance of other wives, turned out in primary shades of pink and green, the smiling consorts. Does it suffice to bask in reflected glory? I imagine how each wife expects a Nobel Prize. It would compensate for the dedicated service she does her husband. Here, the Nobel Prize is no mere dream: Rockefeller has a number of winners amongst its faculty. As a student, Siamon will enter their labs; he will mull over the macrophage (his favourite cell, the big-eater that keeps our immune systems going) and try out ideas over the long lunch tables in the dining room in Founder's Hall. As part of his induction into this elite, Rockefeller's photographer has already produced a photo of Siamon, the like of which I've never seen: his chin has been tilted upwards as though he's heading for the stars.

As the bus winds through Central Park towards the East Side, I dwell on the glory of Rockefeller, this American beacon of bounty and expertise spanned by the Queensboro Bridge where Gatsby's car rode, fenders spread, into the greatest of cities.

I dwell too on dead spaces: the so-called meditation pool, a square of water with a bench, never occupied, on each of its four sides; the artifice of ramrod tulips, transported fully grown on 1 May and set out in precise rows; and the bland faces of the scientists above their white coats. Nothing matters to them very much apart from the next experiment. Their drive and absorption appear detached from domestic turmoil – the province of wives.

Back in our apartment, gratitude to my mother for all she's taken on prevents us from owning how difficult it's become to spend our days together. Adept as I am at hearing what she doesn't say, her resolute stopping-up of reproach speaks to me of my unwillingness to take on her solution to illness. It seems that I have come to the end of my existence as her creation.

What remains in question is Siamon: what my breakdown might do to us. For my part, the responses that came naturally are numbed. I've assumed that he expects me to recover, but what if I don't? What if damage lurks too deep to heal? That's the darker matter, as the bus turns at the end of its cross-town run, passes Rockefeller on York Avenue, and halts at its terminus on 67th Street.

Of late, trust in Siamon has been shaken by his respect for a fellow doctor, the wooden Kay, who set up this double course of shocks. Each time, Siamon would leave me to submit to them while he drove off to the lab. That act of climbing out of the car was like forcing myself to enter a nightmare.

Turning into the gate of Rockefeller and climbing the slope of the campus, I'm approaching Siamon from an estranged position. Some would think estrangement a definition of mental illness, but what I'm seeing is not distorted. I am striving to be a mother, that's clear to all, but to go on acting as a wife and daughter should – civil, controlled – is not a sign of improvement; they are all wrong about that; the lie in this performance corrodes ties. I am maintaining the thinnest semblance of normal, all the while seeing through the façades that sustain that fiction.

Mount the steps to Founder's Hall. Ask for Dr Gordon. 'I'm his wife.'

The receptionist directs me downstairs to the empty dining room while he's called.

And now he's walking towards me in a jacket and tie, a lock of hair falling on his forehead. What I'm not prepared for is how attractive he is, his green eyes alert, looking at me with unexpected intimacy.

'I can't go on,' is all I can say.

He sits down in front of me, takes my hands and says, 'First of all, you *will* get well.' His optimism and the concern in his gaze touch the numbness – a sign that it might not be the end, after all. This is in character: he's a maker of plans.

'Do something with your life,' he says, and he's quick with

ideas: a doctorate for a start. 'I've always thought you could write biography,' he suggests. It's an offer to help me find a sense of purpose equal to his own, like the purpose my mother once nurtured for herself, a purpose it has never occurred to me that I warrant.

'I'm not up to that.' It's beyond me to contemplate flying that high. This is what he wants. He likes accomplished women – looks don't impress him so much as flair. His ambitions affect me like the skyscrapers of New York: can you measure up, they demand. No. Not now.

'For now,' he's considering in his practical way first steps first, 'since something must be done, I think you must leave Dr Kay.' He says he will draw on expertise at Rockefeller, investigate what might be the best treatment of a case like mine that the

In the late sixties it felt like an experiment to combine
motherhood and full-time study

city can offer and will undertake to find an agreeable doctor to replace Dr Kay. It is a breakthrough for us – and for me.

On 10 September, I'm taken aback when the new doctor, Silvano Arieti, orders five more shocks. More?

He will see me when these are done, he says firmly in a book-lined midtown apartment, 103 East 75th, away from the fret of the hospital. 'A patient has to be out of deep depression for therapy to begin.'

Memory loss is a side effect of shock treatment. In the nineties, when I'm writing on Henry James, I will open my copy of *The Tragic Muse* and see marginalia from 1966. A blank. I don't know what that novel's about. I can't re-read it. Nor play Scrabble again.

Throughout these shocks and after, I'm covering Columbia's Latin requirement: a course on Virgil with a bright classicist, Steele Commager, son of the historian Henry Steele Commager, who has recently edited a collection of critical essays on the Roman poet. The Sybil's warning to Aeneas, which at school had carried a reverberation of my mother's underworld, now leaps to life: the meaning of the descent to the Dead. I can't better the translation by Miss Hulston, the Latin teacher at Good Hope, which I'd paced into my body in the school grounds. The words come: 'O Trojan son . . . easy is the descent to Avernus, but to recall the step and pass out to the upper air, this is the undertaking, this the task – *hoc opus, hic labor est.*'

Another memory from an English class comes to join it: Conrad's narrator, Marlow, in *Heart of Darkness*: not his glimpse of savagery – heads on sticks – but that same difficulty of return from the underworld. Marlow struggles to make his way back along the Congo to so-called civilisation. He hopes to leave the heart of darkness yet carries it with him, lodged in the brain.

Eventually, Marlow finds himself back in 'the sepulchral city' amongst faces stupidly oblivious to the savagery beneath the skin of the urban order. To pierce the false façade of civilisation is to find yourself mentally alone, and to be thus alone is to be disturbed. Marlowe has to convince listeners of what he's seen, and at the same time he has to admit how far what he's seen unfits him for normal life: 'I daresay I was not very well at that time.' The 'horror' of this state of mind speaks directly to the urban phantasmagoria of *The Waste Land*. 'Shall I set my lands in order' is a critical question when Eliot was trying to recuperate from a breakdown at the sanatorium of Dr Vittoz in Lausanne.

In 1968, when I'm at last well again and the final sessions with Dr Arieti turn into discussions of Eliot's debt to Dante, I do an extended essay on Eliot. It's a springboard for a biography that I start writing as a doctoral dissertation between 1970 and 1973. And thanks to my mother's intuitive reading I'm prompted to ask a vital question of Eliot's early manuscripts in the Berg Collection at the New York Public Library: when did his religious life start? The answer is resounding; it negates the standard view that religion was a development of Eliot's middle years.

In 1973 the Rhodes Trust in Oxford is impelled by the impact of second-wave feminism to offer opportunities for women, and I apply for a fellowship. At an interview with the great Eliot scholar Helen Gardner I will subdue Eliot's biographical ordeals – his expatriate displacement, his surrender to marriage and subsequent breakdown – to my attempt at dating the fragments that become *The Waste Land*. Though Dame Helen is not entirely pleased with me – she disapproves of mothers in the workplace – she decides that I shall come to her college, St Hilda's, and in time, as a Delegate of Oxford University Press, she ensures publication.

After classes, picking up Anna at a sitter's apartment on
the Upper West Side in the late sixties

So I begin as a biographer. Though my mother's route to
faith is, for me, the road not taken, it's still her writing and taste
in writers that's opening up the path I choose to follow. When
Rhoda Press says, 'I shall rise, and unfurl / Over the curve of
the earth / My white sea wings', she speaks for a woman's
inward power, as did the Brontës and Dickinson. Where we
part is over public utterance.

For 1968, that year of recovery, is also the year of the upris-
ing at Columbia, a catalyst for the first meeting of the Women's
Liberation movement in 1970. This takes place on campus. The
room is so packed that I'm standing on a bench along a wall. I've
heard vehement speeches against apartheid, but nothing like the
torrent of molten rage – white-hot hatred of patriarchy – spew-
ing from the lips of Kate Millett, author of *Sexual Politics*. She
asks women to challenge men's authority and control of the

home, education, law, employment and, above all, the very idea
of what a woman is. Fair enough, but what amazes me is the
naked hatred of men. No more grovelling, no more self-
suppression, no more domestic limitations, no more constricting
our bodies in the artifice of bras, no more chivalry disabling to
our sex. With each assertion, the audience shouts assent.

'Yeahhh . . . Yeahhh . . . Right on!' The time has come for
confrontation. It's them or us.

Is this rage too categoric? Not all men are the same – or are
they, as the dominant order? We're reading *Villette* in Carolyn
Heilbrun's proto-feminist seminar on nineteenth-century fiction, and I think of the tight-lipped schoolmistress Lucy Snowe
containing her fiery nature.

A decade later Emily Dickinson, an avid reader of the
Brontës, reveals 'a Vesuvian face'. Freed from the conventions
of print culture, her poem 'My Life had stood—a Loaded Gun'
marks her explosive power. And although this appears a lone
voice, lava and fire were political currency for activists of her
generation. One of the first French cartoons of feminists in
1848 shows armed women erupting from a volcano, while a
group of young women workers unfurls a banner naming themselves *Vésuviennes*.

Watching Millett perform to 'right on' cries from four hundred women, I hold back. I wouldn't speak in that way. Yet I
have – and at night still do. These cries around me bring back
my giving way in the approach to the underworld, and then,
following my emergence, a recurring dream. For years to come
it moves towards giving way with my mother, a mouth opening ever wider until what comes out of that dark, elongated
hole takes over existence.

When Persephone was carried off into the underworld, did
she cry out to her mother for rescue? Demeter was distraught
to lose her daughter, and devised a plan for her annual return.

What else can a mother do when a daughter is trapped in a dark place?

The head of Siamon's lab has a passing notion to send us to some place in Africa for a spell. That brings a leap of hope, but lasting balm comes from American studies. I do a report on Emily Dickinson's line 'Mine—here—in Vision—and in Veto' and another on the significance of her dashes: I argue against editions that regularise her punctuation, editing out the dashes. It seems to me that she's pushing the words apart, the language of the dominant group, to allow for a muted communication with a reader awakened to unstated experience. There's the visible life – 'I tie my hat, I crease my shawl / Life's little duties do . . . ' – and there's the crucial hidden existence: 'And yet Existence—some way back / Stopped—struck—my ticking—through—'. How passionately I read that in the light of St Luke's. That's how we have to read Dickinson, each reader bringing to a poem her own unvoiced life so as to complete these diagrams of Existence.

Nowadays, at literary festivals, readers ask how long it takes to write this or that biography. How to explain? George Eliot puts it best: 'No retrospect will take us back to the true beginning.' A biography of Emily Dickinson, published in 2010, rose out of my mother's secrecy, seclusion and visionary susceptibilities, and then out of those ten-minute class reports amidst the uprisings at Columbia where, if you had to move on with work, you squeezed apologetically past barricades designed to shut down the university as part of a corrupt military-industrial complex.

I was, you understand, in accord with the anti-power, anti-corporate ethos of the time – you might say that I finally discovered some sort of home in protest: in Dickinson's 'Veto' and Melville's 'No! in thunder' and in the rise of women's voices out of the anti-war demonstrations of sixty-eight.

*

My need for truth was to find an outlet in biography, a genre committed to authenticity. This is what impelled me from the start, as a student in '71, turning over Eliot's unpublished papers in the archives. I had to find Eliot's reality – 'human kind / Cannot bear very much reality' – which he inferred from its antithesis: the 'Unreal city' in its shroud of brown fog. And I had to light up women who appeared in the shadow of solitary genius, and re-conceive them not as passive muses, more as collaborators of sorts. Eliot's first love, Emily Hale, and his first wife, Vivienne, both gifted, both vital to his poetry, had to give in to living – partly living – in his shadow.

If the Eliot biography was in a way my mother's book, the next biography was my own. While researching Eliot in the Berg Collection I looked into Virginia Woolf's diaries (as yet unpublished) for impressions of him in his early years in London. I was often so absorbed by the diary that I would forget my research and go on reading. Like other women in the seventies, I turned to Virginia Woolf as a guide to women, and what gripped me most was an unnoticed sentence at the start of *A Room of One's Own* where she declares her fascination for 'the great problem of the true nature of woman'. In my biography *A Writer's Life*, and in later biographies – including two women who were collaborators of sorts in the art of Henry James – the deep pursuit will be that question Woolf asked about what is obscured in our nature: the authenticity of unuttered thoughts, the pressure to communicate the incommunicable – to say directly, even awkwardly, what's in the mind.

With Anna in our apartment on the Upper West Side, about 1968.
Women's Lib was in the air

With Anna on holiday at Nantucket, summer 1970. I was starting
what became my first biography, *Eliot's Early Years*, and also preparing
to teach composition at Hunter College

14

Lives for Women

Long before the spread of book groups, my mother formed a women's group for reading Shakespeare. It was the same invited set of friends as came together in the sunroom for her private Bible class. Only, they didn't come in a routine way; they fore-gathered, as my mother liked to joke. The verb suggests distant heads of state who come to put their heads together, not Monica knitting booties in fluffy wool and Ren, upright, plaits crossed over her head, dancing through the door. These women were not conscious feminists, though they'd read their Vera Brittain and Olive Schreiner. It's not that they didn't take huge delight in Shakespeare's spirited women, like Beatrice and Rosalind with their quips and repartee, but led by my mother they were more deeply drawn to Desdemona and Cordelia, the wife and the daughter who sustain purity of feeling for a raging husband and a manipulative father.

As they read and discuss, I resist this model of how to be a woman. 'Isn't it self-defeating,' I challenge my mother's friends, 'the pathos of Cordelia, who offers King Lear the love a daughter owes to a father, but who is cast off because she does not play up to the self-importance of a king? And how can Desdemona be so pure as to love a husband who is about to kill her? This is to yield to the crime of violence against women.'

It infuriates me all the more to feel, myself, the appeal of purity, an ideal that transcends life.

'Lear and Othello invite us to pity them in their contrition, but shouldn't we pity their victims more? What Desdemona needed,' I insist, 'what other wives subject to violence need, is a women's refuge.'

My father, with no soupçon of the feminine in his make-up, is never violent. I recall only one slap, when I screamed at the thought of a mouse. It was five in the morning and our father was not amused to be woken by silly children, for Pip stood up in his cot and screamed too. Our father bounded into the nursery, dealt quick slaps all round and retreated back to bed. It didn't hurt.

Bertie Henry, though, the farmer who married my mother's friend Lilian, disciplined his sons. They were sent away to school at an early age, the one stoic, the other seething. Bertie's voice was harsh with a hoarse note at the base. Visiting the farm as a child, I'd hear him: bark, bark – an angry sound. He was uncomprehending when Lilian suffered post-partum depression. Each time she gave birth, Lilian found refuge away from home: her grandmother; her friend Monica. Bertie's logic – for hadn't Lilian pressed him into having children – could not work out why she lost heart, and grew, as she observed to my mother, 'rake-thin'. And yet Lilian is able to love her husband. Her memoir records that he knew how to please a woman, tender to 'the wee breasties', and he trod beside her to the outdoor lavatory at night, when she feared snakes. As a loyal wife she says not a word against him, though her candour allows for silence. I respect this Cordelian purity, 'Love, and be silent', surviving into my mother's generation at the bottom of Africa.

Lilian in her home-sewn, cotton dress has made it to the friends' group, all the way from the farm (two and a half hours by car), to be passed over by my mother when her turn comes to read a passage. 'It's all right, Lil,' she'd say, as though releasing Lilian from an effort that would be too much for her.

Of late, she's taken to calling Lilian 'my practical friend', as though ladling hot porridge at dawn into tin bowls for farm workers who hold out cupped hands precludes the life of the mind. For Lilian is disconcertingly at home in her body, alive to physical response. Children love her intimate motherliness, as I do; her daughters-in-law cleave to her because Lilian stands ready to empathise with whatever it takes to be a wife. Then, too, Lilian attends the Dutch Reformed Church at Piketberg to share her neighbours' occasions with flowers from her garden and fruit from her farm.

So these days of the divide between my mother and me, I'm put out when she praises 'my practical friend'. It comes to me as a sign of her semi-detachment from the individual. To her, we are part of a larger pattern.

As my mother's journey becomes more allegorical, people turn into types. She's travelling through a moral landscape, and encountering people who illustrate or equate with one or other trait. Her multi-sided son is 'fun-loving'. Pip's tendency to break out at the piano with 'Great Balls of Fire' worries our mother. She fears he might become an entertainer like Uncle Eddie, whose stage name is Eddie Gaye.

Pip redeems himself through a more concerted effort than mine to settle in the Promised Land, learn the language and take a graduate degree, after which he returns home as a clinical psychologist. In this he continues to bear the impress of our mother, in his discernments of character. His professional career proves how much she under-rated him when she'd decided, back in his teens, that he should channel his charm into a career

Be-Bop-a-Lula: Pip, fifteen, at the piano jamming with friends, 1960

in hotel management. Her one-time plan for me was to be a nursery-school teacher. This came to her when I took to visiting various cousins at their babies' bath-time. During the day, nannies took care of babies, but the evening bath was the time for hands-on mothering. It was delightful to watch, but this never amounted to an ambition.

Odd, these plans for her children. Can it be that a cultivated imagination becomes deliberate, closed off in certain directions, what Emily Dickinson may have meant by closing the valves of the attention, 'like Stone'? Dickinson's poetically

charged letters, and later the long letters Henry James penned
at the end of a writing day, hardly reflect their correspondents,
who barely exist beyond their assigned roles: Dickinson's
threatening 'Master' or her loyal 'Little Cousins'.

My mother writes often to me in New York, and is relieved
to have letters telling her all is well. A doubt that all may not be
well wakes her sometimes at night, she admits soon after returning home: she caricatures the jolt of waking, '*wakker skrik*',
pithier in Afrikaans.

In April 1968, two years after the asylum visit, there's a pause
in one of her letters. Day-to-day events switch off and she
thinks back to two questions I'd asked during a visit in
July–August 1967. What these questions were I no longer
remember, but their delayed impact after nine months brought
back for her the non-communication as I'd slid towards breakdown. This leads to an attempt to cross our divide.

> The externals of my life here are so well-known to you that
> they do not bear repetition. On the other hand journeyings,
> the 'jungle of the soul', turning and returning, retracing one's
> footsteps to find what is dear and precious – how can that be
> told? . . . I remember precious years; and time-together which
> for me were flawless . . .
>
> I'm sad that I did not answer some of your 'questions'
> when you were last here – the one on the beach, the one on
> the mountainside. Things, meanings, take time to sink into
> me – only long afterwards when I uncover the reality I am
> sad to find that my response missed the need. My timing has
> always been bad[,] for as you know, I am very slow and out-
> of-time generally.

I do know. 'Slow' is her code for the hated barbiturate, which
inflicts this side effect. Even now, it dissipates the questions

themselves in an offer to renew an empathy based in the past. In October 1968 my mother sits alone in her *succah* after a 'young marrieds' class there. Poppies glow against the dark pine branches, and she's pinned up a poster I'd painted in my teens: a copy of Nahum Levin's New Year card with its blessing in 1956. She writes, 'The distant knock of a building-hammer seemed to intensify the silence. Sunlight filtered through the pines and I was surprised by a visitation of the joy of former years. I thought much of you, and retraced my footsteps together with you.' She's missing our talks, 'really one long talk, isn't it, without beginning or end'.

That year she completes her last course towards her degree. Hebrew, ethics, classical culture had all been selected to serve her Bible teaching, but this course, *Nederlandskultuurgeskiedenis*, lectures in Afrikaans on Dutch art and architecture, is something of a spree. She gets a first in the November exam.

Soon after, she takes a room for a fortnight at 25 Arlington Court on the Beach Road at Muizenberg. She always swims at the Far Beach on the great stretches of sand away from the pavilion and promenade. After her first bathe at nine in the morning she starts a letter to me in her old vein. 'At this early hour the human beings are lone, Wordsworthian figures walking towards the horizon.' As she bathes again in the middle of a 'classic' Muizenberg day, warmed by sun and fanned by breezes, and for the third time at low tide in the 'slanting light' at six o'clock, her anticipation of my end-of-year visit quickens.

Wherever I am I think of sharing things with you. I feel you are spending the day with me here. A sort of 'I-Thou' day in which every half an hour or so I break our silence[,] speaking a thought to you. I'm picking every remembered happiness we have shared through the years and storing it for your coming.

Why do I not advance through this opened door? The anticipation of doing so recurs each time we meet, and then there's a retreat on both sides.

'I've *failed*,' she says two or three days after we arrive, lifting her head from the bathroom basin, where she's splashing her face. Her disappointed look over her shoulder holds my gaze as I lean in the doorway, waiting to be her sister once more. Then she drops her head towards the tap again.

My mother cannot hold back her need to convert me – she has become her mission. This means that she must lay before me, again and again, not so much her faith in its visionary aspect but Israel as the answer to the Holocaust, together with an embrace of the community that, like all groups in South Africa – not only racial groups – is closed upon itself. It's as though the shtetl in Lithuania transplanted itself to this land of 'separate development'. Afrikaners keep to themselves; English-speakers in the towns keep to themselves; and Jews likewise. I can't be locked away from other people.

An alarm rings for my mother. This sounds like assimilation.

'The assimilated Jews of Germany, even those who were baptised Christians, found they were categorised as Jews during the Holocaust,' she reminds me. Assimilation is futile; intermarriage a betrayal of who you are.

'Should I keep my feelings for you to myself?' she looks at me worriedly, because she's torn between conviction and her nervous care not to speak in a way she'll regret. 'Even though you reject my feelings, should they never be spoken because there's this risk?'

It is, she says, extraordinary that, all through centuries of persecution, the Jews retained their community through their commitment to the written word – the Word. The scrolls of the Torah and the sages who sifted holy writ in the Talmud provided the core for the community of the faithful clustering about them. And that community was all the closer for threats from outside: Cossacks. Thugs. Nazis. Her father's brother, Berl Pres, his children including my mother's cousin Hannah, a friendly girl aged thirteen (the same age as Anne Frank), together with all the Jews of Plunge, shut up to rot for a fortnight, dead bodies amongst the living. Plunge neighbours collaborating in the kill, and then scavenging the homes of the dead. How can she forget?

Nor does she forget Levin. His presence in her thoughts results in the kind of posthumous visitation she confides, in her casual way, from time to time as I hang about her bedroom.

A fortnight after Levin's death his wife found out about the love affair and shot off one question in the centre of an airletter, with a glaring space above and below: 'Rhoda, what is to be done with your letters to Nahum? Dunia Levin.'

She could not trust herself to reply, my mother confided, but for years afterwards she'd wished to ask forgiveness, both of Dunia Levin and 'the Almighty'. In 1968, eight years after Levin's death, when her guilt was at its sharpest on the eve of the Day of Atonement, she'd set down an unsent note to Dunia regretting the pain she had caused by 'that strange, exalted tie to Nahum'. It then happened one day, in the course of a lunch party, overlooking the sea, that Nahum himself 'reached out' to her with 'a message from the afterlife'.

The message was an instruction to read Psalm XXXII, verses 5 and 10: 'Thou forgavest the iniquity of my sin.' She copies out these words in the original Hebrew, with 'an inrush of thankfulness': 'He that trusteth in the Lord, mercy shall compass him about.'

Improbable as it may seem, my father too visits Rhoda on this matter after his death – or so she tells me. In 1969, at the age of sixty, my father falls ill with Hodgkin's disease, a malignant lymphoma which spread to the lungs. In June I fly with

Anna from New York to be with him, and we are there for three months. During this time he makes a valiant effort to go abroad and officiate as usual at the Maccabiah Games. It does give him a lift to be cheered as he moves, on Pip's arm, around the pool, but after that he collapses and the north-to-south flight home across Africa is a nightmare. My mother and I are shocked to see how wasted he looks in the wheelchair bringing him towards us at the terminal.

On the last Saturday of his life I visit him in Groote Schuur hospital, and as I walk into the oncology ward his face drops. He's sad that my mother hasn't come, even though he knows it's the Sabbath, when it's forbidden to drive. And yet my mother would be the first to say that the law is not inflexible: 'This is a humane faith,' she'd say, 'illness takes precedence over observance.'

I try to explain how heavy her workload is, so that she does need the day of rest, but my father is not consoled. She has been the love of his life and he feels at this moment how it's never been the same for her. To see my cheerful father drop is too much for me. I shed tears in the corridor outside his ward.

A few days later, 4 September, when he lies dying, a delegation from the South African Swimming Union arrives at his bedside, not so much to see him, rather to consult him, as their long-time President, about one of their wrangles. Amongst them is a rival who has tried to oust Harry. He's sporting enough to rise to the occasion and find answers, as though he were at a meeting.

At the last, his left lung fails to function. 'I'm going to roll over and try the other lung,' he tells my mother, who praises his 'incorrigible optimism'.

Siamon flies out for the funeral, and the family regroups at Houw Hoek on a mountain pass for a few quiet days. My mother must take over the reins from a husband who has always protected her, and she finds herself unexpectedly strong, supported by trust in her brothers and above all by her story-telling closeness to Anna, aged four, another in the line of dreamers.

One morning three years later, in 1972, she wakes in alarm, she tells me (and no one else) afterwards. Something brushed her lips. She cried out, and then unmoving lips close to her own reassured her: what she felt was my father's moustache – a famil-iar touch coming upon her from somewhere else. His kiss, she said to me and more than once, confirmed her belief that her love for Levin had quickened her marriage.

Was this a strange illusion, I ask my brother, and he reveals that our father had been upset enough to visit Cille to ask her to stop egging Rhoda on with Levin.

I point out to Pip that our father was practising the old double standard, a different morality for men and women, and Pip gives the usual answer: 'But he loved her alone.'

I think a bit and say to Pip, 'Her love for Levin may have stimulated the competitor in our father, and his surprise to find an unsuspected ardour in Rhoda may have stirred him. I think too that her elation in the early days with Levin, before guilt set in, let off sparks, which excited all of us at home. Do you remember how all four of us would dance to records on the Deccalion?'

In 1973 I fly to England with Anna to take up a research fel-lowship at St Hilda's College. Siamon will remain in New York for a while.

Our move disappoints my mother. This is not the migration she'd hoped for. We will not go to Israel, and neither, except for visits, will we go home. Oxford is an unexpected solution.

My mother accompanies Anna and me in late August 1973, and stays for a few weeks in a hotel while I fix up a house we've

rented. In 1952 London had been, for her, a 'great opportunity', and she's still attached to Auntie Minnie and her family there. But Oxford is alien; we know no one; and allegiance to Israel has turned her against England – for her, now, England is less its literature, more the ruler of Palestine, who turned back homeless survivors of the Holocaust when they tried to land illegally.

I'm relieved when my mother leaves. Her resistance makes it harder to adapt, and this time I'm determined after my retreat from Israel and breakdown in America. It's not only a 'great opportunity'; the welcome at St Hilda's and its green lawns sloping down to the river grow on me. It's astonishing to be planted here.

My mother's youngest brother, Hubert, shares her dim view of this move. After we settle in Oxford he asks with grave emphasis every time we meet, 'And how is *Siamon*?', as though I'd undermined a brilliant career.

Siamon has decided it's right for a couple to 'take turns'. He's urged me to leave behind a 'helper' view of the workplace and become more professional. In the face of uneasy questions from fellow scientists, almost all married men, he's proud to encourage a wife to take off on her own. He has a grant from the American Leukemia Society, which he can bring with him when he eventually joins Anna and me, but his arrangement in Oxford is temporary, and for the next three years he's still centred in his New York lab. For one of these years, we all return to New York. After this, he's appointed to a readership in Oxford's Sir William Dunn School of Pathology, and opens his own lab in 1976.

When my first book, *Eliot's Early Years*, is published by Oxford University Press – the first deeply researched biography of Eliot – with reviews everywhere, Uncle Hubert asks, 'How much did you make?'

'Next to nothing,' I admit. For though this biography still sells steadily, an advance from a university press in 1977 was bound to be small.

Long after, Uncle Hubert's question continues to puzzle me because he cared so for books. Our exchange took place in his library in Johannesburg. Books with fine bindings stood to attention along the shelves, guarding a principle of intrinsic value. It occurs to me only now that my uncle's question may have meant this: if a woman is not the provider for her family, what business has she to move them?

Though the disapproving tone of my uncle's question gets to me, it's distanced by the novelty of a first book and my mother's almost astonished response to the fuel she'd laid down over the years. She calls it 'a little gem'.

Publication seems all the more extraordinary, coming from where I did. A writer's life is hardly thought of at the bottom of Africa. Only someone as gifted as Alan Paton can venture to be a writer; *Cry, the Beloved Country* has the resonance to catch an 'overseas' ear – that magical 'overseas', arbiter of values we can't judge for ourselves. Others my mother used to read were Afrikaners developing a robust vernacular – the *Taal* – for a local readership. Writing also for a local readership are talented black poets and playwrights of the *Drum* generation, a politically defiant magazine coming out of the townships of Johannesburg. Builders on the roads improvise in Xhosa or Zulu, chanting in unison to the beat of the pickaxe; they lift, bend back, let fall – audible, but hardly in print.

Some reviewers are outraged though. These men own Eliot. Who is this female scurrying around, sifting papers? I try (though don't quite manage) to console myself with Virginia Woolf's comic portrait of the gentleman put out to find the housemaid turning over books in his library. But for all that, the change to the UK is working out for me.

It's harder for Anna, aged eight and taking in her grandmother's disturbing clichés: 'the English are cold'; 'their manners put you in your place'. After the stimulus of New York, Anna's bound to feel the regimen of school in North Oxford and the narrow-mindedness of her class teacher who says to me, 'When Anna came she was very American, but now she's all right.' One rule she can't accept is to eat braised liver and onions at school lunch. The headmaster is so determined that she *shall* eat this meat that he sits next to her, waiting for her to put it in her mouth. She can't. They sit there, while the rest of the children go out to play. To escape this punishment she informs the headmaster that she will go home for lunch, and without telling me she sits out each lunch hour near the dustbins at the back of our rented house on Hobson Road. It's a narrow road with no one around, unlike the teeming street life and ethnic mix of the Upper West Side. Poor Anna. Either I'm typing upstairs or away in College. Guilt, compunction about the cost to families, accompanied wives and mothers of my generation, as we dreamt of a new life and made our crossing into the workplace.

St Hilda's was one of the five women's colleges in Oxford. I assume the fellows will share the New York fury over suppression of women. But at lunch, when I speak in this vein, shutters seem to come down over the faces at High Table.

'We are not career women,' says the Principal, Mrs Bennett, evenly, 'we are women with careers.'

Here, the decorum is balm after the blatant misogyny of Columbia. A tutor relates the history of a confrontation in the Senior Common Room. It had been the custom for the younger dons to pour coffee for the senior fellows, 'the Ladies', as Dame Helen Gardner and her contemporaries are called. Until then, the Ladies had dictated how their colleagues should vote at meetings of the governing body. One evening, instead of pouring the coffee, the younger dons just *didn't*. It was a bloodless revolution. That simple breach of manners sufficed as a declaration of independence: an end to the tyranny of the Ladies.

As a newcomer I'm struck by relish of the language as the English turn it around their tongues. Long sentences unfold, each subordinate clause flinging out a consideration or limb of doubt, or advancing with a leap and then coming down with feet on the ground. The English of the Cape is different, its vigour infused with the freshness of Afrikaans. I've come to England as a native speaker, but somehow unprepared for a language played out with so much grace and nuance, such extended diphthongs, such undercurrents of irony. Such ways with words reconfigure the brain, what we take in or give out, inviting a newcomer to partake. This opens up possibilities for speaking and writing I'd not foreseen.

At the same time the English tutors at St Hilda's, Anne Elliott and Celia Sisam, impress me with their absolute integrity and wisdom. They suggest teaching. Eliot is prominent in the Oxford curriculum at this time, when Helen Gardner, the Eliot scholar and leading Lady at St Hilda's, is Merton Professor – the first woman to be appointed to this position.

Eliot's essays offer stimulating topics for discussion: in his essay on Shakespeare, he asks if Othello is '*cheering himself up*' after he strangles his wife, when he presents himself as 'one who loved not wisely but too well'. Eliot points out how Othello 'has ceased to think about Desdemona'.

I lay Eliot's idea of reading before students: 'We must know all of Shakespeare's work in order to know any of it.' The meaning of any one of Shakespeare's plays, Eliot is suggesting, 'is not in itself alone, but in that play in the order in which it was written'.

This resonates for a biographer. I'm bent on seeing the continuity of Eliot's own oeuvre. It comes easily because my mother has shown how single-minded Eliot is, so that if you get the point of any poem you get them all. Finalists doing Eliot as their special author have a growing sense of empowerment, as one poem builds on another. It's the same high-level reading experience as Henry James offers in 'The Figure in the Carpet', which dramatises what makes for a great writer: a pattern suffusing the whole. Eliot, in fact, followed Henry James in calling for an imaginative reader to make a reciprocal effort. Virginia Woolf invites reciprocity in a warmer voice: 'Let books be an equal creation between us.'

I like opening her essays and sharing that invitation with students. The Oxford tutorial seems continuous with a habit of sharing books that had been part of growing up. My mother's bookplate, devised for the many who borrow from the tempting bookshelves in the sunroom, reads: 'I enjoy sharing books as I do my friends, asking only that you treat them well and see them safely home.'

Virginia Woolf's essays offer a trove of rousing questions. Is it difficult to catch Jane Austen 'in the act of greatness'? She spots an instance at a ball in *The Watsons*. I prefer these essays by writers to the rising vogue for critical theory, a thicket of terminology that often turns out to be an elaborate way of stating the obvious. I don't want students to submit to pretentious verbiage; great writing is readable. The reciprocity of the tutorial system, with the individual care practised in Oxford, turns out to be a fulfilling way of life, and it's for real. No longer am I failing to live my mother's dream or trailing in tow.

It's not all easy, of course. At the outset I feel a fraud beside

the fellows with their comprehensive reading, but once a tutorial or class starts the students' beaks are open. Should novels
end conclusively? Is Dickens offering social documents or
something closer to fairy tale? Is *The Waste Land* in any sense
a unified poem? I like the close relationship that the tutorial
invites: searching for answers together. This fulfilment as a
teacher is not unconnected with the past. For all the helpful
models amongst tutors at thirty colleges – I learn from them,
for instance, to select pupils for their capacity to go on developing, rather than fix on the top marks that may prove a
ceiling – my prime model comes from my mother's intentness
as a reader and the eager voices and laughter swelling from her
sunroom.

Moses is her model of the prophet-teacher. In the early, luxurious part of his life (as an adopted son of Pharaoh's daughter),
'he does not know God' – my mother puts this bluntly. It
appeals to her that Moses is not born with spiritual power. Only
when he's alone in the wilderness and spies the burning bush
'everything', Rhoda says, 'becomes clear. A man has found his
vocation; he enters into a relationship with the Supreme Being;
henceforth his powers are not exercised in accordance with his
own passions but are shaped and guided by this over-mastering
relationship.'

For her too this relationship shapes other relations in taking
priority amongst emotional claims. It's for this reason that she
can't always 'hear'. To hear the divine voice, she has to protect
herself from certain kinds of distraction.

We drive from Kloof Road, winding around Lion's Head
toward Kloof Nek. At a gravel rest along the road we park per-
ilously on the edge with a sheer drop of mountain below.
Sunlight slants through the pines and their resin smell mingles
with the sour-sweet tang of protea and other *fynbos*. To return

to this landscape is to find myself too deeply interfused to belong elsewhere.

'I'd like to come back,' I say. Not that I will, but I know from her dream of Klaver that she has it in her to share the fancy.

She turns her head, away from the drop, towards Table Mountain at our back. The late afternoon sun makes its rocky crest glow as though from within. She says nothing. The silence between us lengthens until I start the car, back onto the road, and proceed on our way.

All through the eighties, during these annual end-of-year visits, I write in the dining room from four in the morning till nine, when my mother appears for breakfast. I love those early hours when ideas stir and the dawn rays burst about Lion's Head. I think of biographical leads: Virginia Woolf falling on lives 'like a roll of heavy waters . . . laying bare the pebbles on the shore of the soul', and Charlotte Brontë's wish 'to walk invisible'.

Distance and solitude fill my sails as a biographer with Chaucer's uncompromising advice to shun the crowd in his poem 'Truth': 'Flee from the prees, and dwelle with sothfast-nesse, / Suffyce unto thy good, though it be smal.' Virginia Woolf pounced on this, and I can't resist quoting it in *A Writer's Life*. In this second biography I again ignore academics' non-sensical mantra about 'the death of the author'. Because current literary theory has cast biography into the outer wilderness, to pursue this private writing life feels pleasantly secret, never mentioned in tutorials or lectures. I also ignore the current fash-ion for doorstop compendia of fact. As in *Eliot's Early Years* I'm committed to narrative momentum: a particular story I want to follow. At the same time I'm committed to authenticity and believe that biography could become an art if it treads the tightrope between verifiable fact and the story. At this period of fulltime teaching, everything discussed with pupils – both my own pupils at St Hilda's and those sent from other colleges to 'do' women's writing or American literature or Yeats and Eliot – seems to feed into the private biographic enterprise. One guide is Yeats, who claims that there's an idea to every great life. Yet my sense of what is great, unlike that of Yeats, is anti-heroic: I'm drawn to the lives of the obscure, and think often of three friends who died young. I cherish Virginia Woolf for asking 'What is greatness? What is smallness?' in her essay 'The Art of Biography'.

When my mother called me 'a lucky girl' at my wedding, she saw me as I saw myself, a satellite to a person of distinction, whether it be her poetic or Siamon's scientific imagination. As it turns out, my real luck is to live with a person who urged me to give up the satellite role.

Siamon reminds me of the rational thinker, William Godwin, who wasn't drawn to Mary Wollstonecraft until he read one of her books in 1796. He said it was 'calculated to make a man fall in love with the author'. One of Siamon's undertakings is to be a participant-reader of what I write. All the same, my experience as satellite, rather than as one born to write, has led me to the stories of Vivienne Eliot, Minny Temple and Fenimore, women who lived in the shadow of Eliot and Henry James, cast as satellites to solitary genius yet in actuality central to their works of art. For it was Minny and Fenimore who more than anyone revealed to James what a woman is and what she wants. Such buried lives seem to me marvellously dramatised by James's strange story of drowning Fenimore's dresses in the Venetian lagoon after she committed suicide. This scene, I tell Siamon, will open a biography of these two women and Henry James.

But my mother is displeased to find me in her dining room surrounded by books and paper. 'Why are you working on holiday?' she cries, and later in the day she will report this to family and friends. 'She *never* stops working.'

I don't get the objection. Is aspiration reserved for her, I wonder, and should it be, like hers, under wraps? Privately I admire her silence and concede my limitations, and at the same time try to explain. Writing can't be done in term-time; it has to happen during vacations. But that's not the heart of it, for writing has come to be a lifeline. My mother's irritation when she catches me in the act of writing leaves me cold. There is no way now that she can shake my separate life in the making. It's time now to live and write as I feel I should, true to my own light, not hers.

My mother behaves quite differently when a book comes out. She is celebratory. Like any other mother, she presents copies to friends and dips into reviews. She basks in praise from Monica, the reader she respects above all others. It's as though she makes no connection between a published book and the discipline that goes into its making: the questions we frame for visits to archives, the narrative order, the drafts, notes and verifying of facts; and all along, an eye for likely illustrations. When a book is actually at hand Rhoda reads avidly, and she rereads with delight her own story-telling role in my memoir of three friends, *Shared Lives*, with its extract from her story 'Vignettes of Namaqualand'.

Yet I'm troubled by two private reservations. Am I not using my mother once again for a book? And is it not, if I'm honest, an impertinence, given the quality of her poetic gift, to include her as sideshow of sorts in one chapter, where she offers her mentor-mothering to my schoolfriend Flora, who drinks in every word with her thirst for eloquence, for emotion, for life?

For all that, I'm elated to please my mother by acting in this small way as her channel. A test, a first step if you like, towards fulfilling my childhood destiny, and a pre-echo of the purpose behind the present memoir.

*

Can the figure in the carpet be applied to biography? Might there be an underlying pattern to each life, more visible of course in the lives of the great but discernible – if a biographer has the wit to see it – in 'the lives of the obscure', those lives to whom Virginia Woolf directs us with her feelers for what lies in shadow. The practise of biography compels a biographer to consider her own life and mine, I see, is bound up with my mother's, even as our ways part.

A biographer might say in the last decades of the century, a mother in Cape Town ran seven Bible classes while her daughter in Oxford lectured on women in Victorian fiction and wrote about Charlotte Brontë. So much for fact. Roads not taken beckon in the shadows of lives where purpose, in the routine sense, may be withdrawn and the future does not exist. This mother continued to imagine an impossible migration to a Promised Land embodied in the love of her life; her daughter continued to imagine an impossible return of the native to the Cape of Good Hope. Are we the sum of our acts, or are we our un-acted dreams?

'The story of Abraham in the Bible is the first great biography,' my mother remarks to me. A man called Abram takes a new name, Abraham, the father of Am, people, not any old tribe or nation but *the* People, who must carry his idea of one ethical God – a moral revolution against the idols he smashes, the multiple gods who invite the wanton or brutal acts of the fertility faiths.

Abraham, my mother wants me to hear, is the first in a succession of the Chosen to migrate away from home as an act of faith. She quotes the Hebrew to bring out the original impact of the Lord's command with its insistent repetitions: '*Leh laha m'arze'ha, m'moladit'ha, m'beit aviha*' (Get thee out of thy country, from thy birthplace, from thy father's house). Migration is central to the biographical pattern my mother has dreamt herself into and made her own. This is the tried and tested way for an ordinary person to be transfigured.

Though I have disappointed my mother by refusing to fit my life to this pattern, she and I do cross our divide now and then. I'm in sympathy with her reading of Isaiah's end-of-days prophecy as the highest point in the Bible: an end to violence when arms shall be turned into ploughs and pruning hooks. 'Nation shall not lift up sword against nation neither shall they learn war any more.'

Our disgust with violence is interlinked with agreement on what women could contribute to civilisation in so far as women are biologically formed to nurture life.

'In the eighteenth century, Mary Wollstonecraft saw it as women's mission to outlaw war,' I tell my mother. '"Brutal force has hitherto governed the world,"' I quote her vital message. '"Man accustomed to bow down to power, can seldom divest himself of this barbarous prejudice." She takes up Isaiah's prophecy when she ends, "I sincerely wish to see the bayonet converted into the pruning hook."'

My mother and her group have never read *A Vindication of the Rights of Woman*, a book rediscovered by my generation. My contemporaries, though, are all for rights, and tend to overlook Wollstonecraft's domestic ethos because our current struggle is to escape its constraints. (Siamon has his finger on the political moment when, jokingly, he awards me marks for aspects of marriage, including a D for domesticity – a D was a pleasing badge for a politicised wife in the seventies, even if it wasn't exactly true.) But my mother's generation, I realise, would be in accord with Wollstonecraft's wish for women to draw on their domestic traditions rather than remake themselves as imitation men.

'I'd like to write Mary Wollstonecraft's life,' I confide to my mother. 'I want to stress her commitment to what she calls "the

domestic affections", tenderness, nurture, listening and compromise, qualities that the civilised of both sexes can share.'
Vindication will be more overtly political than my other biographies. A book that has nothing to do with my mother, I might say – and then must concede how deeply she used to concur with the domestic, anti-power, anti-greed values Wollstonecraft put forward for a women's revolution.

My mother, for her part, concedes how unacceptable it is that Jewish tradition from the Middle Ages closed theology to women, and that the ultra-orthodox cut off girls, even now, from higher education. She's excited by a challenge to this from the American writer, Cynthia Ozick, deploring the loss of what women might have contributed to Jewish studies, and books that weren't burnt by the Nazis because they were never written.

My mother has cut out a report of this speech at Bar-Ilan, a religious university in Tel Aviv. The cutting lies on her bedside table, and reading it in full, I wonder what my mother makes of Ozick's dismissal of women's groups. Segregation, she argues, disables women. Putting them at a distance permits rabbis and theologians not to hear what women say.

But why, then, do rabbis appear uncomfortable with my mother, as my brother has noticed? Suitably deferential and self-effacing, she does nothing to jar them. Ozick convinces me that the rabbis' unease cannot be because my mother is a woman speaking to women. Unease is more likely because she does not practise the rabbinic mode of reading; the rabbis do not attempt to seize an authoritative Truth. For them, to engage with the text, the Word, is a religious experience in itself. Reading is to lend the mind to the play of multiple interpretations (some fanciful and even to do with numerology). My mother is out of line, and ahead of her time by several decades, in reading the Torah, the first five books of the Bible, as 'family stories'. She feels the cumulative force of generations in the passage of beliefs and traits from one generation to the next, and she brings out the bonds of parent and child.

Can there be another cause of the rabbis' unease? Can it lie in the very timbre of her voice, even though she conceals her visionary exhilaration? Its source is at the opening of her prayer door to the garden, with a limitless ocean booming to the left, and looming to the right the dark shape of Signal Hill. To silence private visions defers to a religious tradition that gives pre-eminence to the communal over the personal. Within her routines of prayer, observance and teaching, day by day, year by year, her soul's saps pulse unseen.

In teaching, she takes care to offer her groups the scholars' voices: Rabbi Abraham Joshua Heschel at the Jewish Theological Seminary of America, and the German-Jewish philosophers Franz Rosenzweig and Martin Buber. She's a devotee of Buber, and quotes him in conversation. Excessively, to my mind. This rumble of cogitation seems to me to interrupt and dissipate my mother's voice, to alter its very character so that it becomes rather carefully scrupulous. When she speaks in her own voice, the encounters at her prayer door pulse below the surface. That pulse comes through a voice direct, intimate and a little strained – the strain deriving from the barbiturate, which slows her brain, and from a voice slowed deliberately to attend to scholarship. It's as though the speed of intuition races her voice ahead while words follow at a measured, almost formulaic, pace.

When I was a child, she often spoke of the blinded Samson ('O dark, dark, dark, amid the blaze of noon'), as though Milton's *Samson Agonistes* spoke to her own dark night of the soul. By night, when she looked up at the river of stars or surrendered to buffetings by Cape winds, she felt alive, awake, cleansed of dross. She gave me to understand at an early age that only those who undergo unmaking, who experience a kind of hiatus of non-being in their lives, can purify themselves as candidates for regeneration.

As a feminist, I hear her more readily when she trains her eye on the women in the Bible: above all, that promoter of the emotional tie, Ruth, the young widow who famously refuses to be divided from her widowed mother-in-law though they belong with different tribes. My mother exclaims over the moral beauty of this attachment between two women and across the generations.

She also reveres the biblical woman of valour who acts without violence. In Egypt, Pharaoh commands Hebrew midwives to kill male newborns. The midwives can't bring themselves to commit murder, and invent an excuse that Hebrew women give birth quickly, before a midwife arrives. For the midwives it's not a matter of faith ('fearing God', the scriptures say with pious insistence); it's got nothing to do with God. It's the midwife's natural and professional respect for life.

'The midwives can't know God yet,' I hear my mother say, 'not the God who will carry them out of slavery and deliver a code of law.'

But what women feel and do does not much concern the Bible's compilers and scribes when a hero in the making is squarely in their sights. My mother corrects for this wherever she can: 'Pharaoh's plans for the annihilation of the children are defeated by WOMEN.' Her teaching notes spell this out in capitals, and you can hear defiance in her voice.

When she feels her way into the oft-told story of Moses in the bulrushes, she fixes on the word 'placed': a mother placed her baby in her home-made boat-cradle, and then placed the boat among the reeds of the Nile. That act of placing suggests to my mother the 'profound anxiety in the mother's heart', and her care to put the boat down 'as gently and tenderly as she had placed the child in it'.

Then too, when the Egyptian princess decides to adopt the child, there's the valour of his sister Miriam, the little girl who's watching to see what happens and runs to the princess with her offer to find a Hebrew nurse 'for thee', as though she's acting on behalf of Pharaoh's daughter, while naturally she's acting for the baby and his mother. Rhoda admires the diplomacy of 'for thee'.

The bravest woman of valour is Esther, caught between dangerous men. Esther conceals her Hebrew background when the Persian king, Ahashverosh or Ahasuerus (thought to be Xerxes, who ruled in the fifth century BC) chooses her as his queen. It's politic to conceal her background because Haman, the king's vain, boastful functionary, is preparing to massacre her people. The king himself is unreliable, a spoilt show-off with a temper if crossed. In the opening scene of the story that comes down to us through the Bible, he kicks out his first wife, Vashti, when she refuses his summons to exhibit herself to his drunken court. 'Every man should bear rule in his own house,' the king justifies his caprice.

At work in my old top room, I hear an unprecedented din erupt from the sunroom. Rhoda and the quiet housewives in her group are shouting, so that none can be heard. I run along the passage to hear. It's about Vashti. They read her as a feminist rebel. Married young to wilful, unseeing husbands, these loyal, middle-aged wives find themselves at white heat, shoulder to shoulder with Vashti's refusal to be, in the current phrase, a sex object. They see Esther forced to replace her. To the king, she exists only as his choice from a round-up of Persian beauties – 'like men who manage beauty-queen parades', my mother says, trying to quell the shouts.

This is so 'relevant' (as we talk then) to my political passions that I must stay and listen as my mother tells Esther's story: how Esther devises a more effective form of action than Vashti's confrontation. A different kind of theatre, my mother proposes.

At that, we simmer down to lend ourselves to the artistry of Esther as she stages a humane drama of a higher order: an operatic petition of her ruler-husband, risking her life ('if I die, I die') in successive banquet scenes, playing to the king's luxurious taste, as Esther prepares to pit an exposure of her background against Haman's extermination programme. My mother follows the biblical narrator as 'a consummate artist' who paces Esther's story with pauses to quicken the suspense.

The women in Rhoda's home group, Monica and Lilian and Thelma and Mickey and Ida, who live to be mothers, feel in their fibres what Olive Schreiner meant when she said 'men's bodies are our women's works of art'. Rhoda attacks the killer code of heroism by way of Genesis: the Lord breathed into our nostrils 'the breath of life'. From this, she says, 'flows the Hebrew understanding of the sanctity of human life. This was a new value in the world. We know that even the cultured Greeks exposed newborn infants on the roof to test their strength for survival; and their slaves were termed by Aristotle mere "tools with life". Even in the greatest development of pagan culture, we find Plato suggesting that in his ideal city the incurably sick and the mentally ill should be neglected. This seems to show a lack of appreciation of the resources of the human spirit through suffering and affliction.'

Her Moses is decidedly not a hero; he's a man suffering with his people, and struggling to overcome their wickedness and loss of morale as they wander for forty years in the desert.

My mother adds, 'The test of faith is to be steadfast in the

face of worldly failure, because the life of faith is in large measure a struggle with the world.'

'Steadfast' sounds tame, yet it's what she's learnt by holding fast to the lifeline of Psalm XXIII as she teeters over the
abyss.

Given my mother's history of post-partum breakdown, and
mine, following Anna's birth, doctors have warned Siamon and
me that to have another child might be a risk. By the late seventies Anna is twelve and has always longed not to be an only
child. Anna isn't eating, and Siamon and I are of course very
worried about her. We decide that the risk of childbirth will be
worth it if it makes Anna happy – as it does. Then too we are
settled enough in Oxford, with Siamon's lab growing and a lec-
tureship for me at Jesus College, to believe that this time we will
cope better.

This time it happens immediately, at the start of pregnancy.
It's like being switched off. It's an ordeal to get up, and I'm only
thankful that this is happening during the university vacation,
in the spring, between Hilary and Trinity terms. I lie prone,
reading Sherlock Holmes simply to pass the hours. My GP asks
if I really want this baby. I really do, and this time I'm aware
how little content there is to the depression. Siamon says the
one helpful thing: what I'm experiencing, he says, is the impact
of pregnancy hormone, the dramatic change to the body at the
start of pregnancy and after childbirth, to which some women
will be susceptible. I hold on to his promise that the depression
will stop once the hormone has reached a certain level – and so
it does.

The first thing I do after the birth of Olivia, in November
1978, is to shuffle along the corridor at the John Radcliffe hospital in Oxford to a public phone. I can't wait to tell my mother
what a strong, alert child has come into our family. Flying out

to Cape Town three weeks later it's like crossing a fissure with an offering in my arms. This time I will share mothering with my mother. Can we push our divide aside?

She receives Olivia with delight, but though we enjoy the baby together it doesn't budge the divide. With Olivia, it's not

Anna holds her longed-for sister, Olivia. Clockwise from top right: in Oxford; coming to Cape Town – four generations at the gate; with Granny Annie; in the sunroom

the same for her as with Anna. With Anna, she'd replaced me as a mother when I was away in hospital weeks on end. Maternal protectiveness welled up in her for Anna as a baby, and remained firm. She's older and established in her far-off working life when Olivia arrives. She's now a grandmother, and no more. As Olivia grows up, a sturdy child, strong in mind and will, she is not as entranced as Anna by her grandmother's Bible stories. At her children's Bible class, Olivia looks forward most to the butterscotch my mother hands out. When Olivia is a healthy ten-year-old my mother says to her, with the unthinking insensitivity of her own mother, 'When I was your age, I was a thin girl.'

Once, when my mother and I are talking intently during a long car journey, Olivia bites me. She explains later, 'It was to get your attention.' Anna is one of my mother's 'lovely girls'; Olivia (and I) are not, with the result that she can't quite see us.

Rhoda's definition of mankind as 'a family of families' leads her at the age of sixty-two to take action against apartheid. With her woman's eye, she's long noticed that numerous women working in Sea Point have nowhere they can go on their Wednesday or Thursday afternoons off. It's only an afternoon, so there's not enough time to travel home to one of the townships, really a sprawl of shacks, Windermere or Langa, which social engineering has relegated (without lighting, water or police protection against rampant violence) to the periphery of the city. There are men-only bars for blacks in Sea Point, reeking of cheap liquor. When women are off they stay in their rooms: dark, close rooms in back yards.

At length, my mother realises that no one will act on behalf of women workers with no vote. She must act on her own. In the winter of 1979, Rhoda and her cousin Garda, who has

recently moved to Sea Point, distribute leaflets inviting women
to tea one Thursday in July. They also accost 'madams' in the
street, asking them, 'Would you object if your maid is asked to
tea?' Katie Erasmus, my mother's able housekeeper, is in charge
of the food: she bakes delicious scones and cakes, and spreads
them out in her no-fuss manner on long trestle tables in the
Weizmann hall on the Main Road, which has been donated by
the synagogue.

To forestall a Special Branch raid on people crossing the
colour bar in a public hall, Rhoda pays a visit to the Sea Point
Police Station. In tea-rose and pearls, with lipstick, a neat, side
parting to her curly hair and a handbag over her arm, she performs her hesitant 'only a housewife' act – performed so often
that it's almost second nature. Afrikaner policemen, peremptory
and rough with blacks, are brought up to respect white, older
women. They listen politely to my mother assuring them that
all she has in mind is food provision for poor women. No need
to suspect trouble from this fragile lady.

To my mother's astonishment, over three hundred women
turn up. She'd assumed they'd want 'tea and *gesels*' (she uses the
Afrikaans word for chat because street Afrikaans, a local dialect
full of verve and slang, will be the home language for most who
come). It turns out that the women want to use their off time
for courses and activities.

Garda organises the most popular course, in nursing and first
aid. The training by St John Ambulance makes it possible to
find better jobs as carers for the elderly of Sea Point. By the
time the Friendship Club, as it comes to be known, celebrates
its sixth anniversary, two hundred and thirty members have
gained Home Nursing Certificates. Some are proud to be on
duty at rugby and soccer matches, as well as in theatres (as
required by law, wherever crowds gather). My mother offers
Bible study. Lilian sets up a sewing circle; there are knitting,

crochet and embroidery groups; cookery demonstrations; and my mother's neighbour, Anne Rabie, runs yoga and aerobics. Gym-suits discarded by the well-fed matrons of Sea Point hang oddly on the wiry frames of domestic workers.

The Friendship Club, meeting each Wednesday and Thursday, thrives from year to year. A statement to my mother from members at the start of 1980 suggests a motto: 'With Love we serve one another.' Helen Khun accompanies my mother to a concert at the City Hall, one place where races are not divided. Katie September and Betty Rhenoster say that the Club is 'home' to them, and they hope it will 'go on for ever'. Justina Fadana, a quiet, elderly woman with nowhere to live, becomes a permanent guest in Katie's one-time room at 11 Avenue Normandie (when a new room for Katie is built). My mother makes out that Justina is employed by her, since non-whites are not allowed to live in Sea Point, except as servants.

Members are required to pay twenty cents a time, to avoid an atmosphere of charity. All the same, my mother is not shy to elicit donations: one firm supplies cups and saucers; another, off-cuts of fabric for the sewing group. Eventually, there's a choir and group excursions: a hired bus takes a party to Namaqualand each September to see the white, yellow and orange daisies that cover the veld. At an end-of-year party, my mother joins in a country jig called the *tickey draai* (literally, a three-penny turn: a hectic, breathy bobbing and turning to folk music, *boeremusiek*), familiar to Rhoda from the dances her mother had held at Klaver Hotel. My brother is there, and when he sits down at a piano to belt out his party piece, 'Great Balls of Fire', the women abandon their cups and saucers, leap to their feet and dance.

My mother's favourite of all her groups is a children's class each Saturday morning, in a separate room during the service at the Marais Road synagogue. She's especially fond of a little boy, whom she calls 'the professor'. He sucks his thumb while he listens; takes out his thumb to deliver 'a profound question'; and then, satisfied, returns the thumb to his mouth.

One day in 1983, Thelma, the artist in the private Friends' Group, sits in on the children's class. That day, Rhoda relates the 'wonder' story of Jonah, who is swallowed by a whale and spends three days and three nights in the whale's belly before he's spat up on a beach. Jonah has been a runaway from God's mission: to cry out for repentance in the wicked city of Ninevah. Thelma is excited at the way the children respond to the moral nuances, as when, in terror of a storm at sea, Jonah begs the sailors to cast him into the ocean because he's failed in his duty to God, and the sailors, who are heathens, do so unwillingly.

'They know how precious is a human life': Rhoda brings out the sailors' reluctance, implying that you don't have to have faith to be humane.

Jonah does then undertake the Ninevah mission, and the inhabitants do wake up to corruption. Rhoda's telling brings out Jonah's discontent: he's sulking because the Lord forgives Ninevah too readily. For all Jonah's effectiveness as divine agent, he hasn't grasped the higher good of mercy.

Thelma wants this to be a children's book. Rhoda brushes off the idea with her usual deprecation. Thelma insists: she tapes Rhoda telling the story, has it typed, illustrates it, and sends it to Oxford University Press Southern Africa, who publish the book with a commentary for parents and teachers. Having always shunned publication, Rhoda remains passive, at most compliant in the hands of her determined friend, but the press likes the narrative for its closeness to the tone and language of the Bible, and markets it as suitable for both Christian and Jewish readers, 'for in the story of Jonah the Bible reaches a peak of universalist teachings'.

*

The 'runaway basket' filled with unseen poems

In the mid-eighties my mother takes out what Katie calls her 'runaway basket' packed with her poems. At this point she selects seventy poems to put in order as a spiritual autobiography, 'Notes on a Journey'. Here she shows an initiative absent in the run-up to *Jonah*. Over the next few years she reconsiders her choices and reshuffles the order. And all the while her commitment to teaching goes on, thirty-four years in all, from the time Levin inspired her mission in 1955 until she retires from teaching at the age of seventy-two.

On a torn scrap of paper she scribbles: 'So she went on Teaching until her memory began to fail, and time short "to tell of all Thy Works".'

15

Lost and Living Memory

In New York Rhoda (front left) and Basil (centre) meet
Ben Miller (right). Back: Alma Miller, Naomi Press; front: Anna

When my mother is seventy, in 1987, she counts up the years
that separate us: 'Twenty-three years apart divide our lives. The
division between the generations is painful.'

She's confiding her pain about our divide to a cousin, Ben
Miller, a doctor in New York, who lost his family – that is, our
Pres family in Plunge – during the Holocaust. Worse than my

distance in miles, though, is my involvement in a foreign, Oxford world: 'the commitment to our bereft Jewish people is lost in their faraway lives'.

'Bereft.' It's a lament for Ben, who had been lost to sight for many years after the Holocaust until my mother's determined efforts to find a survivor had turned him up in America. It is a lament too for mothers and daughters. And I suppose, the generations passing.

It's also a private lament following Monica's sudden death from heart failure:

> ... my life-long sister-friend Monica, a 61-year friendship beginning at the age of 9 years when I came as a little 'back-velder' from Klaver and found this wonderful gifted child at the head of my class. We met in the Library and ever since we have shared books – indeed shared our lives in every aspect ... In spite of her many gifts, being bereft of a mother from babyhood she chose motherhood.

A mother's duty. A mother's duty was at issue when Monica pressed Rhoda to give up her poetry group in London in 1952. But we, Rhoda's children, were old enough to understand that her deferred longings to see beyond our provincial world did not conflict with her maternal bond. She came back to a town where she had no one to talk to about poetry; no one to guide her as in London. Her predicament, as she confided it to a sister-child, was to alert me ever after to women's un-acted aspirations.

As I write this in the summer of 2013, a one-time neighbour from New York arrives for lunch: Barbara Robey, who still lives on the tenth floor of our apartment block near Columbia University. She has with her a nine-year-old grandson, Sam, whom she's treating to a Harry Potter week in Oxford. As we recall our ways as young mothers, I remember how Barbara once thought to become a doctor. Yes, she confirms, she took pre-med courses at Smith College, where she was advised – this was the fifties, the era of Sylvia Plath – that, for women, such study should not be with a view to a professional career, merely as preparation for educated motherhood.

My mother's expectations were even more subdued in a place where, if a woman worked it was a sign of poverty – almost a stigma, lowering your class, in the way Charlotte Brontë discovered back in the later 1830s, when she went out to earn her living as a governess. I opened my biography of her with the scene of Charlotte left alone on the servants' floor by middle-class employers with whom she'd been accustomed to mix socially as a daughter of a minister. When I came to England in 1973 I was astonished to hear class–conscious remarks about Valerie Fletcher, who, before their marriage, had worked as Eliot's secretary in the fifties. These remarks hinted that the poet married beneath him: a young woman from Leeds who (said an owner of a fine old Cotswold house) drew on *nylon* gloves when a visit came to an end. None of these observers did justice to Mrs Eliot's feat in editing the manuscript of *The Waste Land*. Back in the fifties, my father meant to protect his secretary, Mrs Swan, from prejudice against working women when he'd say, 'highly intelligent, always a lady'. Attitudes to working women changed with the mass entry of middle-class women into the workplace since the seventies. This may make it hard now to fathom the intensity of my mother's longing for 'work-in-the-world' in the early fifties, and what a blessing such work appeared when it washed up at her feet on an after-wave of Levin's mission. So it was that fulfilment as a teacher displaced more unlikely fulfilment as a poet – a dream realised only briefly, with her escape to London.

Siamon was appointed Professor of Cellular Pathology.
He and Olivia visit me at St Hilda's College, Oxford

The twenty-one years between 1952 and 1973 made all the difference for women of the next generation. In 1973, it was unusual but not unthinkable to take off with a child and move on my own to another country when the chance came. Siamon agreed to this. He was ahead of his time in his belief that women should work, and after a while he found a way of joining us in England. Whether it was the right course for a daughter born in New York is another question. On our last night, bags packed, furniture sold, the apartment emptied, Anna, aged eight, stood silently at the window looking out at Riverside Drive and the Hudson River. It's fair to ask whether in that decisive act of migration I did to my daughter what my mother did to me.

Given that past, I hope to free my daughters to bear what fruit they were made to bear, without an obligation to be an extension or a channel. At the same time, I'm convinced that the home education my mother offered, reading aloud and books that awaken empathy, is vital to mothering, and more formative than formal learning.

Anna will grow up to be a teacher like her mother and grandmother before her. When I ask her now what mothering meant to her she reminds me how, at the age of three or four, she used to confiscate my pencil. She didn't want a mother to be preoccupied. She'd have liked a mother who baked cakes, and compensated by baking herself. Later on, she says, 'having a mother who was passionate about her own work' taught her 'to be immersed' in what she does. She thinks a mother should 'see and appreciate' who her daughter is.

Anna ruminates over what she witnessed as a small child: my criticisms of the lifestyle of liberal whites in the face of extreme poverty, aloft in the palaces they've built for themselves on outcrops of mountain, and my feminist anger at the inequalities of Columbia and the workplace. 'Your rebellious streak probably influenced me,' Anna says. 'I am not afraid to tread the path less travelled, to be internally daring. So many people have had mothers who never found their own light. Your family did not like you being outspoken and rebellious, but I did. It led me to feel free to speak out about injustice – to tell my truth plainly whatever the world might say.' I am relieved by these words.

As it turns out, my most memorable experience of mothering will have nothing to do with seeing and speaking out, the ways learnt from my own mother. In fact, it will have nothing to do with experience, but will be – like much mothering – instinctive. It comes about years later, when Olivia has grown up and married: she asks me to be with her when she gives birth.

As she approaches the seventh month of pregnancy there are signs that the baby can't deal with the fluid surrounding him: it's around his lungs and under his scalp. Excess fluid is drained by the foetal surgery unit at University College Hospital in London, and then over the next fortnight the fluid builds up once more. Suddenly, Olivia goes into labour, eight weeks early.

I'm apprehensive, because I'm no expert on childbirth and this is clearly a complicated one.

'I may not be able to help you,' I warn her.

'Just be there for me.'

When she asks for pain relief I leave her side to call the midwife, who takes one look and says, 'Too late. The baby's coming.'

As the contractions lengthen I urge Olivia to cry out if she wants. 'It's all right.'

'Don't waste your energy,' the midwife contradicts. 'Use your breath to push.'

Wrenched though I am by Olivia's pains, it's extraordinary to watch the midwife like a director of a drama. 'Wait – hold your breath. Now pant. Now! *Push.*'

To my surprise, she uses only two fingers to ease out the head, holding the fingers almost still, with minimum intervention. The delicacy of that handwork is exquisite. It could be a work of art: the pulsing of birth against that quiet hand. It's astonishingly quiet: only the concentrated breathing of Olivia, the low-voiced instruction of the midwife and the baby's steady heartbeat (amplified), reassuring us he's not distressed. The consultant, Dr Kendall, and two doctors in his team are ready, waiting at the foot of the bed. The moment the baby emerges, a wool cap is tucked over his head. I'm holding my breath for his cry, and it doesn't come. 'Fortunately, there's no immediate emergency,' Dr Kendall says, and places the small being on

Olivia's abdomen for the briefest look at each other before racing the newborn to intensive care for the ventilation his lungs need.

I feel a rush of delight in this tiny creature, who has held on to life despite the encroaching fluid.

'He's a serious chap,' I say to Olivia's husband Phil, a musician who has stood up to the sight of blood, which he'd thought might shake him.

There's a shower adjoining the delivery room, and as I help Olivia to wash herself down I feel washed clean of my own first childbirth, which had been part of my concern for Olivia. For that scene of uncaring orderlies with a heaving body, exposed to view in a public lift, gets expunged at last by my closeness to my daughter, and by her wanting me there, throughout this ordeal.

Now, when I ask Olivia what mothering means to her, she fixes on an awful night that preceded the birth. 'We had just had the news that our baby was seriously ill, and you stayed up all night watching over me in hospital. To me, on the cusp of motherhood yet feeling more than ever in need of mothering myself, what you did brought home to me what a mother does for her child – and the fact that as mothers, we crave and value our mothers even more.'

Olivia recalls also an exchange we had after Humphrey was born. 'I was afraid I wasn't a good enough mother, and you told me that you yourself didn't always feel selfless – like me, you wanted time for yourself. It relieved and strengthened me to hear this. As a child, I never noticed if your mind wasn't focused on being my mother. I felt that it was. Maybe we are "perfect" mothers already without trying to be perfect.'

As Rhoda enters her seventies, I bring up the question of publication. Her intention is set out in her papers, what she confided

Olivia with me at an interview when
Virginia Woolf: A Writer's Life came out, 1984

to me long ago: 'If this is ever worthy of publication it should be after my death.' But at this point a counter-intention rises, encouraged perhaps by *Jonah*. She brings a typescript of the seventy poems with her when she visits England during the hot summer of 1986. We take her with us to the isle of Harris in the Outer Hebrides where, on impulse, she slips off the side of a boat in her petticoat to bathe in the icy ocean. On an empty beach we pick up the most delicate shells we've ever seen, faint transparent pinks, as though washed up by waters newly divided from dry land.

On our return to Oxford, I suggest we try my publisher, Oxford University Press, which has a strong poetry list built up by Jon Stallworthy, a poet himself. He has been replaced by an editor unknown to me. I write her a covering letter, explaining that my mother has accumulated an oeuvre of poems. We submit them in August; in October, the editor sends a courteous rejection, saying that she finds the choice of words 'overwrought'.

Emily Dickinson too had a belated counter-intention when, in 1883, three years before her death, she sent a sample of her poems to the prestigious Boston publisher Thomas Niles. He replied that he could not 'consume' them. He thought them 'devoid of the true poetical qualities'. She left no comment.

My mother leaves a midnight scribble, dated 28 February 1987, retreating into the modesty of a woman accustomed to living in the shadow of rabbis and theologians. She permits herself to speak in public only as a disciple of Martin Buber. That night, while reading a biography of Buber, she tells herself, 'I have only a limited power of thought. My experience comes from the "encounters" granted me through the epileptic deaths and abysms of my life, and the visionary grace bestowed on me.'

To find her naming her illness is still strange to me. It's not a word she ever says aloud. She has kept a tally of '22 deaths' in all.

That year, 1987, she consults a doctor about lapses of memory. As memory begins to fade, she forgets the ways I'd disappointed her and we come close again.

It's a relief to revert to something like our original tie. The early reversal of the protective mother–daughter relation in our case was peculiar, though it had, for me, its gains. After the independence of my mother's 'work-in-the-world' from the fifties till near the nineties she's dependent on me once more, and this time, to be a daughter tending her ageing mother is in the normal cycle of things. Curiously, this is not a sad turn. There are moments of delight in rediscovering what we share and the deep comfort of closing our divide. I see in her taste and the quality of her mind what has shaped all that's mattered in my life. What's different in this later phase is that my protective feeling for her is not new; it's repetition. And it's this fact of repetition that's threading a pattern in the carpet of our lives.

Though my mother is prone to leave taps running and mislay her glasses more than ever, this appears at first no more than habitual forgetfulness. Some time after she retires from teaching, one morning in the early nineties, Katie finds a poem on the floor next to Rhoda's bed. It appears that retirement has released the poet in her.

> *Tired by the day*
> *The breezes of freedom*
> *blow all around me.*
> *My body like the harp*
> *left idle in the midst*
> *of the morning orchestra*
> *trembles quietly*
> *forgotten by the pains,*
> *by suffering, by necessity.*
> *I listen to the quiet*
> *resonator of the universe*
> *O miracle of love!*
> *Top of a high tree*
> *moved by the song of the birds.*

Her inward and poetic life continues after she's thought to have lost her mind to confusion. Her last poem in May 1993 lays out three possible passages through the lifespan:

> *Some step into the world*
> *stable, strong,*

Some go on long
slow journeyings
or ride on fiery serpents.
Some never seek
but stumbling go
they wade no-ways
until they blench
and fade in the numbering
of death

By 1993 she is, she knows, often 'stumbling', yet at times she's capable of keen enjoyment. In August she accompanies us to Edinburgh and attends the Festival, while I look at a manuscript memoir by Charlotte Brontë's publisher, George Smith, in the National Library of Scotland. We return to London by sleeper, which brings back the overnight trains of her childhood, puffing slowly to Namaqualand, so much so that when I help her out of her compartment on arrival at Euston she thinks we've reached Klaver.

One day in Oxford she wanders out on her own and we can't find her. A secretary at the Sir William Dunn School of Pathology, where Siamon works, spots her looking about vaguely in South Parks Road, and drives her home. She's not distressed. Should I smile at her old-fashioned femininity depending on, and warmed by, the kindness of strangers? So long as you treat her as normal, she's quite at ease, used to her own vagaries and to owning as of old in mildly amused tones: 'I'm im*poss*ible.' At some point, though, she's bound to notice how some are discomfited by oddity.

There is an unsent letter to her youngest brother, after he and his wife have been in Cape Town. When Hubert was little in their Klaver nursery Rhoda had offered him tickeys to kiss her. Now she foresees an oncoming divide.

Midnight
Wednesday May 19th 1993

My dear Hubert,

... When I was sitting and listening to you in the garden
of the Mount Nelson [Hotel] waiting to see you and
Berjulie off at the airport Berj called a taxi and sent me
away. Why?

It's true my memory is impaired, perhaps by the
medication my life-long illness has necessitated – was this a
reason to turn from me even if such impairment was
irritating? Please help me ... – to understand.

A misunderstanding is likely: her sister-in-law probably wished
to spare my mother a journey to the airport, not realising that,
for her, it was not a duty. And then too, undoubtedly, the hotel's
taxi company was safer than a random taxi at the airport. That
said, Berjulie does find muddle off-putting, so it's also likely that
Rhoda's feelers picked this up.

Other unsent letters in 1993 show shifts in crucial relation-
ships. That year, her eldest brother almost dies of septicemia in
the intensive care ward at Groote Schuur Hospital. Her scribble to him is close to prayer:

How shall I thank you enough Basil my beloved brother.
You have blessed me and cared for me all my life long –
May you be helped and upheld and strengthened and
blessed and speedily healed.

Your loving
Sister

Basil recovers and my mother is soothed by his peacefulness as
they sit together on his stoep looking out over Danger Beach

between their old haunts at Muizenberg and the fishing village of Kalk Bay. They are full of the past. 'Klaver ... Klaver ...' The beat of hooves as Daddy gallops off to the farm at dawn. The pony and trap carrying them to their one-room school. Italian engineers arriving to build 'the furrow', and then, by night, when they play their records, the voices of Galli-Curci and Caruso filling the vast spaces of veld.

Another midnight scribble has to do with the shifting tie to her son. There are tensions between them: she has never approved of Pip's 'fun-loving' side, involving poker nights and 'jolling' – a local word for sprees. But now there's also his partner, a dancer with Dulcie Howes (whose fine ballet school

In the early nineties my mother and I revisit her early years
when 'train days' – only three trains a week – brought excitement

trained the choreographer, John Cranko). It appalls Rhoda to discover that Kristin is 'German' – by which she means German antecedents. And yet she needs Pip. It is he who hires cleaners and carers, and who monitors her medication, since she's increasingly unreliable about taking it. He puts up notices around her room, even in her walk-in cupboard, to reassure her of his care, and remind her where she is and where to reach him. He takes her out two evenings a week. They quarrel; they make up. Their bond is more active than mine, with only inter-mittent visits from overseas. He's now the companion I'd been in our childhood. She scribbles worriedly after his heart attack. 'For some time I have been depending on Pip for all social pleasures ... I have recently been conscious of the burden my needs & failing memory have loaded on him.'

Over the ten years of Rhoda's memory loss, the large circle of friends and family gradually falls away until, without Pip, she'd be alone with a succession of paid companions. Lilian now lives in Johannesburg with her daughter Joan. Lilian and Marjorie, my mother's two bridesmaids in 1940, visit when they come to the Cape each summer. I'm there, at home, at the end of the year, and talk turns to the plays of Athol Fugard and the stay-ing power of defiant, multi-racial drama during the bad old days of apartheid at Jo'burg's Market Theatre. We talk past Rhoda; she's left out.

Friday nights remain outwardly the same with the candles, white cloth and two loaves under the prayer cover; and there are guests, most often our father's humorous nephew Arthur and his warm-hearted wife Bernice; or it might be Monica's second son, Ronnie; or Gloria Sandak-Lewin, the top girl in the year ahead of mine at Good Hope, who later attended the Bible classes. Sadly, my mother no longer enjoys Friday nights: the talk is too fast, too full of the present, which is unreal to her, or too full of allusions she no longer recalls. Her manner is nervous, and she fills her gaps with her role as hostess. Arm shaking, she offers dishes repeatedly, cutting across conversation: wouldn't we have more peas, more pineapple pudding? A second later, she urges the same. It's hard to keep some semblance of a dinner party, with vacancy pressing itself upon it to the point of disruption.

'You've offered Pip more already,' I reproach her, as though she can take this in. I break out when she grumbles at Katie whose dinners are, as ever, perfection. Here I am, shouting about South African housewives who take service for granted – no more than a white woman's due. How can she have lost all sense of Katie's need for appreciation, I shout. There's glee in the kitchen, as though my loss of sympathy with my mother relieves the helpers.

I'm convinced that her deepest self is there, even while doctors and carers commiserate over her decline. A carer frets that when she takes Rhoda to the library, she has no interest. In fact, I find her reading all the time, though not newly published books in their bright covers, which the library displays; she's absorbed in *Pride and Prejudice* from her own shelves. Since she can't recall the plot, it's her infinite delight to read Jane Austen for, as it were, the first time.

One day she's walking along the passage at home talking half to herself, half to me. It sounds like a fantastic story of rebellion against her fate, and love for a married man, and running off to a solitary life. There are elements here of her own life but it sounds confused. And then, suddenly, I see.

'Why, you're Jane Eyre.'

She nods a bit impatiently, as though I should have known, and then wanders on in this character.

1994 is the last year she's fit to visit us. Pip arranges for a wheelchair, and we collect her at Heathrow. From Oxford we

Olivia (left) and Anna at their grandmother's, ready for Friday night prayers

take the train to Devon. She will like the track along the sea beyond Exeter and the steep hills at Totnes. We are on our way to the Dartington festival, where I'm to talk on Charlotte Brontë. My mother is in high spirits to be amongst writers, who sit at a communal table for lunch.

'And have you met Jane Austen?' she asks a puzzled novelist across the table.

In a sense, Austen is indeed a present companion to my mother who lives with her, the Brontës and other writers who confide in her across time: 'Reader, I married him' and 'There are not so many men of fortune in the world as there are pretty women to deserve them.'

My mother's visit to Oxford is an opportunity to have her memory investigated, and we ask a team in the university to include her in their research. A research assistant tests her on the days of the week, on which subject she's predictably blank. One day is much like another.

'Do you know who the Pope is?' the researcher persists.

'I'm Jewish,' Rhoda says politely.

If questions were to lend themselves to the patient, rather than expecting the patient to lend herself to the questions, the research might have revealed something worth knowing. If my mother were asked about the gold-smoke approaching her over the veld, or about Yiddish lullabies her father had sung by candlelight, there would have been a response – perhaps too much, for these days my mother is living largely in repeated memories of early childhood. Her shaky hand transcribes 'Klaver' from memory:

> *Across the River*
> *where the long hills lie*
> *side by side with the morning sky*
> *children's voices chipped out of silence,*
> *and as a child's undarkened breast*
> *is pure as the air she breathes*
> *so, free of dross a moment,*
> *the soul receives*
> *Thy Presence.*

Only those who know this primal scene are in a position to reach her; even then, to elicit a meaningful reply, it makes sense to supply a certain amount of information in asking a question, so that memory doesn't seize up in alarm. Since public discussion overrides this, she's at a loss in company. She's a different person – quite her old self – when we are alone.

The research is designed to elicit a preconceived diagnosis of dementia. I'm pressed to say that my mother is 'aggressive'.

'She's tense, anxious all right, as she's always been. Aggressive, no.'

This makes no impression, and I suspect that box gets ticked anyway. I fear an adverse Oxford report will influence my mother's doctors in Cape Town. It's obvious that the doctor in charge has not a clue about her calibre, nor does he recognise what's extraordinary about the memory she retains. Siamon tries to caution the doctor who, unbudged, sends a shuffling reply encased in medical lingo.

Fool I am to subject my mother to research that fails to take in the element of caprice in what we retain or let go. Her retention of her Klaver stories and her indifference to the Pope are not exactly aberrations; they point to a character inaccessible to questionnaires.

I'm resistant to diagnosis because I don't believe that my mother's condition can be defined, given how little we know about the brain. No one has asked if the barbiturate and Epanutin, which she's taken for decades, have finally had the effect she always feared. This is in part a story of a person who's had to struggle against the dulling that makes life livable, even as she finds a poetic subject in the 'abysms' and 'bolts' of illness.

Though my mother never read John Stuart Mill's *The Subjection of Women*, she came to the same conclusion that women's minds are even more vulnerable than their bodies to men who exercise unthinking authority. When I was her sister-child, she'd point out some man as 'a sadist'. Her chilling tone, and even more what she refrained from saying, drew me into the purview of Gothic horror. Her chief horror was the empowered medical man, who 'experiments on patients' or threatens a woman like herself with madness and incarceration.

In the background there was the spectre of Monica's mother –
put away when Monica was a baby – and many others (as Mary
Wollstonecraft testifies in *The Wrongs of Women*) who in one
way or another deviated from marital or maternal norms.

After my mother's post-partum crisis in 1944, she learnt to
conceal her oddity. As her sister, I knew from the age of four
that oddity was bound up with her rarity as an imaginative and
moral being. At the same time I was ashamed of her oddity, as
secretive as everyone else in our family, and often wished for an
ordinary mother. From the fifties to the eighties, the forty years
she was out in the world, she kept herself safe within women's
groups and, latterly, in the black and white women's friendship
club which brought out her freest verve.

In the later nineties Rhoda no longer left home.
With Olivia, then at Cambridge, Pip and Katie Erasmus

My brother does better by our mother. He takes her three times to consult Dr Frances Ames, Professor of Neurology at the University of Cape Town, who is alert to the individuality of memory loss. Dr Ames notes my mother's ploy to avert seizures by 'scrubbing' her palms. 'We should listen to patients,' she reminds her colleagues.

By the mid-nineties, journeys with my mother are fraught with difficulty. We drive for hours to Matjiesfontein to see a bare house, across the road from the railway station, where Olive Schreiner lived as a solitary, nursing her asthma in the dry Karoo air from 1890 to 1894. Here she wrote her *Dreams*, allegories of women to be. From this lone spot, one street ending in the veld, she spoke to the world. My mother is inattentive and finds the cutlery in the hotel unclean. Embarrassingly, she asks again and again for a fork to be replaced.

In December 1996 her brother Hubert dies, and we fly to Johannesburg for the funeral.

Next day we visit her middle brother, Sydney, at his home Inanda House. Sydney shows us around his indigenous garden, televised earlier in the day. It takes most of the morning to walk about the different gardens planted by his wife Victoria, a designer from New York with wonderful flair. Sydney is in his element, talking knowledgeably about trees and plants. He has imported some rare breed of grass, which remains green under a plantation of thick trees. I murmur 'a green thought in a green shade'. He recognises Marvell; he's a reader with his own formidable element of self-taught genius. He and Rhoda are too alike in their originality and self-absorption not to be strained when they are together, yet at a distance, he was attentive, sending her imaginative presents: a puffy chaise longue for reading; a light, warm-lined mac to wrap herself after swims.

That brilliant Highveld morning, where she has what is to be her last meeting with Sydney, she seems to accept his distance and keeps silent. I admire her restraint, for she'd like to reach through their reserve. But she judges correctly: their friction in the nursery and a lifetime's divide have held too long. He treats her with courtesy – 'mind that rock' or 'would you take some tea?' – yet his eyes turn away to his library, his trees, all that fulfilled the promise that had driven him. It was a long-ago vow to his shattered father after the Crash: 'I will save the family.' Whether these were his actual words, I don't know: by the time my mother passed them on, they were intoned as family myth.

Afterwards, my mother is fretful, and so disruptive on the plane coming back that it's impossible to contemplate her leaving home again.

By July–August 1999, my mother can sometimes no longer form a coherent sentence, though an urge to speak never leaves her.

I enter her room and find her wrestling with the phone; she wants to call Sydney, who died in 1997.

'Mommy.' I take the receiver from her, shaking my head. 'I have to tell you he died.'

Her face crumples. '*Don't* say.'

A moment later she's forgotten, and is phoning this brother again.

She's a prisoner in her own house, rattling the front door, locked in case she roams. To relieve this, I drive her to the mountainside gardens at Kirstenbosch, where she can roam freely. 'I'm feeling a little tired. Do you think we might go?' she says almost at once. I take a scenic route back via Hout Bay, but it's now, to her, alarmingly unfamiliar. 'If you don't mind, I think I'd like to go home,' she repeats uneasily all the way. By the time we turn into Avenue Normandie, in time for Friday night, she's so agitated that I'm afraid of her opening the car door and jumping out.

'Help me, help me,' she pleads, 'I'm ill ... ill ... ill.'

Misguidedly, I take her too suddenly off that addictive drug, Valium. She has a day or two of relief and natural happiness, followed by a seizure. 'It hurts,' she says, pointing to a bite at the side of her tongue. As I bend to look, we lock together. At night-time, we're alone in my flat overlooking the sea. I'm ironing, and she's seated near me with a cup of tea and a slice of cake. I open the sliding window and we lean out over a calm ocean beneath what she used to call 'a river of stars'. 'Beautiful,' she breathes. This scene holds in her memory whenever I bring it up, in the same way as she recalls peering into the lit houses on our evening walk in the climbing streets of Fresnaye. The old Rhoda is there when I read from *Poems on the Underground*, which I'd brought her a few years back. I read her favourites: 'Tyger Tyger, burning bright'; Milton's sonnet 'On his blindness'; Byron's 'So we'll go no more a-roving'; and 'O my Luve's like a red, red rose' by Robert Burns. Not twentieth-century poetry because she doesn't care for irony and mockery. Her affinities are still for the Romantics: the Wordsworth of the Immortality Ode with its memory of the child who trails clouds of glory from God, who is our home.

It was a mistake to take her off Valium while my brother, who monitored her pills, was away. She seems unsteady on her feet, and in September, after my return to England, she has three falls. Is her dose of her anticonvulsant drug, Epanutin, too low or too high? Doctors shift the dose this way or that, but she remains on the verge of seizures. The third fall breaks her arm. She can't understand why a cast is put on, and flails about

A last photo of Rhoda, taken by Pip, as they walk on the mountain

trying to rip it off. Instead of simply sedating her until she gets used to it, doctors decide on an operation to put a pin in. What they fail to consider is her state of mind: unfit for an unfamiliar place. After the operation she's wildly agitated in City Hospital, and the pin works loose. A second operation leaves her stupefied.

I fly overnight on Thursday, 30 September. Pip fetches me from the airport at six in the morning and fills me in as we drive through the bright air smelling of the sea.

'She doesn't want to live,' he says.

At home, I find her blank, eyes shut, refusing food.

It's obvious that the doctor, a locum GP, is overdosing her. He fancies a thyroid condition and won't listen when I say that it's not the case; nor does he want to hear about my mother's cramps from unnecessary purges.

'Can she be dying?' I ask. He concedes it could be.

'In that case, I'd like to have another opinion.'

The doctor stiffens unwillingly. My tactlessness does my mother no good. I've let him see how much I detest a know-all whose ego is fragile. The consultant doesn't return my call – she works through GPs, of course.

Something else does my mother no good, something I hide but she will sense. It's the trough a writer can fall into between books. No matter what has come before, it can be daunting to start again with an inchoate mass of material – what Yeats called, in creative terms, 'the dark of the moon'; it's easy to wonder if you can ever approach the full of the moon again. It's a year since I brought out a biography of two women and Henry James, and during this year I've done outlines for two very different subjects, one mysteriously private, Emily Dickinson, and the other a public figure, Mary Wollstonecraft. My New York agent likes the Dickinson proposal; my London agent would prefer to leave it for the time being. The outcome is still uncertain, and to keep the future at bay during the wakeful hours of the night, I tap out a diary on my laptop.

Saturday, 2 October 1999

It was a shock to see her sunk in what looks like a pre-death daze. Beyond speech, immobile, fed by syringe in the corner of a resistant mouth. In the afternoon, just before her onslaught of drugs, she opened her blue eyes – they stared at nothing, unseeing or not naming what she saw. She looked stripped, washed clean of life. At times, there is a hint of recognition – a faint smile in my direction when I said, 'I've been reading your writings on the plane,' and quoted 'Klaver'. A similar quiver back to life when I read aloud from passages she had marked in the psalms: how the Lord will restore thy soul. I speak in her own terms, reminding her that she is 'never alone'.

Mary, the night nurse, aged about fifty, has a round, smooth brown face with a merry smile. She said that she prays 'with your mother' through the night. 'I lay on hands,' she told me. She had wanted to be missionary, not a nursing aid, but there was no money for missionary school in a family of twelve children where the mother didn't work. We agreed that, in our generation, women working has caused problems in family life that didn't exist for our mothers.

This morning, when I came in to see my mother, Mary said she liked my brown Ghost dress. My mother smiled when I spoke to her, though she barely opened her lids. They say she's improved since I came, but it hardly seems so to me. Until now, when people have expected me to be shocked by my mother's condition, I'd felt that the real Rhoda was reachable – it was increasingly difficult, but alone with me, she would respond, even to humour when I read 'will you, won't you, will you, won't you, will you join the dance?'

Monday, 4 October 1999

Yesterday there was a breakthrough of sorts. It may not be due to my presence, alone; more likely to her own resilience and to the tender, skilled nursing of Evie (by day) and Mary (at night). 'Rhodie,' Evie coaxes her to swallow, stroking her arm. 'Do it for me.' Since I came last Thursday my mother had said only 'Sh ... Sh ... ' or 'mm ... mm', which seemed, together with her closely shut, almost pointed lips, a negation of life. But yesterday it was as though she woke up and began to find a few words, though a lot is inarticulate babbling, oddly enough in Afrikaans – '. . . *hy is . . . sy is . . . altyd . . . almal . . . kom weer . . . koer . . . koer*'.

'Koer sounds like a bird's call,' I ventured, but this didn't tell – she wants to shape real words, and make them intelligible. She wants to communicate in Afrikaans, perhaps reverting to her early schooldays.

'*Almal, ja. Ons is almal hier,*' I said, face to face as she lay back on the bed. I was groping for words unused since I left the country in 1964. '*Evie is hier; Mary is hier; jou seun, Pip, kom weer môre, en ek is hier – ek is jou dogter, 'n dogter moet met her moeder wees.*'

She seemed to like this statement of duty, and took it as meant – not bare duty but a condition of being a daughter. '*Ons is familie,*' I repeated, feeling my way into this passage of forgotten words that rolled their own way, it seemed, from ages past.

Once again Rhoda nodded into my eyes, before lapsing into her daze. It's strange to be speaking to my mother in a language we've never used between us, but which appears to be the deepest residual language still in her.

Now and then, she's listening and even smiling when I repeat her name and her past, as though those facts gave her back herself.

'You are Rhoda,' I said, looking into her newly opened eyes. She nodded.

'Rhoda Stella Press from Klaver.' Another nod.

It's extraordinary how fast one's standards change: I was shocked at first; now am pleased to see the smallest improvement: open eyes, clear blue; words, in place of 'sh . . . sh . . . '; the odd smile; the flashes of recognition.

My mother still won't eat, and I've wondered if it is the

body's way of saying that this life should end. My impulse is NO. I want her to go on, to enter into the exchange of words, the taste of ice-cream, the ocean seething since Genesis – all she had before.

5 a.m. Tuesday, 5 October 1999

My mother took food willingly for the first time last night, opening her mouth for the chicken soup and then banana mashed with ice-cream. Yet I'm angry with doctors, who behave with extraordinary authoritarianism when they are in the dark: it was a wrong decision to operate even the first time on a woman in my mother's complex condition. An arm that might heal crooked is less important than a fragile mind.

My brother called in a psychiatrist. He came looking unprofessional, gross, as though he had rolled out of bed. He hardly stopped to speak to me, let alone the patient he'd come to see.

'Is she aggressive?' he asked abruptly. 'I believe she was aggressive.'

He made no attempt to know her; simply sat down at a desk and went into the prescribing routine.

Mary recalls instances where she made a correct diagnosis from experience, which the doctor would ignore. English-speaking doctors trained during apartheid will normally ignore Mary's intelligence, located as it is in a coloured woman who speaks the Afrikaans-English of the meaner streets.

She relishes language, and taught me the latest retort to a person, often older, who doesn't get the point: '*kom reg*', literally 'come right'. She likes my mother rambling in Afrikaans.

'Now you're speaking my language,' she says to her fondly. '*Lekker soppies,*' she smiled into Rhoda's wide eyes as she fed her mushroom soup.

They talk all night. When I can't sleep and pad up the passage towards my mother's room I hear '*asseblief tog . . . sê vir my . . .*' between her brief and urgent breaths.

Over Rhoda's restless body, I asked Mary how she bears the long hours of the night.

'I pray,' she said. 'I want to be something for others. If I'd been a proper nurse, I'd have been running things. This way I am close to people.'

I opened a chest of drawers in my mother's bedroom and found (as remembered) tapes of her classes and a typescript of a talk on Abraham, which opened with God's trials of this chosen man.

When I read this aloud to Rhoda, it roused her from her half-awake look to full attention.

'Like your own life with its trials,' I said, stroking the cast on her right arm. 'You are going through a trial now, and are learning, still, how to live.'

'*Ja,*' she nodded, putting up her hand to stroke my cheek with a tender look. It took me back to childhood, when I was entirely hers. The years of emotional estrangement recede into the wash of time. What's present is Rhoda's noble face – rather thinner, her high nose and white hair on the pillow of the hospital bed Pip hired. I see, sometimes, the girl she was with the dark skin and brown crinkly hair swept back, as that night when she lay on Lou's tweed arm in the dicky of the car and the stars were blown about the sky. There are flashes of her old intentness. These return me to the fullness of a daughter's tie to her mother as author of her being: awareness of others, words, nature and all that makes life quicken. I have the strongest sense of that mentor-mother still here, dimmed (as she's feared) by the pills, but rising again and yet again to the surface, which is why I don't want her to go.

Wednesday, 6 October 1999

The sawbones came yesterday to take out her stitches. When the cast was cut loose we saw a great cut up her arm, still looking raw. The doctor moved the arm rather roughly and my mother cried out 'Agony!'

'Please hold it,' I begged, but he went on with the job, smiling imperturbably.

'She's exaggerating,' he said, and the GP, who was there, backed him.

'But this is a brave woman,' I said tightly. To show fury wouldn't help. 'She never, ever complained of pain.' How easily the helpless are sealed off unknown, as Rhoda was largely unknown throughout her life.

The GP agreed to lessen the dosage, and she did pretty quickly gain animation; in fact, from the afternoon through the night, too much. It's a wall of words. If I say 'Rhoda!' her eyes turn, but almost at once return to their inward fixity. She's trying to say something, and her face at such times gains a meaningful look. There's a long way to go: she has to learn to walk again; and we have to get the medication right so that she doesn't talk all night. I've thought of Iris Murdoch refusing food, and John Bayley accepting this. Was it the humane thing to do, not to prolong so faded a life? Am I doing right by my mother who is unable to speak for herself? I look into her eyes and say, 'Tell me, I have to know as your daughter: are you unhappy?' Before, when I asked that question, she hugged me and indicated that she was happy enough. Now she listens but with some barrier between us. Her sound-language is often unhappy: a lot of 'mm . . . mmm' from tight-pressed lips.

Pip took me to task for taking Rhoda off Valium in his absence last August.

'But she was saying "help, oh help me",' I protested. 'She was having panic attacks. The Valium seemed to be doing no good, and for two days it was bliss.'

'It was a DISASTER,' Pip shouted.

I walked out onto the stoep, paced a bit, then came back to say how much I've regretted this.

'It's my personality,' Pip said apologetically, when he calmed down.

'That's no excuse,' I retorted. I was compelled (though close to tears) to stand up to him.

Friday, 7 October 1999

Rhoda, even in her medicated state, charmed the new day nurse, Lulu (a Xhosa). She has an extraordinary attraction for anyone who serves her – what is it? She looks dignified, leaning back with eyes closed, her white hair swept away from her high nose and forehead. Then she will open clear blue eyes and smile gratefully into the face of a nurse, murmuring 'thank you', even though she can barely speak.

She was her 'real' self for about an hour yesterday afternoon: I read the closing lines of the Immortality Ode: 'To me the meanest flower that blows can give / Thoughts that do often lie too deep for tears.' She gave me that lovely smile of attention, so I read next the sonnet on Westminster Bridge. 'Beautiful' she breathed at 'all that mighty heart is lying still!'

Her well-worn anthology of English poems is inscribed 'Rhoda Stella Press, Good Hope Seminary, 1933'. It's full of notes and underlining, and includes a date, July 1938 [four months after Lou died], next to a heavy line under 'Dear as remembered kisses after death ... and wild with all regret; / O Death in Life, the days that are no more.'

As I read aloud to her, in the late afternoon when the effect of the pills wears off, I mull over the unlikely life of this housewife who 'felt through all this fleshly dress / Bright shoots of everlastingness'. Henry Vaughan speaks to her, and her eye meets Wordsworth's 'inward eye'. She too has seen 'gleams of past existence'. I choose poems that she has underlined – the only words to rouse her. For they speak to a part of her that lies deeper than memories: her intimations of eternity interfused with the face of creation, which for her are not daffodils on verdant English slopes around the Lakes but the harsh, unbroken horizons of Africa.

She completes certain lines, speaking in unison. Together she and the Psalmist walk 'with' their God.

When it comes to human ties, she joins Wordsworth on fraternal love, 'my dear, dear Sister . . . ', as Dorothy had been to him in their youth, when they trod their way above Tintern Abbey in Wales. Rhoda's sedated expression lights up; she looks into my eyes as I read. It's not me she sees, and the 'dear, dear Sister' is not Dorothy, but what she herself has been to Basil, dearest to her from the time he pulled a nail from her foot when he was six and she five years old in the dusty veld where they played.

I say to her GP, 'She remembers more than ninety-nine per cent of your patients ever knew.'

He is not impressed, and smiles kindly as he opens the gate to leave.

Sunday, 9 October 1999

Yesterday, after Evie managed to walk her to the lounge window, she sat on one of the dining-room chairs saying 'beautiful' as she looked out on the stoep, the vine just sprouting, the 'moon-flower' tree and what she called 'my mountain'. It was the pleasure of the patient who's been in bed for weeks, looking out on the world once more.

Pip dropped by this afternoon, on his way to a rugby match.

'Come and sit down,' I said, turning to the dining room.

'I have to make a call,' he said, bringing in the phone, but catching my look of surprise, didn't pick up the receiver. Just then, Evie produced our mother walking towards him.

'You're helping others to help you,' he approved. 'That's what I'm always telling you, Mom, you must help others to help you.' It's a more humorous tone than he sometimes takes with me, as one who's here to do his bidding.

'Speak English!' he pressed Rhoda, though her Afrikaans is idiomatic and rather amazing, as though the different being language brings out had been lurking there since early childhood.

'I'll try then,' she answered with the merest edge. We laughed.

'You're condescending to her, and she hears it,' I said.

He glanced at his watch. 'I'll be late for the match.' She'd been looking his way with delight, and was, I think, taken aback.

'You know that we love each other,' Pip said, kissing her goodbye.

'I don't know about that,' she retorted with a sudden return of spirit.

Later, when I sat on her bed and went over her life, she listened intently. Sometimes she put up her hand to stroke my face or hair. Once she held a strand of my hair, twisting it in a curl, round and round, as she used to make ringlets or curl her own hair while she was thinking. 'Blessings,' she said amidst the broken sentences. 'Goodbye.'

Wednesday, 12 October 1999

Reading my mother's poems and fragments, I'm struck by work a world apart from poems published in the lingering tail of the twentieth century. Their tiny ironies are post–post-Eliot, without the bolt of the 'unattended moments'. Rhoda's poems are visions, trials and prayers like the psalms.

Yesterday, the nurse who stood in for Eve put my mother to bed at four o'clock. She was tired, the nurse claimed. At six I had to stop her forcing pills on my mother's resistant lips. There has to be constant vigilance.

Thursday 13 October 1999

It is 5.45 a.m. and I've been awake since after one, reading Simon Brett's anthology of diarists – unexpected that I find more in Noel Coward and Barbara Pym than in esteemed diarists like Pepys, Evelyn or Fanny Burney (except one entry where she ran from the cries of a beaten dog). Of course I delighted in Virginia Woolf, Katherine Mansfield and Frances Partridge. Muggeridge, a loathsome man. Reading through the night was not a compulsive pleasure; it's become a way of holding off bad thoughts.

At 5.30 I took my coffee to the gate and looked my last on the outlines of Lion's Head and Signal Hill against the lightening sky.

Today, if my mother can walk (supported) to the car, I plan to take her to the sea for a drive. She seemed to like the idea. She's now calling me by name. Sometimes, I catch meaning in the jolting words. That catch at meaning comes from my knowledge of her and her past. No one else could do it, and this makes me uneasy about returning to England tomorrow. One moment she seems on course to modified recovery; another moment she looks dazed and disturbingly still.

I will regret leaving to my own dying day. Her two last words, when I phone from Oxford, are: 'Come home.' Hearing that she's eating well, dressing each morning and managing to walk, I put this off.

Sitting in her dining room with Maria, her companion, on 27 October, she states calmly, 'I think it's time for me to go.' She sinks outside her house four days later, a Sunday. On Monday morning Maria finds her transfigured with 'innocence'; the lines smoothed out, she looks 'like an eighty-year-old child'. She dies on Tuesday 2 November 1999.

Echoes of Kinship

'Souls live on in perpetual echoes,' George Eliot said. Is the end of a life the beginning of that life's reverberation in other lives? A biographer tunes in to echoes in the wake of a life and tests their authenticity. A daughter or son looks for the imprint of a life on the next and following generations. My mother's imprint is clearest on Anna, who at the age of four stood with her grandmother at the prayer door, alive to her 'awakened heart'.

'It was not about words,' she remembers. 'It was a meeting with a wordless self, entirely inward and silent.'

Anna is in India when she hears. She is carrying some of her grandmother's poems, and she sends 'The Priestess' with a fax for the rabbi to read aloud.

She looked after me as a baby when my mother was ill and she was a second mother to me. She gave me the greatest gift it is possible to give: she taught me, as a child, to be attentive the sound of the ocean, to see the mountain, to open my heart, to stand at the door of the sunroom and pray.

She told me stories for hours, late into the night. Under the pink duvet we ate peeled apples and argued about right and wrong through the ancient stories. I was titillated by the Canaanites and their orgies, while Gran was repelled. I could not understand why it was wrong to eat of the tree of knowledge and anyway, if it was God's will to create flawed people, what was he complaining about? I said it was wrong of Abraham to bind his son [for sacrifice], that a parent should put a child before duty, even to God. Gran always took God's side.

I'd thought my mother on course to recovery, and sent my passport for renewal to the South African office in London, with a view to seeing her in December. When she dies, the office won't speed up the process, so I'm not at the funeral.

At eleven in the morning, on Friday 5 November, Rhoda is buried beside Harry in the Jewish cemetery at Pinelands. Berjulie is the first to arrive, all the way from Canada. She does a quick round of family graves and favours Pip with her opinion that our father's shows the most spit and polish. Pip had the forethought to have the stone cleaned. He's helped, he says, by making arrangements. I'm helped by a stranger's meditation on death. My one-time editor and friend, Marie Philip, passed on these words by Harry Scott Holland, a Canon of St Paul's Cathedral, which Marie read, she says, when her mother died:

I have only slipped away into the next room. I am I, and you are you. Whatever we were to each other, that we still are. Call me by my old familiar name, speak to me ... Put no difference in your tone, wear no forced air of solemnity or sorrow. Laugh as we always laughed at the little jokes we enjoyed together ... I am waiting for you, for an interval, somewhere very near ...

That afternoon I walk from the Tube at Marble Arch down Park Lane to Grosvenor House to see my cousin Barbara, eldest daughter to Uncle Hubert, who now lives in New York.

At a quarter to four, the November day is drawing in. Looking up at the bare trees of Hyde Park against the darkening sky, I see a world without my mother. Do I want to live in it? But of course, I do.

'Do you miss Uncle Hubert?' I ask Barbara.

'Terribly. I look for men who can teach me things. I've been going out with a man who is well-educated, who meets my train with bagels and cheese, who's even Jewish, but he spends his time raising money for Harvard. Why not raise money for the poor? I can't connect with him. I see men with this quality or that, but no one who has them all like my father.'

That evening, at a family Friday night, I see my mother's last remaining brother, Basil, who is eighty-four today. He has the long jawline of the Presses and likes to tell a story against himself. As a schoolboy, he relates, he asked my mother to help him with an English essay. She wrote the introduction and conclusion, and Basil filled in the sandwich. His master's comment was 'very good at the start and finish, but *poorish* in the middle.' When he and my mother were together, she'd be talking, she'd remember, while Basil would be thoughtfully munching leftovers from the fridge. He played up this Pooh Bear character, and played down his wisdom.

'Pooh was a bear of enormous brain,' he'd recite with relish when I was a child.

'Of enormous *what*?' I fill in, as he nods the cue.

'Well, he ate a lot.'

My mother adored 'my big brother Basil' for his stability, the opposite of her delicate frame and excitable imagination. Basil, immaculate in a blue tie and dark, well-cut suit, is not too well, and in London to consult a cardiologist. Yet he's serene, as my mother would say, admiring a temperament unlike her own.

'You still have an uncle,' he says as I bend to kiss him.

Next day, preparing lunch for friends, I switch on the radio this Saturday morning: it's Classic FM's hit parade.

'This was number one in 1916,' the announcer says, breaking the countdown with a curiosity. 'Caruso in *Santa Lucia*.'

Crackling through the old record, the great voice rises over the veld, rises and falls, and fountains higher, as Rhoda lifts her head in her candlelit room.

The day after the funeral, something strange happens to Anna in India. She's thinking of her gran, wishing she'd been with her, when an unknown Norwegian woman approaches with a box. It's a surprise, this woman says. Inside is a white and gold kitten, which a friend had sent to comfort Anna. The kitten, chosen from strays at an animal sanctuary, had been on a thirteen-hour bus journey.

'I took him home,' Anna relates over the phone, 'and tried to give him food and drink but he refused to take more than a sip or two. An hour later he had what looked like an epileptic fit or heart attack, and reminded of Gran, I held him on my heart, willing him to live. But fifteen minutes later it happened again – and again and again. Four times he recovered and slept, and the fifth time died in my arms. I dug a hole between the sea and the river, and I felt the body freeze into an empty shell as I carried the kitten wrapped in a shawl to his grave.'

On the phone, Anna and I agree, as Anna puts it, that 'Gran formed us, she made us who we are, and I still feel her living inside me. I feel her now, a part of me.' Their closeness resounds in a startling comeback of her grandmother's voice almost two years later. On Anna's birthday, 9 August 2001, I'm away from home when she switches on the answering machine and to her amazement hears, she reports, 'a birthday message from my departed Gran. The machine went "... crackle, crackle ... I want to find Anna. I want to wish her a happy birthday."'

Anna concedes a logical explanation, that the answering machine was retrieving a message from the distant past. 'But even so, the timing was a coincidence.'

The message stirs Anna to say what she believes. 'I feel that we are always here, in one form or another, that our spirit is never born and never dies. So, if we miss someone who has passed, we can simply become still and feel the spirit of that person within the silence of the heart. We can learn to commune with the dead, as my dear grandmother reached out to me.'

I too have received a message of sorts. On Friday 19 November 1999, seventeen days after Rhoda's death, Maria phones to report a curious incident. When she moved my mother's desk, it collapsed, including the shelf of books at the back. One paperback, *The Bible and the Common Reader* by Mary Ellen Chase, a teacher at Smith College, fell open at the back flyleaf. And there, on that page, is an undated letter to me. My mother pencilled it on Rocklands beach, rocky, shelly, strewn with brown fronds of seaweed, where she used to swim, in the company of six diehards, throughout the winter. The icy water woke her from hated drugs. Towards the end her voice blends with an echo of the fourteenth-century visionary, Dame Julian of Norwich, who bore the scourge of the Black Death saying, 'All shall be well, and all manner of thing shall be well.'

Dearest Lyn –

When it's so exquisite as it was at Rocklands this morning I long to share it with someone & think of you – the sea was so serene & crystal with one ship on the horizon. I thought of Sirkka too & the spiritual joy that is

part of her lake-bathe. I thought of death & suddenly
heard across the sea & calm horizon all was well. The dark
background to life disappeared – this was Reality.

Have I a right to comfort? It would have been right to heal
our divide by yielding to what's wise in the scriptures. Would
it? I think back to one Day of Atonement when I'm fourteen,
standing beside her in Sea Point. I'm bored and privately at odds
with the dressy, sidelined girls, while the men sway (a gesture of
fervour traditionally reserved for males) and chant, 'Our Father,
our King, we have sinned before Thee.' The three Schiff sisters
make an entrance, flouncing down the aisle in new spring outfits with cinched waists and stiff petticoats. They apologise
profusely as they press their way into the front row, visible to
men. My mind flicks to iced cakes in the window of Maison
Mayfair on the Main Road; to youth leaders in the Movement,
where my mother has sent me to learn more about Our People;
and to one in particular with green eyes and a country accent
who dances in brown slippers because, people say, he's too poor
to afford shoes. They say he came first in matric. It's like the
start of a story to be so poor and brainy. The Movement urges
members to go to Israel, and my mother has promised to take
me when she visits someone very special at the end of the year.

'Our Father, our King, we have sinned before thee,' the
cantor laments in Hebrew with elaborate musical embellish-
ments. '*Hetanu lefanehah.*' The closely packed congregation takes
up the lament. '*Selag lanu, kaper lanu.*' Forgive us, let us atone.

She stands still in her plain dress and hat, absorbed in prayer
through all the hours of the fast. Her prayer book is open to the
list of sins: we have made false promises, we have been wanton,
we have corrupted, we have spread gossip, we have bad-
mouthed others. My mother fancies the prayer book's verbal
picture of 'running to do evil'. Not just evil, but running to do

it. Glancing my way, her finger points to the sin of the stiff-necked.

In 2003, my mother's friend Lilian Henry comes to England to stay with Vanessa, her adored granddaughter. At eighty-six, she travels alone by bus to Oxford. She brings the best gift ever: a typescript memoir of a youth shared with my mother, and filled with comic stories of the characters she lived amongst on Piketberg Mountain. She has a flair for stories, which I imagine comes from her Irish parents. At the dark end of a winter day we walk arm in arm through the rumbling bus station, and kiss goodbye as if for the last time.

'Another kiss for your mother,' she says.

Rhoda called Hubert's youngest daughter 'a story-book girl'. Linda was a child-reader of old-fashioned children's books. In 2006, as Linda Press Wulf, she writes a novel for children called *The Night of the Burning*. It's the story of Linda's mother-in-law Devorah Lehrman, who, aged twelve, is telling her story as a terrified survivor of a pogrom by Cossacks and neighbours on the Polish–Russian border. She becomes one of a number of orphans whom Isaac Ochberg ('Daddy Ochberg') transports from Poland to Oranjia. This was 1922, twenty years before my mother ran the library at Oranjia, but Linda imagines my mother into that scene under her second, preferred name. 'Once a week the library was opened by blue-eyed Miss Stella, who loved books as intensely as I did. As she walked down the orphanage corridor with her keys, calling to us like the Pied Piper, children rushed to choose the book they would borrow but especially to hear the stories she read aloud.'

As it happened, my mother never read stories aloud in the library – there was no time because so many orphans were lining up to check out books and receive their kiss. Her reading aloud is Linda's own memory of sitting beside her aunt in the sunroom as she introduced old-fashioned home girls, *Emily of New Moon* or *Little Women*, to a smiley blonde child, her little tongue curling excitedly around her lisp. The novel's dedication is in part 'For my Aunty Rhoda in the book-lined house on Avenue Normandie.'

Other echoes resonate from Rhoda's meeting with Sirkka Anttila, the Finnish sybil who in the summer of 1952 sent her on her way with awakened purpose. In late March 2002 Siamon attends an immunological conference in Oulu, in northern Finland, and on an impulse, he hunts up Sirkka's phone number in Helsinki.

The bold vigour of Sirkka's voice bursts out. 'All my inner life same with Rhoda. Not to be separated. All inner existence. Precious moments – all light Rhoda. Now, near to death, one only thankful and conscious. Brain is ischaemic, not to write or work, but still sense of humour and deeply conscious of life, death, eternity. Some way at home already.'

Sirkka, now eighty-four, lives on her own in Kallio, meaning hilltop, and (as I saw later) the flat is indeed on a hill overlooking the city. Sirkka's bedroom looks the other way, towards a church: a small, bare room with an iron bedstead. The flat is filled with Finnish folk art, including the three painted spindles Sirkka, aged twenty, rescued by night from behind the Russian lines during the Winter War. There's a portrait of her with her one-time husband Touko Markkanen, both in black and smouldering: two forceful characters. Touko had a hunchback, and Sirkka took to him the same year, 1953, as my mother sent her *The Little Locksmith*. Here are Sirkka's own publications: her '*mystikko*' poems, *Näkymättömän hymy*; a diary following her conversion to the Russian Orthodox church, when she entered, for a time, the Heinvesi Monastery of

Valamo; and a diary from the Winter War period, September 1939 to March 1940, published in 2000. Books lining the walls have the look of books that are looked at.

Still on the line to Siamon, Sirkka turns to these shelves. 'Books full of Jewish things sent by Rhoda.' She opens a copy of Buber's *I and Thou* sent from New York in 1966, and reads aloud the inscription: '"My sister Sirkka, Sirkka my dear and near one, I had a dark summer during which I have written to you, but none of these letters can be sent." Hey-hey.'

The final echoes are brief – a voice urging my mother to go alone into the arctic wilderness of Pallastunturi. 'Rhoda ... Rhoda ... Choice of life. Focus. Lapland. Boots.'

In the summer of 2004 I hear that Sirkka can no longer live unaided and has moved to a kind of sanatorium in the woods. That August I suggest coming to see her.

Dear Sirkka,

　　You may not remember me, the daughter of your 'sister'-friend, Rhoda. I found your letters to her, and would like to bring them to you, if I may. If you can put up with a visitor, I'd very much like to visit and read to you from these poetic letters (I understand that your eyesight is not good), and place them in your archive at the Finnish Literature Society.

　　I have lovely memories of staying with you in your lake place at Ukonvuori when your children were small, and your reading the *Kalevela* aloud in a rocking chair in front of the fire.

　　　　　　　　　　　　　Hoping we may see each other,
　　　　　　　　　　　　　　　　　　　Lyndall

On Sunday 29 August Sirkka's daughter, Saara Markkanen, who is my mother's goddaughter, takes me to her mother's flat.

It's about to be sold, and this is the last day or two, Saara says, that the flat is still intact. From there we drive to the sanatorium. On the way Saara warns me that Sirkka can no longer recognise visitors, not even her daughter.

The architecture, not drawing attention to itself, is extraordinary with light filtering through the leaves of the woods. Sirkka, whom I last saw in 1964, is seated at a table, grey of course, but her high cheekbones and slanting dark eyes are familiar. They look hard at me, and then at the photograph of my mother that I place in front of her. Suddenly her eyes light up and a smile of wonder breaks upon her face. I put down the letters on the table and as I read a few extracts aloud she beams, not speaking but strongly present. Then she tires and is led off to her room. Her mother's awakening is so unexpected to Saara that she's in tears.

Sirkka's papers are in the Finnish National Archives. I page through the Finnish of Sirkka's pocket diary until I come upon my mother's name on Wednesday 23 July 1952. The archivist, Anna Makkonen, translates Sirkka's first sight of Rhoda in the gallery: '*I met a woman writer at the Ateneum. Dark, wearing glasses, intelligent sensibility.*' There's our old address, 11 Avenue Normandie, Cape Town, and our old phone number, 46376 – I can hear her dialling Mrs Bass, the fishmonger, and her tired voice giving the order.

Amongst Sirkka's papers are my mother's letters. Weird to open a box in Helsinki and find her hand. '*I shall never forget that blessed time with you in Finland which shall live forever reincarnated perhaps as one of those gleams that grace a moment in future lives.*' That was at the end of 1958, when Sirkka gave birth to her twins, Antti and Anna.

Since Sirkka died, Saara and I keep in touch. 'You write vividly, as your mother did to mine,' I email her in 2008. 'My mother used to read aloud parts of Sirkka's letters. Her English, my mother said, was "vibrant", injecting something Finnish into English, which made us feel our language afresh ... I remember when you were born, and Sirkka sent a photo of you propped on her shoulder with her dark head turned tenderly towards you.'

As godmother, my mother kept Saara's drawings which, she told Sirkka, 'bring her close to me (leaning against my knees almost, with her hands in my lap in preparation for a story)', and she pored over the photos showing 'the shape of Saara's lovely head, her intense narrowed eyes' that came in fat envelopes with Finnish stamps. 'She sounds such a clever little girl whose way of being is so precious to me that I dare not speak of it,' she wrote to Sirkka in 1958 when Saara was three.

Mothering like this is universal, and yet it was rare for Saara and me to be daughters of women who lived for an infinity beyond human ties. In this sense our mothers were solitary and insistently obscure. Their triumph was to be the obverse of a celebrity who, like Emily Dickinson's frog, tells his name the livelong June to a surrounding Bog. A month after Sirkka and my mother part, Sirkka reveals herself as one who glides by in a silence where she's nothing. Life is 'moving nothingness'. So she puts it, on 7 September 1952, to Rhoda in London. Dickinson's sassy voice echoes behind them: 'I'm Nobody! Who are you? Are you – Nobody – too? Why then there's a pair of us.' Only when we accept nothingness, Sirkka adds, 'one is free to smile'.

A package from Japan arrives one day. In it are two landscapes. The artist, Yoshiko Aya, explains that the paintings are inspired by my mother's poems: 'Dawn' is based on the poem 'Klaver', and 'Morning Sky' on 'The Priestess'. Can this be another Meeting of my mother with a stranger, kin of her soul, from a far-off land?

It so happened that, twenty years ago, a graduate student from Tokyo came to St Hilda's College in Oxford. She was Atsuko Hayakawa from Tsuda College, founded by Madame Tsuda on the model of St Hilda's. As a very young woman, Tsuda had been one of the first students at St Hilda's after the college for women was founded in 1893. Atsuko brought me a miniature of a group of intrepid Japanese girls in search of education, standing in their kimonos at the prow of a vessel outward bound on its long way to the West. Tsuda is the smallest in the row of girls who lean ahead in their keenness to learn. Atsuko herself had been a pupil of Virginia Woolf's Japanese translator, and in Oxford she completed an insightful and delicately-worded thesis on Woolf's short fiction. Atsuko has since become a professor at Tsuda College, where she teaches a translation course.

During 2012 Atsuko returned to Oxford on sabbatical. When I talked of my mother, she asked if she might have copies of two poems. And this is how Yoshiko Aya came to read these poems, translated by Atsuko, her friend. Aya's vistas of dream-like light are Japanese landscapes with subtle colours, brush strokes and untouched space, cooler than Africa yet Aya's sky is tinged with the gold-smoke that crossed the veld to my mother as a child.

Ours is a dispersed generation. When we sailed to New York in 1965 we knew no one. By 2010, a number of younger cousins have settled there. Basil's daughter Jennifer, married to a New Yorker, has a party at Sotheby's, where she works. It's largely a family party for the publication of my new biography: a book on Emily Dickinson. Barbara comes, lovelier than ever. She has a weekly programme on local radio, discussing Jewish issues with a rabbi. Her brother Donald is accompanied by his partner John. Don is making a fold-out family tree, a work of intricate discovery. Uncle Sydney's daughter Caroline, a reader with tastes close to mine, manages a downtown newspaper. And Fran Miller, a teacher, comes, the daughter of my mother's long-lost cousin Ben, the only one from the Old Country to survive the Holocaust.

I stay with Jen in her apartment on East 79th Street. After the party, we look at a photo of my mother and Basil, who died in July 2003. They sit on his stoep looking out on False Bay. There's that glow in Rhoda's face whenever she's with him. 'Their love had no dross in it,' I murmur to Jen, 'no bad thought ever, though they were so different.'

Jen waits with me at the corner as we signal for a cab. I'm off to Penn Station to catch the train to Albany, and there, a limo from the summer writing course at Bennington College will take me into Vermont. Every June, for the last eleven years, I've travelled north along the Hudson River, recalling each time how Henry James made this journey by boat to visit his Albany grandmother. James, aged two, would hear, through the night, the hoots and churnings of the river traffic.

'Your father loved family tales,' I say to Jen as a cab pulls over to the sidewalk. I bung my case in the boot while the driver waits at the stop light for the midtown traffic roaring down Lexington Avenue.

'Those tales,' Jen says. 'Don has discovered that, in 1894, at the station when our grandfather left, his father, Benjamin, tried to wrest the ticket from his son. He thought he should go instead.'

The traffic light is changing. The cab revs.

Suddenly I remember something my mother said, her idea that her father, at the age of fifteen or sixteen, had a breakdown before he took off. If that happened, it would have added to the distress of the scene. Benjamin, she said, fainted at the station. It was not in his nature to leave home and he would never see his son again.

*

Tales make life, make us what we are. These days I tell tales to Olivia's son, the same as my mother told to me. Humphrey is in the neonatal ward at University College Hospital in London for his first five months. Then he goes to Great Ormond Street, where an Australian surgeon, Miss Cross, undertakes a long operation on a stomach that has yet to mature.

'When you're a big boy,' I tell him, 'you'll go to Cherry Tree Wood, and there will be . . . ' and I picture the world he's not yet seen. 'Shall I tell you about the Bad Rabbit?' Humphrey's lips part, revealing his first tooth, as Peter Rabbit crunch-crunches on a carrot in Mr McGregor's garden. His serious eyes fix on mine as Mr McGregor comes on the scene, waving a rake and shouting, 'Stop, thief!' Then Humph smiles when I pant with Peter, 'huh, huh, huh', as he makes a dash for his mother's burrow. A new life quickens to the age-old tale of risk and home.

Glossary

bather bathing costume or swimsuit

coloured people of mixed race. In the apartheid hierarchy, the 'coloureds', as they were called, were second-class citizens who came between the whites and the third class, known as 'natives' – the black descendants of Bantu-speaking peoples, Xhosa, Zulu, Sotho etc

dennepits pine nuts

dicky a minute, unroofed back seat to a car, carved out of its boot. It held two windblown passengers, tightly pressed. Dickies were packed with partying boys and girls in Cape Town in the thirties and forties

dorp small village, sometimes used affectionately or pejoratively as a place of no importance

fynbos the indigenous flora of the Cape of Good Hope, with thousands of species unique to the region

gits a revision of 'gats' which is a euphemism for God in the context of surprise or disturbance. The closest English equivalent would be 'golly'. (Afrikaans, pronounced with a soft 'g'. With thanks to Anita Visser)

impi military platoon (Zulu)

joller a hedonist given to sprees

kiddush grace before meals, always recited by a male, on the Sabbath eve and on holy days

klaver clover. Because the dorp had this name, it's fair to surmise that clover grew easily in the region. It was one of our grandfather's crops. The correct (Afrikaans) spelling is

Klawer, but the place name was spelt Klaver by English
speakers, including our family, in the first half of the twentieth century. Either way, the pronunciation is the same

kloof narrow passage between two mountain peaks

melktert milk tart, a Dutch South African delicacy

mielie corn on the cob

Nederlandskultuurgeskiedenis Dutch cultural history

Olifantsrivier Elephant river, so called in the eighteenth century
by the first colonial explorers of the north-west Cape, who
saw elephants bathing there. No elephants remained in my
grandparents' time

ozeret literally, servant, but intending to convey a sense of
domestic drudge

riempies leather thongs

sabra native-born Israeli

shaliah (plural *shlihot*) emissary (Hebrew)

shtetl Yiddish for a small Jewish village in Lithuania, the
Ukraine and other areas of north-eastern Europe

skiet and donder shoot and rough-up, as in low-grade films and
novels from overseas, marketed to the violent townships. The
literal translation of *donder* is 'thunder', so that the meaning
is somewhat stronger than 'rough up'

stoep veranda

tackies plimsolls or trainers

tickeys three-penny bits

Notes

1. 'Sister'

3 *'dwelt among the untrodden ways'*: 'She dwelt among the untrodden ways' is one of Wordsworth's Lucy poems (1799). Both this poem and 'Strange fits of passion' are about a dead woman who was true to her untrammelled nature, like the poet's beloved sister Dorothy.

4 *'Colossal substance of Immortality'*: Emily Dickinson, 'The Soul's Superior instants'.

5 *'Great Balls of Fire'*: A rock 'n' roll number performed by Jerry Lee Lewis.

2. Mothers

21 *Kausanai forest*: Simon Schama opens up the fate of his own Plunge family in *The Story of the Jews*, BBC 2, November 2013.

27 *the windy shore at Muizenberg*: It was on this beach that the British landed in 1795 and took the Cape colony from the Dutch.

28 *I know by heart*: Robert Louis Stevenson, 'The Swing', 'Where Go the Boats' and 'The Land of Counterpane', from *A Child's Garden of Verses* (1913).

3. 'Illness Was My Teacher'

29 *the Gardens*: The oldest part of Cape Town. Gardens were planted by the Dutch East India Company when it took over the Cape in the seventeenth century, to provide a refreshment station and citrus for sailors during long, scurvy-plagued voyages around Africa to the spice islands of Batavia and Java.

36 *Rhodes's thatched cottage*: Empire builder Cecil John Rhodes bought the cottage and died there, aged forty-four, in 1902.

4. Orphans and Stories

43 *Jock of the Bushveld*: A 1907 South African classic by Sir Percy FitzPatrick (1862–1931), about the adventures of his dog near Graskop in the Transvaal. These had been bedtime stories for his children; his friend Kipling urged him to turn them into what became an instant bestseller, never out of print.

54 *James James Morrison Morrison Weatherby George Dupree*: 'Disobedience', from *When We Were Very Young* (1924).

5. The Silent Past

60 *'clothes spread wide . . .'*: *Hamlet*, Act IV, scene vii. John Everett Millais painted *Ophelia* in 1851–2.

68 *. . . silent, bare*: Wordsworth's sonnet, 'Composed upon Westminster Bridge,

September 3, 1802'. At some later date, Rhoda pencilled 'epilepsy' in the margin.

68 *Wilfred Harris*: In his *Neuritis and Neuralgia* (OUP, 1926), he prescribes a strong drug, luminal, a derivative of veronal, for epilepsy in cases where bromide treatment fails. Virginia Woolf was given veronal during a mental breakdown in 1913.

6. 'Only a Housewife'

85 *Caledon*: Named after the Second Earl of Caledon, governor of the Cape Colony 1807–11.

87 *burly, shaggy bears*: 'Lines and Squares', from *When We Were Very Young* (1924).

87 *'crying with all . . .'*: 'Rice Pudding', from *When We Were Very Young* (1924).

93 *'had humoured, or softened . . .'*: The late Lady Elliott, mother of the three daughters in *Persuasion*.

7. School versus Home

114 *'worsted God'*: Emily Dickinson, 'A little East of Jordan' (*c.* early 1860).

8. 'Lapp Heights'

123 *Rainbow Valley*: By L. M. Montgomery (1919). One of the sequels to *Anne of Green Gables*.

9. Free in London

144 *'Finland'*: Published at the same time, October 1952, in *Finlandia* as 'Saalinen – Finland'. See p. 129.

145 *'Distrust the clouds . . .'*: 'Voice and Vision', from a City Lit anthology.

10. Mother to Daughter

165 *Marie Bashkirtseff's diary*: Marie Bashkirtseff (1858–84) was a Ukrainian-born diarist, painter and sculptor who wrote about the struggles of women artists and contributed to a feminist newspaper in France. Her painting, *The Studio*, pictures herself in an all-women studio. She died of TB at the age of twenty-five.

167 *Ideal Marriage*: By the Dutch gynaecologist Theodoor Hendrik van de Velde (1873–1937). Despite the condescension, the manual was popular with women for dispelling ignorance.

11. At the Crossroad

179 *Muriel Spark's word*: *Loitering with Intent* (1981; reissued Virago 2007).

12. Dividing Dreams

194 *"The Hound of Heaven"*: By the English poet Francis Thompson (1893).

13. The Way Down

7 *Ben-Zion Goldberg*: His papers (including what I prepared on St Augustine, Rousseau and Nietzsche) are in the library of the Herbert D. Katz Center for

Judaic Studies at the University of Pennsylvania, www.library.upenn. edu/cajs/goldberg.html.

228 *made to have a fit*: Electro-convulsive therapy was first developed in Italy, in 1938, by Ugo Cerletti. According to Lisa Appignanesi in *Mad, Bad and Sad* (Virago, 2008), p. 367, he had seen pigs in a slaughterhouse become 'more manageable and less agitated when an electric prod was administered. Since the idea, later disproved, that epileptics didn't develop "schizophrenia", it was thought that if epileptic-like convulsions could be administered in patients, this would stop or ameliorate other forms of mental illness.' Some established figures in psychiatry claim that 'producing a fit and then unconsciousness' helps in some cases. This is a current opinion. Back in the mid-twentieth century, when Sylvia Plath had shock treatment following a suicide attempt, doctors believed more in its curative possibilities, and doctors believed that it helped in my case.

14. Lives for Women

245 *'I-Thou'*: *I and Thou* (1923), by the philosopher Martin Buber.

247 *Hannah, a friendly girl*: Recalled as a schoolmate by Jacob Bunka, the sole Plunge Jew to survive (because he was away in the Red Army). A wood-carver, Bunka (born 1923) was interviewed by Olivia Gordon for *Psychologies* magazine in 2006, and he appears in Simon Schama's BBC 2 documentary *The History of the Jews* (2013).

261 *'Nation shall not . . .'*: Isaiah 2:2–4.

262 *a challenge to this*: A speech reported in the *Jerusalem Post*, 8 August 1978.

266 *'men's bodies are . . .'*: Olive Schreiner, *Woman and Labour* (1913).

273 *reshuffles the order*: At first, she appears to have planned five sections: Childhood; Diary in Hell; Heaven is Here; Failure and Fall; Work in the World; with a coda Beyond Death: A Message. Then she decides on an unbroken sequence to cover her years from twenty-seven to her present age of seventy-two, shuffles the order and calls it variously 'Notes on a Journey', 'Records of a Journey' or 'Diary: Notes, Poems and Letters', or 'A Grandmother's Journey'. The epigraph is from Psalm 73, verse 28: 'That I may tell of all Thy Works', written in Hebrew – *l'saper col malhoteha*.

273 *"to tell of all Thy Works"*: Psalms 73:28.

15. Lost and Living Memory

298 *'will you, won't you, will you . . .'*: 'The Song of the Mock Turtle', from Lewis Carroll, *Alice in Wonderland* (1865).

303 *'Dear as remembered kisses . . .'*: Tennyson, 'Tears, Idle Tears' (1847).

Acknowledgements

This book is dedicated to my brother Philip (Pip) Getz, who provided an abundance of memories, points of view, photographs and translations of Hebrew letters.

Our mother was to be the focus, and I'd meant to be no more than a channel for scenes and experiences on which her poems draw. It was Lennie Goodings, publisher of Virago, who transformed this into a mother and daughter story. It was stimulating to have a reader respond with so sure a touch. I've been fortunate too to work once more with the editor Zoe Gullen.

Another thanks is for the imaginative empathy that fuels writing: this came from the literary agent Isobel Dixon, and in a different way from my daughter Anna Gordon, who read chapters at an early stage. Anna and my other daughter, Olivia Gordon, wrote passages that are included verbatim. Olivia, a journalist, provided details and photos from her visit to Plunge, Lithuania, in 2006, as well as her thoughts on motherhood. Her son Humphrey Clark, braving a traumatic start to life, has made his own special contribution to this book.

Atsuko Hayakawa translated two of my mother's poems into Japanese, and they inspired landscapes by the artist Yoshiko Aya. Their creative responses have been an unexpected gift.

Yet another unexpected pleasure was meeting Paula Deitz, editor of the *Hudson Review*. I was amazed by the alacrity with which she asked for an excerpt.

I am grateful to the Stellenbosch Institute for Advanced

Study (STIAS). The setting, privacy and good company offered ideal conditions for writing.

I should also like to thank the following for their help with memories, facts and material: Phillis Warshaw; Marie Philip of David Philip Publishers in South Africa; Naomi Press; Linda Press Wulf; Donald Press; Caroline Press; Suzanne Press; Victoria Press; Jennifer Roth; Annette Kessler; Garda Fig (for memories of the Black and White Friendship Club during many years of apartheid); Phillippa Cheifitz; Shirley Gelcer; Sylvia Magid; Tony Shapiro; Maria Bjat; Saara Markkanen; Anna Makkonen at the Finnish National Archives; Paula Alves (for kindly allowing me to see her flat in Maida Vale, where my mother lodged in 1952); Clare Bateman; Nicola Maye Goldberg; Milton Shain; the Gitlin Library in Cape Town (for an issue of the *South African Jewish Chronicle* of May 1955); and Professor Rachel Salmon of Bar-Ilan University, who explained about rabbinic reading. I took in Simon Schama's admirable stress on the Word in *The Story of the Jews*, shown on BBC 2 in 2013, as well as his record of what happened to the Jews of Plunge in July 1941. Above all, I'm grateful for a vivid memoir by my mother's life-long friend, Lilian Henry.

Georges Borchard, my New York agent, noted that 'Siamon disappeared' at a critical point. He was right, as always. There are no adequate words to thank Siamon for his tolerance of this challenge, and for his readiness to be amused and touched as each chapter unfolded. His character in this book and in an earlier memoir, *Shared Lives*, speaks for itself.